Prophet of Orthodoxy

Russell Sparkes has studied Chesterton's works for many years. He is a contributor to the *Chesterton Review*, and has spoken on Chesterton's ideas to conferences both in the UK and abroad. For the last two years he has been working with the Centre for Faith & Culture at Westminster College, Oxford to establish a branch of the International Chesterton Institute in Britain.

Russell Sparkes was born into a Catholic family in 1955. Educated at Hertford College, he is married with two daughters. His previous book, *The Ethical Investor*, was also published by HarperCollins.

'*Orthodoxy, The Thing* and *The Everlasting Man* are among the great books of the age.' Graham Greene

'Chesterton was importantly and consistently on the side of the angels ... his ideas were fundamentally Christian and Catholic. He did more than any man of his time to maintain the existence of the important minority in the modern world.' T.S. Eliot

'Chesterton – a man of colossal genius.' Bernard Shaw

'GKC was a kind of Christian liberator letting in fresh air.' Dorothy L. Sayers

'Both in his prose and his verse he sees, as few writers have, the world about him as full of sacramental signs or symbols.' W.H. Auden

'I have the highest admiration for Chesterton's writings. Some of the chapters of *Orthodoxy* shook me up profoundly.' Andre Gide

'After reading *The Everlasting Man* for the first time I saw the Christian outline of history set out in a form that seemed to me to make sense ... It was this book which helped me most become a Christian.' C.S. Lewis

'Chesterton is so happy that one might almost believe that he has found God.' Kafka

'He wrote like an angel and was as cunning as an old fox in his raids on the hen-runs of Atheism.' Colin Morris

'Chesterton was not merely a theologian. He was theology.' D. Davies, *Church of England Newspaper*

'Chesterton was one of the deepest thinkers who ever existed.' E. Gilson

'C.S. Lewis was the heir to Chesterton ... the two writers dominated the world of English Christian writing in the twentieth century.' *Church Times*

'If every other line he wrote should disappear from circulation, Catholic posterity would still owe him an imperishable debt of gratitude, so long as a copy of *The Everlasting Man* enriched its libraries.' Mgr Ronald Knox

'A devoted son of the Holy Church and gifted defender of the Catholic Faith.' Cardinal Pacelli (Pope Pius XII)

'Chesterton is quite right. Take away God and what is left, what do men become? What sort of world are we reduced to living in?' Albino Luciani (Pope John Paul I)

PROPHET
of ORTHODOXY

The Wisdom of G.K. Chesterton

Edited by
Russell Sparkes

Fount
An Imprint of HarperCollins*Publishers*

Fount Paperbacks is an Imprint of
HarperCollins*Religious*
Part of HarperCollins*Publishers*
77–85 Fulham Palace Road, London W6 8JB

First published in 1997 by
Fount Paperbacks

3 5 7 9 10 8 6 4 2

Russell Sparkes has asserted the moral right
to be identified as the compiler of this work

A catalogue record for this book is
available from the British Library

0 00 628 0374

Printed and bound in Great Britain by
Caledonian International Book Manufacturing Ltd, Glasgow

Dedication

To Father Ian Boyd, Editor since 1974 of the *Chesterton Review* which has so increased our understanding of Chesterton; also to the memory of Maisie Ward and Dorothy Collins who preserved so much for posterity.

Acknowledgements

To Messrs A.P. Watt, as literary executors of the Chesterton Estate, to reproduce the works of G. K. Chesterton.

To the *Chesterton Review* for permission to reproduce the Homily of Emmet, Cardinal Carter.

To Messrs HarperCollins for permission to reproduce the Letter to Chesterton by Albino Luciani, translated from the Italian by Isobel Quigley.

Contents

Part Three: Major Writings

Postscript

Homily on Chesterton

*Extracted from Homily given in Toronto Cathedral,
18 September 1994 by Emmet, Cardinal Carter,
former Archbishop of Toronto*

I acknowledge the difficulty in talking about a man who has not been enrolled among the saints of the Church. The Second Vatican Council has told us that a homily should be about spiritual things and that we should avoid panegyrics. But I have no difficulty in turning my mind and my thoughts in that direction, and I hope that you will join me in this contemplation. Indeed, it would not scandalize me if the Sacred Congregation were to take the first steps for the beatification of Gilbert Chesterton. Speaking only for myself, I find in his history much that speaks to me of God and of eternal verities.

In this super-secularized world, it is not hard for us to acknowledge that the welfare of the Church is closely linked to the health and condition of the Catholic literary world. Alas, I say this with a heavy heart, because I mourn the absence today of outstanding leaders of Chesterton's calibre.

When challenged about his conversion, Chesterton was extraordinarily frank. He admitted that the turning-point was not something outstandingly intellectual, as was the case with Newman. You will recall that Newman found such a turning-point in St Augustine's insight. Augustine felt that he must turn to Christianity because that was where he had to find the answer to the presentation of the religion of the world in the *Secarus judicat orbis terrarum*. This remains our great boast; we are the only Catholic Church. When it was Chesterton's turn, he once again seemed to turn the shyness of the retiring English Catholic on its head. To the astonishment of his inter-locutor, he said that he became a Catholic because of the Sacrament of Penance. When pressed, he said that the Catholic Church was the only one which made the absolute claim to be able to forgive sin. When we think of it, this is a most powerful argument, not so much because the sacrament does give us relief, but because of the insight that only the Catholic Church could be so bold, and almost arrogant, as to make such a claim.

When I first became a priest and was empowered to administer this sacrament, I was, in the beginning, rather hesi-tant to do so – almost to the point of embarrassment. Who was I to say the words of reconciliation: 'May Our Lord Jesus Christ absolve you; and, by virtue of His authority, I absolve you of all your sins in the name of the Father, of the Son and of the Holy Spirit.' Who was I to dare to say that? Then, of course, it came to me that it was not I, but the Church that was speaking. And the Church claimed this right by virtue of what the Lord Himself had said, 'Whose sins you shall forgive they are forgiven.' This He said to the apostles and to their successors. And, again, He solved the problems that were to come to the Church with His instruction, *Dic Ecclesiae*, as it is written in the Gospel.

I have omitted many names that I could have mentioned as part of this literary leadership, but I do believe that Chesterton stands out among the great Catholic writers. Like St Paul who once wrote in tears, I mourn the failure in literary leadership which characterizes the world today. We seem much more intent on dissent that we are on proclaiming the glories of our faith. So let us not forget those who lead us at this crucial historical turning-point and whose work is still there for us to recall. I congratulate *The Review* for finding many of the unpublished writings of Chesterton, and also for giving us so many insights into his works. But, above all, I thank the Good Lord who sent us the leadership that we had in these days and the figure who was chief among them, G.K. Chesterton. May his memory never dim, and, above all, may we have the courage to follow his bravery and example.

Introduction

GKC – The Making of a Man

G.K. Chesterton was one of the most prolific authors who ever lived. His literary fame is without doubt. Such imaginative fiction as *The Man Who Was Thursday* and *The Napoleon of Notting Hill* are continually in print, not to mention the popularity of Father Brown. However, what has been forgotten is his reputation as one of the greatest Christian apologists this century, a man recognized as such by C.S. Lewis among many others.

In part, this neglect was due to fashion; in part, Chesterton's warnings of the insidious moral effects of free market capitalism seemed dated after the Second World War given the rise of the welfare state and the real ideological threat from Communism. In contrast, our post-Modernist world increasingly resembles that of the early part of the century so that GKC's writings now seem prophetic rather than antiquated. Like the Edwardians, we have global competition and only one dominant ideology – that of free markets and personal choice.

The spirit of modern society is troubled, and many of our usual guides no longer seem to work. The collapse of Communism and the approaching millennium have led to increasing recognition of the need for ethics in politics, business and society generally, but modern man seems to have lost the ability, or the confidence, to tackle them. In contrast, these were issues Chesterton repeatedly addressed. It seemed timely, therefore, to make his work in this area available to a new generation, and this has been my aim in researching, editing and writing this book.

GKC is a very personal writer, both in style and content. It is customary in such an anthology to include a brief summary of the author's life, but this would not do him justice, nor would it aid the reader to get the most out of his writings. I have therefore chosen to spotlight a few incidents or periods which made the man and shaped the writer. The aim is simply to assist the reader in understanding how Chesterton developed his clear vision of the purpose and sanity of life.

It is worth noting that he wrote at a time when certain authors were known by their initials. Stevenson became 'RLS', and Shaw 'GBS', so it is not surprising that Gilbert Keith Chesterton was and is known as 'GKC'. This only seemed to happen to those taken in some mysterious way to the public's heart. Despite his popularity, no one ever called Wells 'HGW'!

Youth

> Bowing down in blind credulity, as is my custom before mere authority and the tradition of the elders, superstitiously swallowing a story I could not test at the time by experiment of private judgement, I am firmly of the opinion that I was born on the 29 of May 1874 on Campden Hill, Kensington.

The opening sentence of Chesterton's *Autobiography*, from which I have extracted only a part, is surely one of the classics of literature which deserves to be as well known as the first lines of *Pride and Prejudice*. In Chesterton there is always the pleasure of feeling humour bubbling up throughout all his work, rather like a mountain spring bubbling up through a rock. Here, of course, he is indirectly teasing critics who accused him of credulously swallowing the doctrines of the Roman Catholic Church by pointing out how little we know, even of such things as our own birth.

In fact the young Gilbert was born into an association which blossomed with the great British Empire, and with the extinction of that institution came under eclipse – the respectable middle class. His father, Edward, carried on the family estate agency business founded by his own grand-father. Unlike current social economic groupings, their position in society was not based on money. There was a sense of tradition, of carrying on the family business without the urge to expand which possessed later generations. Good manners and correct speech were essential. Avoiding the vulgarity of the servant classes a must. As he reminisced in the *Autobiography*:

> At the age of three or four I screamed for a hat
> hanging on a peg, and at last in convulsions of fury
> uttered the awful words, 'If you don't give it me, I'll say
> 'at.' I felt sure that would lay all my relations prostrate
> for miles around.

Bourgeois virtues certainly, but based on the honesty and sense of duty which enabled a small country to become the economic centre of the world, and to rule a huge empire. If truth be told, class for Gilbert was always a foreign language. (It is *inter alia* a means of communication.) He knew the rules, but never understood why. GKC once went up to the grand-daughter of the Duke of Argyll saying: 'We are all members of the jolly old middle class, aren't we?' This means that he is one of the very few British writers who can be genuinely called 'classless' – a fact which enabled him to get to know ordinary people in a way impossible for most other writers of the time. Orwell found that he remained 'a gent' in the workhouse; he could get to know tramps, but had problems with the respectable working class. Chesterton was without this inhibiting shyness of knowing that they were his social inferiors; in return they loved him, as his huge funeral procession in Beaconsfield showed.

As regards religious belief, we may say that the late Victorians instilled into their children a deep and pervasive sense of Christian morality, even as their own belief in its source foundered. (In the Edwardian period this was to lead to trouble.) A true child of his time, when GKC left school he was an agnostic, with little religious belief, and still less formal religious practice. His gods were popular poets such as Swinburne and Whitman. His childhood was happy, and at the age of five this happiness was augmented by the arrival of his brother Cecil – 'We always argued, but never quarrelled.' Chesterton was also lucky enough to have a deep sense of wonder, almost awe, at the world. This childlike attribute stayed with him throughout his life except for the depressed years of his late adolescence.

At the age of nine he was sent to St Paul's, one of the great public schools of England. Since it is based in London for day-boys, rather than boarders, it is less well known than certain others. Yet its consistent reputation for academic excellence has attracted some of the sharpest young minds in the country. When GKC tells us he was a dunce at school, it is against this background that we should consider it. Yet in many ways he *was* a dunce: tall, untidy, always lost in thought. The sort of dreamer who is not punished for not doing his set work because his reasons are so innocent. He drifted through his school years without making much of an impact.

There is a story of an American psychology major who pretended to be insane in order to investigate conditions in asylums. Confirmed as mad by a panel of famous doctors and professors, he had been committed for less than an hour when the inmates came up to him saying: 'What are you doing in here – you are sane.' Likewise, Gilbert was able to deceive his teachers, but not his peers. When he was fifteen some of the brightest boys of the form created a Junior Debating Club, and made him President. People like Edmund Bentley and Lucian Oldershaw were to remain some of his closest friends. Among this group were two Jewish brothers, Maurice and Lawrence Solomon. They stayed lifelong friends of GKC's, Lawrence later moving out to Beaconsfield with him. The boys not only held debates but published a journal, and the quality of the writing eventually attracted the attention of the Headmaster, who promoted Chesterton to the privileges of the Sixth Form. (When he left the school the Headmaster came to Mrs Chesterton saying: 'Six foot of genius. Cherish him, Mrs Chesterton, cherish him.')

A crucial omission from his schooldays was the fact that he never learned how to structure and organize work – with grave consequences for later life. Chesterton was blessed with a powerful brain, capable of huge exertions and of producing a great volume of high quality work at high speed. Perhaps it was an artistic temperament, but he would probably have lived longer had he learned self-discipline at school. Work for him was usually something to be done at the last minute, and with a kind of romantic cavalry charge at it.

Decadence and Despair

Gilbert left school aged eighteen in the summer of 1892, and for the next three years just drifted. He studied art in a desultory way at the Slade School of Art, and attended a few lectures on English Literature at University College, London. Yet little real work was done, and no exams were passed. Such lacklustre aimlessness is foreign to the GKC we know, yet was a symptom of the doubt, fear and depression raging within him. Puberty came late to Chesterton, and with it he lost the magical and secure kingdom of childhood. Into the void came near madness.

He was a natural cartoonist, able to depict and describe a man in a few rough lines. For example, there is a sketch 'When the Revolution Happens – Bernard Shaw refuses to drink the blood of Aristocrats' which has Shaw tied to a tumbril. Yet what is brilliant is the way the artist has caught Shaw leaning back in a posture which shows that he feels he is above all this nonsense. It seems quite likely that Chesterton could have made a very successful career as a cartoonist, if he had so chosen. Unfortunately, cartooning is a natural gift which cannot be taught. He could not develop this talent at the Slade, and was not interested in what was on offer. In consequence he wasted his time at art school in idle chatter, and absorbed some dubious ideas circulating at the time. The 1890s in art was the period of the Decadence, an art form heavily influenced by symbolism, sensuality and the occult. On the continent Baudelaire worshipped the 'Flowers of Evil', while writers like Huysman advocated both twisted sexuality and Satanism. Beardsley's sinuous drawings that hint at perversion and torture are well known, but for the full debased sensuality you need to see Redon or Klimt, whose canvases have much more of an erotic charge. There was also a clear philosophy, as enunciated by Oscar Wilde.

For the first time in Western history the great canon of meaning in art was dropped, and 'art for art's sake' became the rule. The overall philosophy was nihilistic, i.e. that there is no meaning in life, and that therefore the selfish pursuit of pleasure, as in Ancient Rome, was the only sensible option. The restless Gilbert absorbed these ideas, but found that indulging sexual and sadistic fantasies, in imagination at least, only made him feel more depressed and uncertain. (It has been alleged that his notebooks contained obscene drawings of naked women, but I know of no proof of this.) Simultaneous experiments with the ouija board and occult philosophy merely made things worse. In his own words:

> There is something truly menacing in the thought of how quickly I could imagine the maddest, when I had never committed the mildest crime ... there was a time when I had reached that condition of moral anarchy within, in which a man says in the words of Wilde, that 'Atys with the bloodstained knife were better than the thing I am'. I have never felt the faintest temptation to the particular madness of Wilde; but I could at this time imagine the worst and wildest disproportions of more normal passion; the point is that the whole mood was overpowered and oppressed with a sort of congestion of imagination ... I had an overpowering impulse to record or draw horrible ideas and images; plunging deeper and deeper as in a blind spiritual suicide.

The saints have often described their struggle with evil as physical in its violence, as we can hear from a more modern voice. The Trappist monk and well-known religious writer Thomas Merton went through a similar experience to that of Chesterton. In 1936, having spent his first year at university in pursuit of pleasure, and abandoning his studies in favour of nightclubs and pornographic literature, he found the world suddenly collapsing in on him. He retired to a hotel bedroom with a window:

> That window! It was huge. It seemed to go right down to the floor. Maybe the force of gravity would

draw the whole bed, with me on it, to the edge of that abyss, and spill me headlong into the emptiness. And far, far away in my mind was a dry mocking voice that said: 'What if you threw yourself out of that window?' ... now my life was dominated by something I had never known before: fear. It was humiliating, this strange self-conscious watchfulness. It was a humiliation I had deserved more than I knew. I had refused to pay any attention to the moral laws upon which all our vitality and sanity depend: and now I was reduced to the condition of a silly old woman.
Elected Silence

This mental illness, and its cure, was the same as GKC's. The phrase 'moral anarchy' is the crucial one; loosing his passions from moral restraint did not bring happiness, but misery and despair. This is surely true for all of us, but for the spiritually aware the struggle seems greater. Milton described the Devil as 'darkness visible', and Chesterton claimed to have met him. His state of mind is well described in the poem is addressed to E.C. Bentley, 'A Cloud was on the Minds of Men' which forms the preface of the nightmarish novel, *The Man Who Was Thursday*. That eerie and disturbing essay *The Diabolist* (page 133) is wonderfully descriptive writing of his sense of temptation, of having to choose between two very different paths. Set in the grounds of a university, in the twilight lit by a bonfire, the diabolist comes to him:

Why do you care about morality? I glanced at his face quickly. He thrust out his neck as he had a trick of doing; and so brought his face abruptly into the light of the bonfire like a face in the footlights. His long chin and high cheek-bones were lit up infernally from underneath, so that he looked like a fiend staring down into the flaming pit. I had an unmeaning sense of being tempted in a wilderness, and even as I passed a burst of red sparks broke past. A common, harmless atheist would have denied that religion produced humility or joy ... but he admitted both. He only said, 'But shall I not find in evil a life of its own? Granted that for every woman I ruin one of those sparks will go out: will not the expanding pleasure of ruin? ... What you call evil I call good.'

Gilbert felt that 'that quiet conversation was by far the most terrible thing that ever happened to me in my life'. *The Diabolist* is probably based on Sir John Hankin. A very clever man, and a colossal pessimist; a man of literary talent who found literature so meaningless that he could only write clever superficial comedies of manners – which were very successful. It was almost inevitable that such a man, who expressed his contempt for the artists' colony of Bedford Park, where he lived, by always wearing evening dress, should kill himself, which he did in 1909. According to GKC's *Autobiography*: 'He was a pessimist, which is something more atheistic than an atheist; he was a fundamental sceptic, that is a man without fundamentals. He was one who disbelieved in Man much more than he did in God.'

Chesterton's sanity, and his life's purpose, hung in the balance. What saved him was a sense of wonder and joy at the existence of the world: 'I hung on to the remains of religion by one thin thread of thanksgiving,' expressed not in conventional terms of religion, but in the poetry of Browning and Stevenson, 'Browning's "God must be glad one loves his world so much", or Stevenson's "belief in the ultimate decency of things"'. The young Chesterton chose morality, sanity and orthodoxy: 'I am becoming orthodox, because I have come, rightly or wrongly, after stretching my brain til it bursts, to the old belief that heresy is worse than sin.'

It took the next five years of spiritual exploring, as he explains in *Orthodoxy*, to find that this vision or personal philosophy was the orthodox vision of the Christian Church as expressed in the Apostles' Creed. But such positive convictions remained with GKC for the rest of his life, and he became recognized as a great optimist, perhaps the only genuinely optimistic thinker our gloomy century has produced. This episode is probably the most important in Chesterton's life. He had experienced spiritual horror, but was eventually able to find his way out of the abyss. Such knowledge made him a safe guide for others. Sanity lay not in decadence and abnormality, but in the orthodox teachings of Christianity and the ordinary good things of life. In the final words of 'A Cloud Was on the Mind of Men':

> Between us, by the peace of God, such truth can now be
>   told;
> Yea, there is strength in striking root, and good in growing
>   old.
> We have found common things at last, and marriage and a
>   creed,
> And I may safely write it now, and you may safely read.

Nevertheless, this period also left its mental scars. GKC had felt the reality of evil, and throughout his life he was able to describe it for others. You can see that in the powerful evocation of evil in many of the Father Brown stories: for example the blasted and desecrated graveyard in *The Honour of Israel Gow*, the frozen forest of *The Sign of the Broken Sword*, the human bat in *The Dagger With Wings*. It can also be felt in the bizarre edge of many of his drawings. Over the next few years he wrestled with the Book of Job, the one book of the Old Testament which most explicitly tackles this subject. (Look at the references to the Book of Job in Chesterton's early *Speaker* articles, on a variety of unrelated topics, or in his *Browning*.)

Convinced of the reality of evil, Chesterton regarded as innocents progressive thinkers such as Wells and Shaw who denied its existence. After Auschwitz and the gulag, who can deny that he was right? Yet this knowledge did not make him world-weary, unlike the Existentialists who emerged when these horrors became evident after the Second World War. As GKC saw, the only convincing explanation for the presence of evil in the world was the Christian doctrine of the Fall of Man. Shaw and Wells denied the existence of both God and evil, and planned the creation of a heaven on earth. But their plans were built on a swamp of ignorance which let in such sewer rats as Hitler and Stalin.

The Wild Knight of Fleet Street

> Nothing looks more neat and regular than a newspaper, with its parallel columns, its mechanical printing, its detailed facts, its responsible polysyllabic leading articles. Nothing, as a matter of fact, goes every night through more agonies of adventure, more hairbreadth escapes, desperate expedients, crucial councils, random compromises, or barely averted catastrophes ... it gives all its organizers a gasp of relief every morning to see that it has come out at all; that it has come out without the leading article upside down, or the Pope congratulated on discovering the North Pole. *The Real Journalist*

In 1895/96 two strong forces came together to jolt Gilbert out of his depression; the first was work, and the second love. Christianity has always known that work is a good thing in itself which is vital for sanity, the monkish dictum *laborare est orare* (to work is to pray) merely being the mirror image of the old English saying, 'the Devil makes work for idle hands to do'. In September 1895 GKC went to work for a small publisher called Rodway, a specialist in the occult. Like many such, this was located in Bloomsbury near the British Museum. Within six months, however, he left to join the much larger firm of Fisher Unwin, where he was to stay until 1901. They were based in Paternoster Buildings in the City, just behind St Paul's Cathedral. Chesterton was a man who saw the significance of things; I am sure that his spirits lifted when he left the shadow of the occult for Our Father's Mansion.

The young publisher lacked many of the most basic office skills, being disorganized and hopelessly untidy. Offices at that time used a mechanical means of reproduction called the cyclostyle, using solvents and ink. In letters Gilbert describes himself as black with cyclostyling ink. He also had the schoolboy's ability to look like a mess in the most expensive of clothes, his buttons often undone. (Office workers then wore elegant frock coats and a top hat.) Yet he was enthusiastic, had a deep love of literature, and a brilliant memory. GKC later claimed to have read ten thousand novels in this time. When twenty years later Fr O'Connor challenged him to describe the plot of one, his reply was absolutely right!

He wrote occasional book reviews for *The Bookman* over this period, but the real breakthrough as a writer occurred at the turn of the century. Like many a creative artist, GKC suddenly obtained 'lift-off' which took him from obscurity to the first rank of English letters. Cecil Chesterton (GKC's brother) wrote 'In the autumn of the year 1899 no one outside his circle had heard of G.K. Chesterton. In the spring of 1900 everyone was asking everyone else – who is GKC?' Partly fortune smiled on him, although we should note that, as will be explained in the next section, he had something to work hard for, and he did. In October 1899 he was finally commissioned to write a major article for *The Bookman* on Poussin. The style is unique and unmistakable:

> Poussin and his school multiplied nymphs and satyrs
> with the recurrence of an endless wall-paper, till a
> bacchanal has become as respectable as a bishop and
> the god of love is too vulgar for a valentine ... This is
> the strange feeling of sadness evoked by the groups
> and landscapes of Poussin ... For this is the second
> death of the gods – a death after resurrection. And
> when a god dies, it dies eternally.

The young writer had found his voice, and never lost it. This review, right at the start of his writing career, illustrates GKC's instinctive vision and awareness; art criticism was in its youth in the 1890s, and it is doubtful if Chesterton knew that Poussin painted from little models rather than from life. Yet he had picked up the essence of Poussin's art, its strange, dead, lifelessness. GKC now burst on to the national stage. In the autumn of 1899 his best friend Bentley was taken on as a writer for a radical Liberal magazine called *The Speaker*. In late 1899 Britain invaded the Boer Republic of South Africa, and virtually the whole country approved in a wave of im- perialist fervour. Only *The Speaker* and the small group around it were against. Bentley persuaded the Editor, short of hands, to commission his friend Chesterton.

The latter argued that what was at stake was not the so-called 'White Man's burden', i.e. the imperialist's self- appointed duty to conquer and bring civilization to native peoples, but rather the covert desire by some vested financial interests to obtain certain assets, particularly gold mines. He questioned the morality of the war, and raged against the means of winning it. (We should not forget that when the Boers turned to guerrilla warfare in 1900 after the defeat of their regular army, the British forces invented concentration camps to intern their women and children. They were not deliberately designed as death camps, but thousands did die there of disease.) Chesterton's attacks were the stronger for being so clearly based on morality; they were never mere political diatribe. In May 1900 for example:

> 'My country right or wrong' is a thing which no patriot would think of saying except in a desperate case. It is like saying, 'My mother drunk or sober' ... What have we done, and where have we wandered, that we should talk as if we have never done anything more intelligent than found colonies and kick niggers? We are the children of light, and it is we who sit in darkness.

An American correspondent noted that 'Chesterton was the one British writer, utterly unknown before, who built up a great reputation through determined and persistent opposition to British policy.'

The year 1900 saw the publication, financed by his father, of a book of poems called *The Wild Knight*. Containing 'The Donkey', 'The Praise of Dust', and 'By the Babe Unborn' (see pages 99–101) it attracted the praise of Kipling. Chesterton was now in demand both as a journalist and a writer. His best articles from *The Speaker* were reprinted in book form as *The Defendant* in 1901. He started to write regularly for both *The Speaker* and the *Daily News*. In 1902 the latter became a regular Saturday column which lasted until 1913. By 1905 he had two weekly columns, including one in the *Illustrated London News* which lasted until his death in 1936, as well as frequent reviews and other articles. Chesterton loved the sheer romance of Fleet Street.

He also loved the lifestyle of the journalist. He would spend his evenings debating politics, history, English literature and religion with his friends such as Bentley, a journalist on *The Telegraph*, Hilaire Belloc, and his own brother Cecil, who had also become a journalist. Then as the witching hour of the deadline approached, intense thought would produce the required copy. Thought was assisted by copious intakes of food and drink. Charles Masterman recalled later: 'Chesterton used to sit writing his articles in a Fleet Street cafe, sampling and mixing a terrible conjunction of drinks, while many waiters hovered about, partly in awe … one day the head waiter spoke, "Your friend," he whispered, "he very clever man, he sit and laugh, and then he write, and then he laugh at what he write."'

It may seem strange to us that such a natural writer as G.K. Chesterton did not hit his stride until the age of nearly twenty-seven. Maturity, physical and psychological, came late to him. Yet again we should be wary of applying modern standards to the late nineteenth century. People generally did mature much later then. Whether it was the lack of the hormones in the processed food which they did not eat; or whether it was the lack of sexual imagery from the television they did not watch, is difficult to say. (It is a hard fact that the average age for the onset of menstruation for girls has fallen from sixteen in the 1890s to twelve now.) For Gilbert there was another reason; his mind was like an enormous and powerful engine which needed a period of running-in before it would operate at full capacity.

God Made Thee Mightily, My Love

Literary and journalistic success came at just the right time for Gilbert, for he needed the money which came with it. Then as now a junior job in publishing is not a path to riches. In 1900, after four years' work, Fisher Unwin were paying him £60 a year in salary ($290 p.a. at the then exchange rate). The value of money has fallen sharply in the twentieth century; a pound in 1900 was worth 61 times its debased descendant of 1996. Yet £60 a year (£3,660 p.a. in 1996 terms) was little more than an allowance which let Gilbert live at home with his parents, and not much more.

In the summer of 1896 GKC was taken along to a small debating club in Bedford Park. This was one of the first purpose-built 'urban villages', with its own village green and carefully designed street layout, unlike the jerry-building which characterized most of the late Victorian expansion of London. It still stands just above Turnham Green in west London. Rents were low, which attracted a large Bohemian element – Yeats and his family lived there for a while. Cheap housing also attracted the genteel poor, including the widowed family of a diamond merchant called Blogg. There were three daughters, all of whom were forced by financial necessity to go out to work. Lucian Oldershaw formed an attachment to the youngest daughter, Ethel; Gilbert fell instantly in love with the eldest daughter, Frances. He was 22, she was 27 years old. Frances could not be called beautiful, but she had a pleasing face with a wistful charm that matured into a quiet dignity. She was also a little woman, five feet two inches tall, weighing no more than eight stones (112 pounds). Gilbert was a tall man, six feet two inches in height, fairly thin at this time, and weighing around eleven stones (154 pounds).

For two years he courted his new love, regularly walking the two-and-a-half miles from Kensington to Bedford Park, before proposing to her in St James Park in the summer of 1898. Mrs Blogg was not impressed with this 'opinionated scarecrow'. She was even less impressed with his negligible income. Protocol demanded that no respectable married woman should work, so they would have to live on his income – impossible on £60 a year. She stated that as a minimum they would need £300 a year to live on, and £500 to be comfortable. No wedding was possible until these figures were reached.

Rebasing them to current values does not make them seem too high: in 1996 terms the targets are £18,300–£30,500 a year, or $28,000–$47,000. Yet inflation only reflects general trends; in 1900 income tax was minimal, and house prices and servants cheap. A middle-class couple could live very well on £500 a year. Anyway, the need to earn money is the other reason for the extraordinary step forward GKC made in those years. Only in 1901 did his earnings from *The Speaker*, *Daily News*, and other writing reach the magic £500 mark, and on 28 June 1901 they were married. It is a curious fact that no biographer seems to have noticed that this was also Frances' thirty-second birthday.

The recent success of *Shadowlands*, the love story of C.S. Lewis and Joy Davidman, shows the public's re-awakening to the fact that there is more to love than mere sexual attraction. Perhaps our grandmothers really could teach us a thing or two. From this perspective the romance of Gilbert and Frances is a great love story. Gilbert was totally dependent on her, while she for her part quietly supported this man whose genius was so great and yet so unbalanced. Immanuel Kant is generally regarded as one of the most profound thinkers of the Western tradition. It is reported that as he wrestled with the *Critique of Pure Reason*, he ordered his servants to prepare identical meals at the identical time each day. He needed the minimum of distraction in the outer world to focus as much of his mind as possible on the inner one. Chesterton was a poetic visionary rather than a professional philosopher, but his needs were the same. Frances had to handle *everything* for her absent-minded husband. There is the well-known story that he once sent her a telegram: 'Am in Market Harborough. Where ought I to be?'

In his *Autobiography* Chesterton deplored the tendency visible even then:

> There seems to be a much more vivid interest in the lives of such literary men than in their literary works. Any amount is written and rewritten about the romance of Mr and Mrs Browning ... but I rather doubt whether Browning is reread, or whether Mrs Browning is read at all.

He himself started his career with the study of Browning, and this was followed by several more great writers. Of his *Dickens* Kate Pellegrini, Dickens' daughter, said that this was one of the best things ever written on her father. Yet in all GKC's literary biographies the work comes first, and the life is only used to illuminate the mind of its creator. I am sure that he would have laughed heartily at the modern treatment of literary figures which seems obsessed with their sex lives. One would have thought that most writers have fairly ordinary sex lives in practice, if not in their imagination – think of poor D. H. Lawrence.

Yet we must briefly look at the intimate details of the Chestertons' marriage to examine one accusation made against it. Shortly after Frances was safely buried in 1938 (Gilbert had died in 1936), Ada Chesterton (Cecil's widow) published a book *The Chestertons* which alleged that Gilbert had never really loved Frances, but married her when rejected by her sister Gertrude, the 'girl with red hair' according to Ada. Unfortunately, Gertrude's hair was yellow, and Lucian Oldenshaw, who married the other sister Ethel, told Maisie Ward that this story was complete nonsense.

Ada was a thoroughly modern woman, a Communist and a woman who supported herself by her own journalism at a time when such feminine independence was very rare. Relations between her and Frances (a Victorian lady, and both words are used advisedly) were never good. Frances treasured her privacy, and asked Gilbert to keep her out of the *Autobiography*: 'a lady artist touched on as lightly as possible in this very Victorian narrative.' Unlike the reticent Frances, Ada was pushy, forceful, and resembled Edith Sitwell in a striking ugliness. While she was an able writer, she was also naturally quarrelsome, and Gilbert, who hated any kind of disagreement, eventually had to fire her from the management of *GK's Weekly* in the 1920s for making a nuisance of herself. *The Chestertons* was her revenge on both of them. Maynard, a friend of Cecil's, called it 'that amusing but unreliable and malicious book of Cecil's widow'.

Ada went on to say that on their wedding night Frances shied from his embraces, and the wedding was never consummated, leaving Gilbert a life of pseudo-monastic frustration. It is hard to see how Ada could have known. She only married his brother Cecil in 1917 on the day the latter marched off to the Front. (Since he died there in 1918 it is quite possible that *her* marriage was never consummated.) This cannot be true for Gilbert and Frances. Frances underwent an agonizing operation to enable her to have children, while all who knew the Chestertons remarked how devoted they were to each other. 'We were always lovers,' Frances remarked after his death, and her own death two years later was from the kind of cancer known to result from depression following the death of a loved one. In Victorian terms, she died of a broken heart.

I cannot see how anyone who has read Gilbert's letters and Frances' diary can believe for a moment that theirs was a marriage based on convention and mutual suspicion, rather than love and respect. It is also psychologically impossible. Chesterton was always himself; it is inconceivable to imagine him living a lie. Yet the greatest testament to their marriage is Gilbert's love poetry. He dedicated the wonderful introduction to *The Ballad of the White Horse* to her (see page 109). I will quote one other example:

> God made thee mightily, my love,
> He stretched His hands out of His rest
> And lit the stars of east and west
> Brooding o'er darkness like a dove.
> God made thee mightily, my love.
>
> God made thee patiently, my sweet,
> Out of all stars He chose a star,
> He made it red with sunset bar

And green with greeting for thy feet.
God made thee mightily, my sweet.

Voice of Orthodoxy

My first impulse to write, and almost my first impulse
to think, was a revolt of disgust with the Decadents
and the aesthetic pessimism of the 'nineties ...
I thought that all the wit and wisdom in the world was
banded together to slander and depress the world ...
then above all, everyone claiming intelligence insisted
on 'Art for art's sake' ... I started to think it out, and
the more I thought of it, the more certain I grew that
the whole thing was a fallacy; that art could not exist
from, still less in opposition to, life; especially the life of
the soul which is salvation; and that great art never had
been so much detached from conscience and
common sense. *Milton and Merry England*

Chesterton was determined to remain a journalist all his
life, but right from the beginning he also had a message to
communicate; he was an essayist, never a mere 'reporter' of
facts. In 1902 he was given a great opportunity to set out his
stall. The publishing firm of Macmillan was producing a pres-
tigious series called 'English Men of Letters'. Contributors
tended to be old and distinguished – Anthony Trollope had
written *Thackeray* for them – and it was a gamble entrusting
Browning to such a young and newly established writer. They
were not happy with the manuscript. Editor Stephen Gwynn
later reminisced:

Old Mr Craik, the Senior partner, sent for me and I
found him in white fury, with Chesterton's proofs
corrected in pencil; or rather not corrected in pencil;

there were still thirteen errors uncorrected on one page; mostly in quotations from Browning. A selection from a Scotch ballad had been quoted from memory and three of the four lines were wrong. I wrote to Chesterton saying that the firm thought the book was going to 'disgrace' them ... But the book was a huge success.

Browning was the perfect start for GKC's literary career, 'a sensation' which immediately established him in the first rank of the literary establishment. A poet Chesterton knew and loved, he too had ceaselessly turned over in his mind questions of love and faith, death and morality, the visible decline of religion which started in his lifetime. We see this in Browning's poems such as *Abt Vogler*, *Rabbi Ben Ezra*, or *Bishop Blougram's Apology*. In Bishop Blougram's words:

> What if the breaks themselves should prove at last,
> The most consummate of contrivances
> And so we stumble at truth's very test!
> All we gained then by our unbelief
> Is a life of doubt diversified by faith,
> For one of faith diversified by doubt
> We called the chess-board white – we call it black.

The book illustrated the worst aspects of GKC's writing – his lack of concern over detail. He knew Browning well and quoted from memory without bothering to check that his memory was accurate. Yet if there were thousands of people who could check quotations, none of them had GKC's unique vision, the ability to get to the heart of Browning, a notoriously obscure writer. Browning is principally difficult because of his invention of, and love for, the 'dramatic monologue' and his passion for detailed observation. In GKC's words:

If a man had gone up to Browning and asked him with all the solemnity of the eccentric, 'Do you think life is worth living?', it is interesting to conjecture what his answer might have been … under the influence of the orthodox rationalist theologian he would have said, 'Existence is justified by its manifest design, its manifest adaption of means to ends', or in other words, 'Existence is justified by its completeness' … if he had answered the question 'Is life worth living?' with the real vital answer that awaited it in his soul, he would have said as likely as not, 'Crimson toadstools in Hampshire'.

In other words, Browning would have immediately seen in his mind a picture of the things which made life worth living to him, a mental picture of the intense happiness and joy he had felt seeing toadstools growing in a field, and tried to capture the immediacy of this in words. In this way Browning is a verbal Impressionist. GKC understood both the vision and Browning's way of expressing it. Yet even in this book Chesterton keeps coming back to moral and even theological thought. Discussing Browning's epic poem *The Ring and the Book* (surely a source of inspiration for *The Ballad of the White Horse*) he writes:

The author of the Book of Job says 'I will show you the relations between man and heaven by a tale of primeval sorrows and the voice of God out of whirlwind.' Virgil says, 'I will show you the relations of man to heaven by the tale of the greatest people and the founding of the most wonderful city in the world.' Dante says, 'I will show you the relations of man to heaven by uncovering the very machinery of the spiritual universe, and letting you hear, as I have heard, the roaring of the mills of God' … Browning says,

'I will show you the relations of man to heaven by telling you a story out of a dirty Italian book of criminal trials from which I select one of the meanest and most completely forgotten.'

The success of *Browning*, however, placed him in a dilemma – should he continue his career as a journalist, or switch to literature? Shaw advised him to move from journalism to more lucrative books and plays, assuring him that with his literary talent celebrity and financial success was assured. The only recorded disagreement of any substance between Gilbert and Frances was over his profession. She would have liked him to pursue what she considered the more respectable career of a writer. Chesterton resisted fiercely; all his life he insisted on being called a journalist. Edmund Bentley, one of his best friends and a *Daily Telegraph* journalist himself, wrote:

> Although there was so much he could do with his pen, he could be nothing with his whole heart but a journalist. What he meant by being a journalist was being engaged in direct democratic appeal to the reading public about disputed or disputable questions of any sort or kind ... GKC, then, was a journalist in this sense also, that he made a living by writing for the Press ... to live in this way was his deliberate choice, there can be no doubt of that, for it was a hard life, and a much easier one lay to hand as a writer of books.

In other words, he demanded to be a journalist in order to write for as wide a circle of readers as possible; he hated the idea of being stuck in a literary ghetto. The sheer milieu of journalism and the atmosphere of Fleet Street he found invigorating, as it kept him in touch with the concerns of ordinary people and the events, including political decrees, which affected them. He also passionately believed that he had something to say to the people, a moral message in a world going to the asylum if not to the dogs; the idea of Chesterton as a prophet is not far-fetched. Ideas cascaded from him. Thus while the popular image of a journalist is sometimes the caricature of somebody too lazy to do anything else, the opposite was true for GKC. He literally worked himself to death in order to express joy in the world, and to help the poor and helpless.

His solution to the dilemma facing him was typical – he would do both! From 1902 to 1914 he produced, without exaggeration, the work of three men. To start with, he had more than enough to do as a full-time journalist, his columns for the *Daily News* and the *Illustrated News*, as well as regular articles for such magazines as *The Speaker, The Clarion*, and *The Eye-Witness*. Then there were the literary works, fiction such as *The Napoleon of Notting Hill* (1904), *The Man Who Was Thursday* (1908), *The Ball and The Cross* (1910), and the Father Brown stories from 1911, plus literary criticism: *Browning* (1903); *Charles Dickens* (1906); *George Bernard Shaw* (1909), or *The Victorian Age in Literature* (1912). Finally, from 1903 the prophet awoke, first in the pages of *The Clarion*, and then in book form: *Heretics* (1905); *Orthodoxy* (1908), *What's Wrong With the World* (1910), the latter a development of his social views. Not to mention a major poetic epic – *The Ballad of the White Horse* (1911).

Truly, one's head spins merely thinking of the immense effort required to achieve this. And we should not forget that these works came from the man who spent much of his time debating political and religious ideas and issues, and that they were written in haste to meet a deadline. In view of all this, its overall quality is astonishing. Yet this productivity did take its toll of him. The great brain was a powerful engine, but required constant fuel. He therefore ate and drank constantly, in an absent-minded sort of way. He absorbed vast quantities of alcohol, mostly beer, not to alter mood or protect himself from reality, but simply to give him the energy to go on. (There is no account ever of GKC being drunk.)

Quite apart from its psychological qualities, alcohol's prime physiological effect is as a food. By 1902 he already had a double chin and rounded features, the 11-stone (154 pounds) man who had proposed to Frances was now a 16-stone giant (224 pounds). A man of 6 feet 2 inches in height can carry significant extra weight without visible effect, but by 1906 Shaw was calling him 'The Young Man Mountain, a large abounding gigantically cherubic person', and the 16 stones was nearer 18 (252 pounds). This weight did not seem to stop him being vigorous and active, but continued pressure pushed it toward 20 stones (280 pounds) by 1911, when his face became bloated and shiny; he was obviously ill. In fact, such huge abuse of his body by gross overwork and excessive eating would probably have killed him in 1909 if Frances had not dragged him off to live in the countryside at Beaconsfield, a small town 20 miles west of London.

The Strange Death of Liberal England

GKC made his reputation as a young and ardent Liberal, but political idealism is hard to sustain once a party is in power, as the Liberals were from 1906. He became increasingly disenchanted. He couldn't bear the hypocrisy of practical politics.

> I remember going to a great Liberal club, and walking about in a large crowded room, somewhere at the end of which a bald gentleman with a beard was reading from a manuscript in a low voice. It was hardly unreasonable that we did not listen to him ... Next morning I saw in the front of my Liberal paper in gigantic headlines the phrase 'Lord Spencer unfurls the Banner'...the contrast between what that orator

was to the people who heard him, and what he was to the thousands of newspaper readers who did not hear him, was so huge a hiatus and disproportion that I do not think I ever quite got over it.

He also deplored the way the new government sold honours to raise money for the party coffers. Hilaire Belloc had become a Liberal MP in 1906, but quickly became disillusioned. Along with Cecil Chesterton he argued that the whole business of party politics was nothing but a charade designed to allow the ruling plutocracy (i.e. the rich) to dominate and exploit the poor. Since the ordinary papers were not interested in this thesis, the two of them founded their own magazine in 1911 called the *Eye-Witness* (later the *New Witness*) with Belloc the editor for a year, followed by Cecil.

Yet Gilbert's problems with the Liberal party were deeper, more philosophical and moral. Lloyd George was starting to lay down the basis of what became known as the welfare state. While the theory was to help the poor, the practical effect was to bully them. Chesterton was outraged that the State gave itself powers to remove children from their families, and that poor children were forced to have their hair cut off for fear of infection with lice, something never done at Eton. GKC always thought that madness was normally the mind becoming obsessed and overwhelmed by one idea to the exclusion of that balance which is sanity. Both these ideas are well set out in his articles 'The Mad Official' (see page 153) and 'The Urchin's Hair', the latter a brief extract from a book published in 1910, *What's Wrong With the World*. He was not yet a Catholic, but shared the viewpoint of the 1890 encyclical *Rerum Novarum* that the State serves to support the family, and not the other way round.

Yet what finally destroyed GKC's trust in the Liberal faith of his youth was the celebrated Marconi Scandal of 1912. It also, in his eyes, cost him his beloved brother.

> It is the fashion to divide recent history into Pre-War and Post-War conditions. I believe it is almost as essential to divide them into the Pre-Marconi and Post Marconi days ... [there is] the legend that we denounced certain Cabinet ministers because they gambled on the Stock Exchange ... The charge against the Marconi ministers was that they received a tip, or were 'let in on the ground floor' as the financial phrase goes, by a government contractor whose contract was at the time being considered by the Government. *Autobiography*

The facts of the matter were these: on 7 March 1912 the Postmaster General, Sir Herbert Samuel, awarded an enormous contract to the Marconi Company to build telegraph stations around the Empire; this was done in confidence and not public knowledge. The Managing Director of the Marconi Company, Godfrey Isaacs, decided to increase the share capital of its 55 per cent-owned subsidiary, the American Marconi Company (AMC). Godfrey issued new shares in AMC at par value of $5 (£1.06) to his brother, the Attorney General (Sir Rufus Isaacs), the Chancellor of the Exchequer (Lloyd George), and the Chief Whip (the Master of Elibank). The new AMC shares came to the stock market on 18 April at a price of £3.25, treble their nominal value. They rose to £4, at which point the politicians sold.

City rumours of these activities led to accusations in the House of Commons, and a major Parliamentary debate on the subject on 11 October 1912. Sir Rufus and Lloyd George both denied that they had bought shares in 'that company' which had just won the contract with the Government. Full details did not emerge until a Parliamentary Inquiry examined ministers in 1913. Asked why he had not even mentioned his AMC dealings in the debate, Chancellor Lloyd George scratched his head and replied, 'There was no time on a Friday afternoon.' In June 1913 Parliament voted on a motion 'that this House regrets the transactions of certain of its ministers in the shares of the Marconi Company of America, and the want of frankness displayed by Ministers in their communications on the subject to the House.' Voting was on strict party lines, and the motion was rejected. Under present-day law there is no doubt that the parties were guilty of a number of criminal offences under the 1987 Financial Services Act, as well as the ultimate political crime of lying to the House of Commons!

This scandal, and its rumour-driven nature, was meat and drink to the *Eye-Witness*. In January 1913 Cecil Chesterton went too far and accused Godfrey Isaacs of dishonest share promotion, for which there was no real evidence. Isaacs then took out a writ for criminal libel, a criminal offence for which the punishment included prison and hard labour. The cocky Cecil ignored Gilbert's pleas to back down and settle, and when the matter went to court he was humiliated. (Belloc avoided appearing as a witness.) Counsel for the prosecution was Sir Edward Carson, a brutal and formidable advocate. (Seventeen years before, his ruthless questioning had pierced the wit and self-confidence of Oscar Wilde, leaving him broken in the dock.) He tormented Cecil as a witness, forcing him to stammer, hesitate, and then withdraw most of his allegations. While the subsequent fine of £100 was less severe than it could have been, both Cecil and his family felt keenly that he had lost honour. To vindicate himself, he volunteered for the Western Front in 1916 at the age of 37, dying there two years later. Gilbert was devastated by Cecil's death, and blamed the Isaacs brothers for it.

In 1906 the Liberal party won a landslide victory in the General Election, but it never won a clear victory thereafter. The historian George Dangerfield devoted his book *The Strange Death of Liberal England* to asking why. While Prime Minister Asquith was beset with problems regarding Ireland

and trade union unrest, so had been Gladstone. For Chesterton the answer was a moral one: 'If my Victorian uncles had known, they would have been horrified and not amused; they would have put a stop to it somehow.' The old Liberals had advocated individual freedom based on the bedrock of a deep personal responsibility, the new Liberals merely saw freedom as an opportunity for personal enrichment. Foolishly they ignored the damage done to the respect by the governed for the governors. History may say that political worship of individual freedom and 'choice' has done similar damage in the 1990s.

History has certainly demonstrated the correctness of GKC's suspicions about Lloyd George and his circle. It was 50 years before the sheer scale of his speculations became apparent, and in particular, the way he and his henchman Maundy Gregory had sold peerages on a scale unknown even to the corrupt eighteenth century. The normally restrained *Oxford History of England* says of Lloyd George (known as 'The Goat'):

> He himself gave hostages to fortune (never in fact impounded) by the irregularity of his private life. He was the first prime minister since Walpole to leave office flagrantly richer than he entered it, the first since the Duke of Grafton to live openly with his mistress. Essentially his devious methods sprang from his nature. He could do things no other way.

The Road to Zion ...

Chesterton has sometimes been accused of being an anti-Semite, but this does not stand close examination. Anti-Semitism can be defined as a deep hatred of Jews, often coupled with a conspiracy theory about how they have deprived the theorist of his just deserts. Chesterton was totally unlike this; with the brief exception of the Isaacs brothers in the anguish of Cecil's death, he never hated anyone in his life. Throughout his life he had many Jewish friends, starting with the Solomon brothers at St Paul's. He met the original of Father Brown, Fr O'Connor, in Yorkshire following repeated visits to a Jewish friend there, Francis Steinthal. Not to mention GKC's friendship with one of the most celebrated Jewish writers of the day, Israel Zwangwill.

Why then has Chesterton been regarded as anti-Semitic? Partly because he contributed to the *Eye-Witness*, both of whose main lights, Cecil Chesterton and Hilaire Belloc, *were* openly anti-Semitic, although the unsubtle Cecil was much more blatant. (Belloc's 1922 book on *The Jews* begins: 'It is the thesis of this book that the continued presence of the Jewish nation intermixed with other nations alien to it presents a permanent problem of the gravest character.' In 1916 Cecil advocated putting rich Jews in concentration camps.) Belloc in particular was such a strong personality and influence on Gilbert that I think that most of Chesterton's anti-Semitic remarks were unconsciously picked up from the former, and thoughtlessly repeated. Offensive, yes; made with malicious aforethought, no. Margaret Halford was a Jewish actress who retired from the stage to live in Beaconsfield; she wrote later:

> I'm a stiff necked viper on the Jewish question ... I'd have foregone the pleasure of a personal friendship if his true attitude had not become so manifest ... the benevolence and love in the air were unmistakable, and irresistible.

More importantly, however, the one group he did persistently attack were the plutocrats, the men of new money who had come to dominate society in the Edwardian period. For a deep traditionalist like him, these *nouveau-riches* were buying up and undermining the historic roots of Old England.

They were not part of the social landscape. Unlike the old aristocracy they were replacing, they had no sense of responsibilities and duties. He disliked them more when they were foreigners, and the most obviously foreign were some of the great Jewish bankers and industrialists. Yet while he occasionally uses the word 'Jew' in a way which sends shudders down a modern spine, he only ever uses it thus when he sees them as the rich and powerful taking away what has always belonged to the people. A good example comes from an extract from the *Song of Quoodle* (a dog):

> They haven't got no noses,
> The fallen sons of Eve;
> Even the smell of roses
> Is not what they supposes;
> But more than the mind discloses
> And more than men believe.
>
> They haven't got no noses,
> They cannot even tell
> When door and darkness closes
> The park a Jew encloses,
> Where even the Law of Moses
> Will let you steal a smell.

This poem was based on a real incident. Although, as he was the first to state, this was only carrying on the aristocratic policy of enclosing common land which had brought the agricultural population to starvation over the two preceding centuries. Yet to repeat, this does not make him an anti-Semite; what he hated about these men was their new money, and the way they used it, not the fact that they were Jewish. In 1911 he gave a lecture to the Jewish Society in the East End. The *Jewish Chronicle* reported: 'Mr Chesterton said that speaking generally, as with most other communities, poor Jews were nice and the rich were nasty.' Chesterton never attacked the poor and the weak, which included the great mass of Jewish people. Many of them were recent immigrants, having fled the horrors of pogroms in Tsarist Russia, living in poverty in areas like London's East End. Contemporary Jewish writers such as Dr Eder made similar attacks, accusing rich Jews such as the Rothschilds of betraying their poor co-religionists in their haste to assimilate into the English aristocracy.

Chesterton's youth had also left him with a nose for moral evil. In 1930s Britain world-weariness and appeasement made criticism of Germany highly unpopular. GKC, however, was one of the first to point out in 1933 the horrors of Hitlerism, at a time when most people in the country refused to believe that such things could be possible. This is yet another example of Chesterton's great insight. There is also his biting satire on Goering, when that individual had just taken over as German minister of justice in 1933. Rabbi Wise, a leader of American Jewry, stated: 'I deeply respected him. When Hitlerism came, he was one of the first to speak out with the directness and frankness of a great and unabashed spirit'. In 1934 GKC wrote:

> The Germans will find it very difficult to cut up their culture on a principle of anti-Semitic amputation. They will find it difficult to persuade any German, let alone any European who is fond of Germany, that Schiller is a poet and Heine is not, that Goethe is a critic and Lessing is not ... [this is] the Prussian great illusion of pride, for which thousands of Jews have recently been rabbled or ruined or driven from their homes ... I am certainly not enough of an anti-Semite to say that it served them right.

The late twentieth century has developed the doctrine of political correctness, racism being one of its most heinous sins. Yet the meaning of the term has broadened; it once referred to hating a certain group of people, physically attacking them, denying them a decent job or housing, as in the late unlamented apartheid regime of South Africa. No Christian would argue with this defence of human rights. Yet it is now used to state that no negative remarks may be made about any ethnic group, even in jest, or whether factually correct. History will judge whether this is the late twentieth century's great contribution to the moral advancement of mankind, or just a temporary fashion. Chesterton might well have described the mindset of political correctness as 'totalitarian', and this constriction of language has some resemblance to 'Newspeak' in Orwell's *1984*. Indeed, it could be argued that political correctness is an 'ethic of resentment', a brooding on the real or imagined wrongs done to certain groups in the past, and as such opposed to the Christian aim of forgiveness. In GKC's words: 'Love makes everything lovely; hate concentrates itself on the one thing hated.'

We must remember that Chesterton was a man of his time, and that Edwardian society thought it only natural to poke fun at strangers, and we cannot condemn him for holding such attitudes. (The Edwardians would, of course, have closed down most of our media on the grounds of pornography, imprisoned homosexuals, and regarded our abortions as a crime against humanity.) The Weiner Library is the UK's main centre for the study of anti-Semitism and examination of the Holocaust. In my opinion their observations on Chesterton are spot on:

> The difference between social and philosophical
> anti-Semitism is something which is not fully
> understood … With Chesterton we've never thought
> of a man who was seriously anti-Semitic on either
> count. He was a man who played along, and for that
> he must pay a price … He was not an enemy, and

when the real testing time came along he showed
what side he was on.

One last thought. Chesterton was a convinced Zionist,
demanding a national homeland for Jewish people. Advanced
views for 1910, and ones that looked even more unrealistic
than most of his ideas at this time. On a visit to Palestine in
1920 he again met Dr Eder, with whom he had campaigned
in Britain for the Zionist cause, the latter taking him to see
Chaim Weizman, the first President of the future Israel. The
first recognition that the creation of a Jewish state in Palestine
was a practical possibility was the Balfour Declaration in
1917, a letter from the former British Prime Minister Arthur
Balfour. Until 1918 Palestine was part of the devoutly Muslim
Ottoman (Turkish) empire. The Jewish population was tiny
and Jewish immigration would not have been encouraged.
(In fact, given the corruption and brutality of the Ottomans
no one in their right mind would have wanted to live in
Turkish-ruled Palestine, except possibly T.E. Lawrence.)
Palestine was conquered by General Allenby in the Great
War, after which Britain was given a League of Nations
mandate to administer it. Only at that point did Jewish immigration become a real possibility. Chesterton was acquainted
with Balfour, and it seems likely that he was an influence on
Balfour's thinking. If GKC is accused of anti-Semitism we
should also remember that he made a contribution to the
foundation of the State of Israel.

... And the Path to Rome

The move to Beaconsfield in 1909 reduced some of the pres-
sures on Gilbert, but it could not stop them. Once his weight
exceeded 18 stones (252 pounds) in 1911, he began to suffer
from gout and water retention, his whole body becoming

puffed up and swollen. The mind too was reeling from the catastrophe of Marconi. He had been brought up with an unquestioning faith in Liberalism, which had collapsed. Worse still, his beloved brother had lost his reputation in the libel court. The greater catastrophe of the outbreak of the Great War in August 1914 was the final straw. Chesterton saw, unlike many of his contemporaries, that this would not be a brief glorious affair as was generally thought, but: 'a war of defence, by its nature one from which a man comes back battered and bleeding and boasting only that he is not dead.'

The strain was too much, and he totally collapsed in November 1914. Initially the illness was physical: a mixture of bronchitis, heart strain and gout. (Not only was Gilbert grossly overweight, but also a heavy cigar smoker.) Total rest eased the situation until Christmas Eve 1914, when he slipped into unconsciousness. The exact cause of this is unknown, but it fits the Victorian diagnosis of 'brain fever''' Death seemed near over the next three months, but by Easter recovery was clearly under way, and by June 1915 convalescence was almost complete.

Shaw wrote to him:'You have carried out a theory of mine that every man of genius has a critical illness at forty, Nature's object being to make him go to bed for several months. Sometimes Nature overdoes it: Schiller and Mozart died.' Immediately after his reception into the Catholic Church GKC wrote a sonnet called 'The Convert', whose final line is: 'Because I am Lazarus and I live.' We may wonder whether this reflects awareness of how close to death he had come. Chesterton also lost a lot of weight during this illness, coming down to around 16 stones (224 pounds), which explains the renewed physical vigour he showed over the next ten years: a visit to Ireland in 1918, Palestine in 1919–20, the US in 1920 and 1930, as well as journeys to Poland and Rome.

Chesterton's illness confronted Frances with a moral dilemma. Before lapsing into unconsciousness, Gilbert mentioned being buried in Kensal Green cemetery – but that was mainly, although not exclusively, a Roman Catholic burial ground, and strongly associated with the Catholic Church. While there had been rumours for years that Chesterton was considering leaving the Church of England for Roman Catholicism, partly due to his keen friendship with Fr O'Connor, he had said nothing to her. Matters worsened in the spring of 1915 when Fr O'Connor appeared at Beaconsfield, plainly expecting to admit Gilbert into the Church and possibly administer the last rites. Although the priest was a good friend of them both, Frances refused to let him see the invalid, and he had to leave. When Chesterton recovered, he refused to discuss the subject, although he had told Fr O'Connor in 1912 that he was thinking of converting to Rome, but was held back by Frances. She was a devout Anglo-Catholic, a part of the Church of England, which under the influence of Newman in the 1830s, had re-introduced much Catholic ritual back into Anglican usage.

The detective priest Father Brown is probably GKC's best-known fictional creation. His origins were thus. In 1909 the Chestertons were visiting Fr O'Connor in Yorkshire when, after dinner one evening, Gilbert mentioned certain morbid fantasies to the priest; to his surprise the latter knew far more about them than he did. Shortly afterwards GKC met two Cambridge undergraduates who mused aloud what a sheltered life a priest must lead. This gave him the idea for the first Father Brown story, *The Blue Cross*. This incident also set him thinking about the depths of his own soul, and whether he had really cleansed them:

> It brought me in a manner face to face once more with those morbid but vivid problems of the soul, to which I have earlier alluded and gave me a great and growing sense that I had not found any real spiritual solution of them … That the Catholic Church knew

more about good than I did was easy to believe. That
she knew more about evil than I did seemed
incredible.

Like many obviously good people, Chesterton always had a
deep sense of his own sinfulness. Whenever he was asked later
why he had converted to Rome, the reply was always the
same, 'for my sins'. He was not joking. Such humility is a sure
touchstone of deep spiritual worth. He always felt that the
world should be: 'taken with gratitude, and not for granted ...
I never saw the two sides of this truth stated together
anywhere, until I happened to open the Penny Catechism, and
read the words, "The two sins against Hope are presumption
and despair."' He was later to say that joining the Catholic
Church was the most important act of his life, and it was
something which he agonized about for over ten years, until it
was achieved in 1922. It was not just a question of personal
scruples, but ties of friends and family also held him back.

Quite apart from Frances herself, he had a number of deep
friendships with Anglo-Catholics who were bound to feel let
down if he crossed over to Rome. What he had learned from
Frances was how actually to practise a religion, as opposed to
theorizing about it. From Anglo-Catholic priests like Conrad
Noel and Percy Dearmer, he learned about the sacraments,
and the purpose of liturgy, and also gained a deep devotion
to Mary. The key role of Anglo-Catholicism in deepening
Chesterton's understanding of Christianity has been little
explored; most of his biographers have been literary men to
whom it is of little interest, while earlier Roman Catholic
authors like Maisie Ward tended to down play it. Conrad
Noel was the priest who married Gilbert and Frances in
1901. According to the *Autobiography*:

the Anglo-Catholic group ... was in fact a very fine
body of men, to which I for one shall always feel a

gratitude like that of my brother and the blind man in the Scripture ... When Conrad Noel first appeared on the horizon of my brother and myself, my brother was frankly anti-religious and I had no religion except the very haziest religiosity.

Many Anglo-Catholics were also active in campaigning for better conditions for the poor via the Christian Social Union. GKC later wrote a little poem which seems to satirize them: 'And so they sing a lot of hymns, to help the Unemployed.' This impression is a mistake which ignores the traditional English habit of teasing the things which we love. The *Autobiography* describes them thus: 'good friends and very gay companions.' He also had his family, as well as his friends, to contend with.

Although Gilbert was baptized into the Church of England, he was brought up by his parents as a Unitarian, like themselves. This eighteenth-century sect was a typical product of the Enlightenment. It denied the Godhead of Christ, and replaced the Trinity by the Unity of a creator God. By the late nineteenth century its creative energies were running thin, so that Unitarianism became little more than a group of normally prosperous and well-educated people obeying a code of good behaviour. In other words, it came to resemble an ethical society, the opposite extreme from the dogmas and rituals of Roman Catholicism. The Chesterton family were scandalized in 1911 when Cecil became a Catholic. GKC adored his father, 'Mr Ed', and I think it highly likely that a desire not to offend his father delayed his own conversion more than worrying about Frances. It is noteworthy that Gilbert's own conversion occurred in July 1922, four months after Mr Ed's death, and four years before Frances was ready to follow him.

Finally, while Chesterton never worried what people thought about him personally, he was very aware of having an audience of ordinary people who listened to him, whom he did not want to alienate. While Cardinal Hume is a national figure enjoying universal respect, people forget how recently Catholicism in the UK has joined the mainstream of British life. Until the 1960s this was not so, with the Catholic Church still viewed by many as an alien element built on the backs of the poor Irish. It was still regarded as vaguely disrespectable at the beginning of this century. People felt that it was their patriotic duty to support the Church of England, not this monolithic edifice with its ghetto mentality and Irish priests. Intellectuals particularly were convinced that Rome demanded a man's conscience as part of the entry fee.

The *Autobiography* reports Johnston Stephen saying:

> The only little difficulty that I have about joining the
> Catholic Church is that I do not think that I believe in
> God. All the rest of the Catholic system, so obviously
> right and so obviously superior to anything else, that I
> cannot imagine anyone having any doubt about it ...
> he was gratified when I told him that real Catholics are
> intelligent enough to have this difficulty; and that
> St Thomas Aquinas practically begins his whole
> argument by saying, 'Is there any God? Apparently not.'

This was probably also Chesterton's own position from his discovery of orthodoxy in 1900 until his own severe illness in 1914. But that and Cecil's death were the kind of deep shock which forces a man to look into the depths of his being. Gilbert increasingly took counsel from his friends Maurice Baring and Fr Ronald Knox, both of whom had been through a conversion experience themselves. Chesterton later wrote in a little booklet, *The Catholic Church and Conversion*:

The convert is a man who discovers the truth, deepens his knowledge and understanding, and then finds he is gripped by it and tries to run away. He has come too near to the truth, and has forgotten that truth is a magnet, with the powers of attraction and repulsion ... To a certain extent it is a fear which attaches to all sharp irreversible decisions; it is suggested in all the old jokes about the shakiness of the bridegroom at the wedding or the recruit who takes the King's shilling [i.e. joins the army] and gets drunk partly to celebrate, partly also to forget.

Anglo-Catholicism had helped him see the coherent and consistent scheme of thought which lay behind Christian belief. Yet while it contained much of the truth, it left out other parts. Chesterton also saw that it was in a difficult position, for the truths which he and the Anglo-Catholic movement most loved were not always accepted by the Church of England, of which the movement was a part. There seemed only one institution which both possessed an authority which had safeguarded truth right from the early days of the Church, and which also had a vast but complete system of belief. For a mind like GKC's, which saw truth as an interlocking puzzle of manifold truths reflecting different aspects of a transcendent and incarnate reality, joining the Catholic Church was almost predestined.

Long afterwards I found what I meant stated much better by a Catholic writer: 'God is not infinite; He is the synthesis of infinity and boundary.' ... the other teachers were always men of one idea, even when their one idea was universality ... I have only found one creed that could not be satisfied with a truth, but only with the Truth, which is made of a million such truths and yet is one.

The last piece of the jigsaw was the visit to Jerusalem in 1920. He arrived expecting a modern city, and found a medieval town which reminded him of the crusaders who had fought to get there, and to bring the Cross with them. Visiting the key sites of the New Testament also made him reconsider the gospels and the nature of the historical Jesus. These deliberations were to appear as the subject of one of his greatest books, *The Everlasting Man*, a few years later. It enabled him finally to slough off any remaining Unitarian inhibitions. He saw plainly that Jesus was no minor Jewish prophet, still less the social reformer proclaimed in his youth. Madman yes; blasphemer yes; or someone more than human. On the way back to England he and his companions stopped at the Italian port of Brindisi, where they entered a small and undistinguished Catholic chapel. There he bowed to Mary: 'It was in front of a gilded and very gaudy little image of her in the port of Brindisi that I promised the thing that I would do, if I returned to my own land.'

On Sunday 30 July 1922 Fr O'Connor admitted Gilbert Keith Chesterton into the Catholic Church. At this time Beaconsfield had no Catholic church, so the ceremony took place in a little shed which was part of the Railway Hotel. I doubt if GKC noticed. Frances wept throughout the ceremony. The *Autobiography* ends with a description of how as a child he had seen the figure of a man with a golden key in his toy theatre:

> But I know that he who is called Pontifex, the Builder of the Bridge, is also called Claviger, the Bearer of the Key; and that such keys were given to him to bind and loose when he was a small fisher in a far province, beside a small and almost secret sea.

Of course, one of the earliest titles of the Papacy is that of Pontiff, builder of bridges between this world and the next. Gilbert had come home. (See also the poem 'The Convert' on page 114.)

The Dumb Ox

In 1920 the post-war economic boom came to an end, and Britain slipped into a depressed economic state that persisted until the Second World War. There were no 'Roaring Twenties' here. Although prices had doubled during the Great War, a mistaken economic policy of restoring the pound to its pre-war value against the dollar made many industries uncompetitive. At the same time, the technological boost given by the war resulted in the rapid growth of new industries such as artificial fibres and consumer electricals, particularly in the United States; Britain's traditional heavy industries such as shipbuilding and mining found themselves left behind. The result was high unemployment and union militancy throughout the 'twenties; 1926 saw the only General Strike in British history. In short, money was tight throughout the twenties, with the thirties even worse as the Great Depression hit.

When Cecil went off to war in 1917 he entrusted his little magazine to his brother. When he did not come back, Gilbert felt it a sacred duty to ensure the *New Witness*'s survival. Paper was cheap and money abundant before the Great War. Many literary and philosophical magazines flourished then: *The Speaker*, Shaw's mouthpiece the *New Age*, *The Atheneum* as well as the *New Witness*. All fell on hard times during the war, and few survived it. The *New Witness* was in dire financial straits when GKC took over, and the changing intellectual climate after the Armistice in 1918 meant that sales continued to drop. It finally went under in 1923. To revive it against this economic background was a Labour of Sisyphis, but Gilbert was determined to do so. To achieve this he used up the family fortune inherited from Mr Ed, and went on fund-raising trips to the US in 1920 and 1930.

Finally, in 1925 the magazine was re-launched under the title of *GK's Weekly*. Chesterton hated the title, but was advised by Shaw that his was the only name to make anyone buy it. Until his death he was both its Editor and main writer, the latter usually requiring a fifteen-hundred-word leader article and a major piece of two thousand words. Cecil's pugnacious nature and vehement and vitriolic opinions made him an asset to a satirical magazine. Brisk, hard-working and decisive, he possessed the management skills an editor needs, and an owner/editor needs in spades. Gilbert Chesterton in contrast had no managerial skills, and the magazine lurched from crisis to crisis. It was persistently loss-making, and GKC had to raid his limited coffers to keep it going, which often involved writing yet another book review or Father Brown story.

Maisie Ward was aware of the colossal drain, physical, emotional and financial, which the magazine represented:

> Who can blame Frances Chesterton if she desired to withdraw her husband from quarrels that shattered the peace of mind of the dearest being in her world, a person to whom her whole life was dedicated ... was it worthwhile? ... he would have been a lesser man had he abandoned it. And yet at moments imagining the poetry, the philosophy that might have been ours – another *White Horse*, another *Everlasting Man* – I am tempted to wish that these years had not been sacrificed to the paper which enshrined his brother's memory.

It is probably true that the effort required to produce and sustain the magazine shortened GKC's life, and it is certainly true that the two-year gap between the expiry of the *New Witness* and the launch of *GK's Weekly* saw the creation of two of his best works: *St Francis* and *The Everlasting Man*. Gilbert himself never doubted: 'In the end it will not greatly matter whether we wrote well or ill, but it will greatly matter on which side we fought.' He wanted to preserve his brother's memory, and also he wanted a platform to speak to the ordinary man or woman. Not only had most of the independent magazines gone out of business, but Fleet Street itself was a very different place.

Around 1900 the Harmsworth Brothers had copied William Randolph Hearst's invention in San Francisco of the 'yellow press' and brought it to Britain. Sensationalist stories and huge headlines built large circulations which were attractive to advertisers and politicians alike. By the 1920s the British Press was dominated by the Harmsworth group on the one hand, centred on the *Daily Mail* and the *Daily Mirror*, and Beaverbrook Newspapers on the other, with its *Daily Express* flagship. These newspaper barons demanded that their writers toe the party line, which GKC refused to do. They then blacklisted him from writing for any of their papers, i.e. most of Fleet Street. He could have written for other papers on travel and literature – the *Daily Telegraph* sponsored the visit to Palestine – but he was not interested in surrendering his independence and in 'writing articles on the back of advertisements'.

Dorothy Collins was GKC's secretary over the last ten years of his life. She noted how hard he worked, writing thirteen to fourteen thousand words each week on top of the regular magazine articles which were needed. Each day he would start writing at 10.30 and, with two breaks, continue into the early hours of the morning. In the second half of the 'twenties his weight ballooned again, always a bad sign. In photographs he often looks exhausted. GKC's friend and translator into French was the Belgian professor Cammaerts, who described him carrying out his labours like a ploughman:

> Every new sentence was a new furrow; when he had reached the end of it, he turned his horse's head around and started another, indifferent to the weather … When he was too tired to go on ploughing, he sat

under a hedge at the top of the hill and surveyed the landscape of his memory and dreamed of Browning and Dickens and Cobbett and Francis and Thomas – of all those who, by deed or word, had helped to keep his furrows straight.

I would say that the image is almost right: for it is not the ploughman who does the really heavy work, but the steady strength of the horse or ox which drives the plough forward. Dr Johnson is a well known influence on Chesterton, but perhaps he was most inspired by a 'dumb ox', the nickname of the great medieval philosopher St Thomas Aquinas. Tall and of great physical bulk, Aquinas obtained the name because his great intellectual powers seemed to develop relatively late. Fellow students at the newly opened University of Paris noticed how he attended lectures, but never said anything. (In reality, he probably saw through the teaching he was given, but had not yet found the answers he sought.) Yet once Aquinas began to teach in his late twenties, his genius was immediately recognized, and he spent the rest of his life developing the teachings of the Church.

In fact, Aquinas deserved the name 'dumb ox' in another way. He put himself into the traces of the intellectual plough, and ceaselessly laboured in these fields, doing the work of many men. He died, probably of exhaustion, aged fifty. Aquinas' whole life was totally focused on God; his amanuensis Br Reginald stated that: 'His marvellous science was far less due to the power of his genius than to the efficacy of his prayer'. Or as Aquinas himself said, 'It is holiness using natural talents to witness to the truth and spending itself to make truth reign supreme.'

Chesterton physically was another 'dumb ox', his great mind also slow to show what it could do. Once he joined the Catholic Church, he too willingly put himself into harness and fought in its colours for the truth. For the rest of his life, as well as his normal output of books and articles, he forced his exhausted body to defend the faith in print, to give regular lectures for the Catholic Evidence Guild, and to help raise money for it. As a young and rapidly growing church, the Catholic Church in England was desperately short of funds. Since there was no Catholic church in Beaconsfield, the Chestertons helped build one from their own scanty resources. As Fr Knox was to say in his memorial address in the great requiem Mass held in Westminster Abbey, 'his health had begun to decline, and he was overworked, partly through our fault'.

Chesterton's last masterpiece was his 1933 book on St Thomas, a book nobody else could have written. He brings the medieval philosopher alive, and cuts through the complexity of his thought to reveal its importance and eternal relevance. The distinguished contemporary expert on Thomas, Etienne Gilson, bowed down before it:

> I consider it as being without possible comparison the best book ever written on St Thomas. Nothing short of genius can account for such achievement ... the few readers who have spent twenty or thirty years in study of St Thomas cannot fail to perceive that the so-called wit of Chesterton has put their scholarship to shame. He has grasped all that which they had tried to demonstrate, and he has said all that which they were more or less clumsily attempting to express in academic formulas.

I mentioned before the physical and mental similarities between the two men. It is almost inconceivable to see how Chesterton, with no philosophic training and in such a short period of time, could have written *St Thomas Aquinas*. He was exhausted himself, in his late fifties, heavily overweight, plagued with heart trouble and bronchitis. Nor was he free to concentrate on the great medieval master; there were the three weekly essays to produce for the *Illustrated London News* and *GK's Weekly*, as well as all the loathsome management tasks for the latter. It seems to me that the only possible answer lies in the words of Cardinal Newman: '*cor ad cor loquitur*' – one heart speaking to another.

By the 1930s GKC had become a prophet of orthodoxy and of the meaning of life against the decadents and pessimists who had returned in the wake on the Great War. 'I have read modern poems obviously meant to make grass something merely scrubby and purely repugnant like an unshaven chin.' The BBC discovered that he was a natural radio broadcaster, and he appeared frequently from 1932. By 1934 he was ill with heart fatigue, bronchitis and chronic exhaustion – he frequently fell asleep – yet he continued to work. His last major work was a broadcast in March 1936 called *The Spice of Life*. (An extract is printed on pages 217–20.) In it he attacks modern poets like T.S. Eliot for their obsession with misery and insignificance:

> You have to be happy in those quiet moments when you remember that you are alive; not in those noisy moments when you forget ... T.S. Eliot has described [modern pessimism] in *The Hollow Men*: 'This is the way the world ends, not with a bang but with a whimper.' Now forgive me if I say, in my old-world fashion, that I'm damned if I ever felt like that ... I say to the young pessimists: And they may end with a whimper, but we will end with a bang.

Anyone can be positive in health and prosperity; but surely the measure of a man is how he copes with misfortune, ill-health, old age and the prospect of his own death. Compare the voice of the dying GKC with that of H.G. Wells in his final work, *Mind at the End of its Tether*, published nine years later. The former apostle of progress now denied his earlier optimism, saying that, 'there is no shape of things to come'. (The book was written in 1944 before the public had heard of the atomic bomb.) The prospect of his own death oppressed Wells and filled his thoughts, and he now expanded this soapbox pessimism to the planet as a whole: 'This world is at the end of its tether. The end of everything we call life is close at hand and cannot be evaded.'

In the spring of 1936 Chesterton became weaker and weaker; a visit to Lourdes was tried, but to no avail; it was obvious he was dying. Dorothy Collins requested the newspapers not to bother the family. It is a sign of the enormous respect in which GKC was held by Fleet Street that they complied. As he lay dying on 14 June 1936 the Dominican priest Vincent McNabb paid Chesterton the honour of singing over him the *Salve Regina,* the great medieval hymn which is sung over dying members of the Dominican order. A song to the Virgin (in English it begins 'Hail holy queen, mother of mercy'), it was appropriate given Gilbert's devotion to Our Lady. Cardinal Pacelli, the future Pope Pius XII, sent a telegram: 'Holy Father deeply grieved death of Mr Gilbert Keith Chesterton. Devoted son of Holy Church, gifted Defender of Catholic Faith. His Holiness offers paternal sympathy to people of England.'

No man can accurately record his own death, but Chesterton came near in *St Thomas Aquinas:*

> his strange end came upon him with great strides ... those men must have known that a great mind was still labouring like a great mill in the midst of them ... It must have resembled some mighty modern engine, shaking the ramshackle building in which it is for the moment enclosed ... In the world of that mind there was a wheel of angels, and a wheel of plants or of animals; but there was also a just and intelligible order

of all things, a sane authority and a self-respecting liberty, and a hundred answers to a hundred questions in the complexity of ethics or economics ... But there must have been a moment, when men knew that the thunderous mill of thought had stopped suddenly; and that after the shock of stillness that wheel would shake the world no more; there was nothing now within that hollow house but a great hill of clay.

The Importance of Chesterton

The Sleep of Reason Bringeth Forth Monsters

There is something very wrong with the twentieth century. Yet its most distinctive characteristic is rarely commented upon – its abnormal pessimism. We must be the most miserable inhabitants of Western Europe since the Black Death. The fourteenth century had reason to feel despair after that plague. The last inhabitants of the Roman Empire had a right to lament in the fifth century as the barbarian hordes emerged to wreck everything. To weep and wail after catastrophe is understandable; to do so in the midst of technological advance and material abundance seems perverse. Western civilization, now including North America of course, was built upon action and optimism, upon the enquiring mind, ever since the pioneering work of the Ancient Greeks. Only the twentieth century has had both the folly and the colossal egotism to turn its back on the past, and choose choice and unreason. But then, as GKC reminds us: 'when men stop believing in God, they don't start believing in nothing; they believe in anything.'

Much of this pessimism derives from the miserable outlook of the so-called 'thinkers' of the day, a process which started at the end of the nineteenth century with writers like Ibsen and Hardy. Twentieth-century art and literature has been dominated by such gloom about life, calling it pointless, meaningless, vacant. The author/artist feels alone and in despair. Chesterton watched this process from its beginning:

> Hardy became a sort of village atheist brooding and blaspheming over the village idiot ... [he] has the honour of inventing a new sort of game which may be called the extravagance of depression. The placing of the weak lover and his new love in such a place that they actually see the black flag announcing that Tess has been hanged is utterly inexcusable in art and probability; it is a cruel practical joke. But it is a practical joke at which even its author cannot brighten up enough to laugh. *The Victorian Age in Literature*

T.S. Eliot declaimed that men cannot bear too much reality, a fitting motto for a culture built on media escapism and drugs: legal and prescribed. On the contrary, if the concept of sanity means anything, it surely consists of knowing and working with reality. We seem to be denying our intellectual birthright. Chesterton is the only great literary figure that this century has produced without this taint that I can think of. *Orthodoxy* starts with the author's aim: 'the desirability of an active and imaginative life.' When in the 1950s a psychiatrist was asked how he defined sanity, his reply was: 'If you want to know sanity, read Chesterton!' The one thing GKC really hated was pessimism. As he wrote in his notebooks: 'Is a man proud of losing his hearing, eyesight, or sense of smell? What shall we say of him who prides himself on beginning as an intellectual cripple and ending as an intellectual corpse?' This unique optimism is the first and the greatest reason to read Chesterton.

In this he is like C.S. Lewis, who called his spiritual autobiography *Surprised By Joy*. The shy don and the boisterous journalist could not have been further apart in terms of personality, but both were recognized and recognizable by their joy in life. In accordance with the teachings of the Church, and the traditional wisdom of most other cultures, Chesterton and Lewis scorned the 'fool's gold' offered by the worship of greed, of material possessions and of sensuality. Both found that self-restraint and the attempt to live a moral life were hard work, but infinitely worthwhile.

GKC often uses the analogy of a complicated key and a complex mechanism; when the right key is inserted, the mechanism turns and everything goes into its correct order. He sees morality as that key to sanity. As both Chesterton and Merton, and many others, have found, self-indulgence leads to the disintegration of the personality, and greater and more frequent indulgence in the drug of immediate gratification in order to keep the personal demons at bay. But this merely feeds and strengthens them, leading to ultimate degradation. Adopting a course of humility and obedience, in contrast, leads to things falling back into place; the sense of constant mental anguish disappears, and is replaced by a sense of joy and of being at ease with the world – in other words – *sanity*.

GKC was an intuitive and instinctive thinker, a poet rather than a philosopher. Yet we should not imagine from this that there was anything trivial about him. In Dr Johnson's words, he believed that 'The business of a poet is to examine not the individual but the species; to remark general properties and large appearances. He does not number the streaks of the tulip.' All his life he showed the classic traits of genius: universality and foresight. Of his universality let it be merely said that other talents have seen the elements of themselves they most want in Chesterton, be it as essayist, thinker, novelist, poet or debater. Yet all these talents added up seem too much to have come from one man. Another aspect is completeness; unlike ordinary mortals a genius appears to spring into being fully made. Lesser creatures learn their trade; a genius merely becomes aware of what he can do. When Chesterton described St Francis in these terms, he also described himself:

> He was a character ... a humorist especially in the old English sense of a man always in his humour, going his own way and doing what nobody else would have done ... the most familiar example is Dr Johnson ... the atmosphere can only be defined by a sort of antithesis; the act is always unexpected, and never inappropriate ... It is surprisingly and yet inevitably individual. *St Francis*

Chesterton adored Dr Johnson, that great writer of the eighteenth century, and often characterized him in debate. Like Johnson, he had a distinctive pithy style which lent itself to filling books of aphorisms. He also shared with the Doctor a natural and highly quotable wit, coupled with a strong moral sense, a rare combination. (On his second trip to the US in 1930 GKC debated the topic of science and religion in New York with the acclaimed lawyer Clarence Darrow, victor of the 1921 'monkey trial'. At one moment the microphone failed, at which point Chesterton bellowed out 'Science, you see, *is not* infallible,' to universal laughter.)

The Enlightenment of the eighteenth century saw philosophers such as David Hume deny for the first time that there was any such thing as objective morality. When he heard this Johnson replied, 'If he does really think that there is no distinction between virtue and vice, why, Sir, when he leaves our houses let us count our spoons.' Both the message and the tone could have been GKC's. Perhaps the greatest similarity was a view of life based on common sense and acceptance of the native understanding of ordinary people. Johnson: 'About things on which the public thinks long, it commonly attains to think right.'

Chesterton's admiration for Dr Johnson is well known. What is less well known is how both men stand in that peculiarly English tradition of the conservative revolutionary. The line starts right at the birth of English as a language, with William Langland and his great poem *Piers Plowman*, in the fourteenth century, and goes on to include Bunyan, and William Cobbett – a not undistinguished list. A revolutionary since the author is disgusted at the society in which he finds himself and which he desires to change; a conservative since his beliefs are based on morals rather than politics or class envy, and he looks back to the past for inspiration. Compare GKC's tone with that of Langland, writing about 1360.

> And in the apparel of a poor man and a pilgrim's likeness
> Many times has God been met among poor people.
> And in a friar's frock once was he found
> But it is far ago in St Francis' time.

The Democracy of Language

Anthony Burgess once noted: 'He wrote too well, too sincerely and vigorously to earn a mere niche in a museum.' Richard Ingrams is a well-known British writer who was for many years the Editor of *Private Eye*, a kind of spiritual descendant of the *Eye-Witness*. He makes the good point that:

> Chesterton is often spoken of as a neglected writer whose books have long been unavailable since his death. But judging by the frequency with which he is quoted by all sorts of people – generally speaking, a good test – he has never been neglected, nor is it even the case that his books are out of print.

The democratic aspect of this would have delighted GKC, who shackled himself to the treadmill of journalism in order to make his work available to the man or woman in the street. A literary establishment advocating welfarism, pessimism and free love may do its best to ignore him. But ignore him you cannot; as Ingrams says, the democratic process of language ensures that his thoughts remain buoyant among us, and ordinary people continue to buy his books. Chesterton is without doubt the twentieth century's most important creator of aphorisms; like Dr Johnson, the combination of wit and insight makes them irresistible. (I counted 56 references to GKC in *The Faber Book of Aphorisms*; Shaw got 10, and Wells and Orwell nil.) To take just a few lines from *What's Wrong With the World*:

> If a thing is worth doing, it is worth doing badly.
>
> The only true free thinker is he whose intellect is as much free from the future as from the past.
>
> The Christian ideal has not been tried and found wanting. It has been found difficult; and left untried.
>
> There is one metaphor of which the moderns are very fond; they are always saying, 'You can't put the clock back'. The simple and obvious answer is, 'You can'. A clock, being a piece of human construction, can be restored by the finger to any hour. In the same way society, being a piece of human construction, can be reconstructed upon any plan that has ever existed.
>
> There is another proverb, 'As you have made your bed so must you lie on it', which again is simply a lie. If I have made my bed uncomfortable, please God I will make it again.

Chesterton's literary criticism is not respectable in most academic circles. A modern GKC might argue that current literary scholarship increasingly seems to resemble the hieratic system of ancient Egypt, or the mandarins of old China, with able minds pouring over commentaries on older studies of the dust-ridden classics written thousands of years before. Chesterton was totally unlike this; when he wrote *Browning* he did not spend years following the well-known 'slughorn' controversy between Professor Lucifer and Dr Munchhausen. He simply read and reread Browning until he could get into his mind, until he could see the world as Browning saw it.

Academics, with few exceptions, have always hated this approach. (An important exception is Harold Bloom, Professor of Humanities at Yale, who praises GKC highly in his recent book, *The Western Canon*. This is understandable since Bloom is trying to isolate books and ideas which are canonical, i.e. have helped define Western culture.) When Chesterton's works on Browning, Dickens and Stevenson appeared, they were all acclaimed by people who knew these authors and their works. Yet they are rarely quoted in modern academic studies on the subjects. But this was always GKC's method, which explains the overwhelming freshness of his work. For example, it is a now commonplace observation that truly great works of fiction cannot be transposed to television – too much of subtlety is lost. The second- and third-rate work much better. Not a well-known opinion seventy years ago, but here is Chesterton: 'The worst novel makes the best play.' The ubiquity of his aphorisms is a sign that the public loves Chesterton even if the critics do not. Another is that popular genre – the detective story.

In Julian Symon's history of crime and detective stories, *Bloody Murder*, the doyen of British crime writers rates Father Brown highly: 'It seemed to me still that the best of these tales are among the finest short crime stories ever written.' Julian Symons also notes, like many others, the author's unique ability to make the world seem a different place, but self-evident once we have arrived there: 'The very merit of Chesterton is his ability to ignore such things (the usual mechanics), to leave out everything extraneous to the single theme he wants to develop, and yet to provide a clue that is blindingly obvious once we have accepted the premises of the story and the character of Father Brown.'

The Father Brown stories were immensely popular when they came out, and have always stayed in print. The little shabby priest is unique, for he is an expert on morals rather than on the residue of cigar ash or the minutiae of railway timetables. Critics have sometimes complained about the arbitrariness of the solutions, but this misses the point. Chesterton founded no school of priestly detectives, unlike all the imitators of Conan Doyle or Agatha Christie. The reason for this was not the complexity of his plots, which were not difficult, or the intricate construction of his stories, for they were loose. No, although there is some brilliant macabre scene-setting in many of the Father Brown stories, they present little technical difficulty in analysing and in attempting to copy. What does make imitation impossible is the fact that the key to the stories is the moral insight of the detective. Father Brown says: 'When I tried to imagine the state of mind in which a thing could be done, I always realized that I might have done it under certain mental conditions, and not others; and not generally the obvious ones. And then, of course, I knew who really had done it.'

GKC described him as 'a Catholic priest [of] external simplicity and internal subtlety ... his commonplace exterior was meant to contrast with his unexpected vigilance'. Whereas Sherlock Holmes and Sexton Blake and many others were amateurs, Father Brown is a professional who is good at what he does. Malefactors give clues which to him are obvious that things are not what they seem, and the rest is easy. For example, the very first story in the canon, *The Blue Cross*, partly depends on this. The priest unmasks Flambeau the jewel thief who is dressed up as another priest; the words and the man do not match, and the little priest knows it.

Portraits in Miniature

The most natural reason to read any author is that he is enjoyable to read, and it is a bonus if he can make the reader think. GKC could easily do both, and normally did. He was not a great novelist in the Victorian sense: 'I could not be a novelist; because I really like to see ideas or notions wrestling naked, as it were, and not dressed up in a masquerade as men and women.' In purely literary terms, his genius was probably best expressed in the form of the essay.

Essays seem to have fallen out of favour now, although they should be distinguished from the newspaper articles with which we are all so familiar. Ever since Francis Bacon brought the genre to the English language in the 1620s they have had certain defining rules: essays should be short, they should bear the deep personal imprint of the author, and they should be well crafted. We can still read Dr Johnson or Lamb, Emerson or Thoreau with great pleasure after a hundred years or more. As Virginia Woolf wrote in *The Modern Essay*: 'A good essay must have this permanent quality about it.' Reading last week's newspaper articles in contrast is often tedious since they are so concerned with the ephemeral excitement of the week's news. Like mayflies they may shine brightly but briefly.

Graham Greene once wrote with a smile that the literary audience of the 1930s rejected Chesterton on the grounds that his style was too difficult, whilst simultaneously worshipping the obscurity of James Joyce. In truth there is something of the eighteen century about Chesterton, not in the sense of archaic language, but in terms of style. Like Dr Johnson he writes in periods, in long sentences with interlocking clauses separated by colons and semicolons. Or, as he describes Stevenson: 'taking up two or more elements, or two or more reins of the subject in hand so that he combines, implicates and contrasts them … he will be found to have established the work of two sentences in the space of one.'

Modern prose, perhaps reflecting the unthinking speed at which we work, think and live, tends to be linear, consisting of short sentences developing one idea. Chesterton often plays with two or three ideas at once, and it is not uncommon for an argument to be interrupted by the odd joke, with the style resembling a fugue, or spokes radiating out from a hub. In this he simply reflects the older vigour of speech which we find in the conversation of Johnson, for example. As the *Autobiography* says: 'That was a race which dealt in periods. My father told me of a fellow clerk of his youth, who took leave of the tavern with a stately array of thanks: "Tell Mrs Bayfield that the steak was excellent; the potatoes done to a turn; in short, a dinner fit for an Emperor."'

All his life GKC had a profound mistrust of experts. In his opinion they tended to focus on one aspect of life to the exclusion of all else. We might say that not only could they not see the wood for the trees, they could not see the tree for the leaf. The problem arises when they apply the certainty they feel for their subject to the world as a whole. Intellectual fashion takes over, but history is littered with the corpses of such dead enthusiasms. The year 1897 was Queen Victoria's Diamond Jubilee, and a wave of imperialist fervour then shook the country. This looks obviously absurd to us now, but Chesterton was one of the few to say so at the time.

In contrast to the foolish expert, he had a deep and persistent trust in the basic common sense of ordinary people. GKC always considered tradition to be such common sense refined by time. Chesterton felt that ordinary proverbs and sayings expressed truths which the intellectual élite did not want to know. He therefore desired to know and be in regular contact with ordinary people, and this was one of the reasons for his insistence on being a journalist. In contrast to the narrow expert he knew that truth is but a reflection of an infinite reality. Rather like a master of mystic tradition, he uses paradox to make us question our conventional wisdom.

Mystics sometimes talk of the need in the spiritual life to differentiate between the map and the territory. What looks like unrelated points, or even contradiction, may in fact reflect the reality of three dimensions. Chesterton's great vision saw traces of a higher order in the world in which we live, but he struggled to express this in the limits of human language. Paradox was one way of achieving this, analogy was another. (After all, had not the greatest teacher of all used parables?)

Hilaire Belloc put it thus:

> He made men see what they had never seen before. He made them know. [by] His unique, his capital genius for illustration by parallel, by example, is his peculiar mark ... No one in the whole course of English letters had his amazing – I would almost say supernatural – capacity for parallelism ... [it] consists in the illustration of some unperceived truth by its exact consonance with the reflection of a truth already known and perceived.' *On the Place of Gilbert Chesterton in English Letters*

In Ronald Knox's words: 'He had the artist's eye which could suddenly see in some quite familiar object a new value; he had the poet's intuition which suddenly detects in the tritest of phrases, a wealth of new meanings and of possibilities.' Or in a descriptive phrase from the novel *The Napoleon of Notting Hill*: 'There is a law written in the darkest of the books of life, and it is this: "If you look at a thing nine hundred and ninety-nine times you are perfectly safe; if you look at it the thousandth time, you are in frightful danger of seeing it for the first time."' As GKC wrote of Cobbett describing the latter's denunciation of the horrors of the Industrial Revolution when they were just beginning: 'He saw what we see, but he saw it when it was not there.'

Reading and rereading Chesterton I have been struck by at least three elements of Chesterton's genius as a writer. Firstly, there is his almost supernatural insight, the ability to see through a mass of detail to get to the heart of the matter. This occurs not only in fields such as literature where he was an acknowledged expert, but in areas like economics or medical ethics where he certainly was not. Before the First World War leaders of popular opinion like Wells and Shaw prophesied univeral progress, the triumph of peace and democracy. Here is GKC in the *Daily News* in February 1905:

> The earnest freethinkers need not worry themselves
> too much about the persecutions of the past. Before
> the Liberal idea is dead or triumphant, we shall see
> wars and persecutions the like of which the World has
> never seen. They need not reserve their tears for the
> victims of Bonner or Claverhouse.[1] They may weep
> for themselves and their children.

Secondly, his wonderful memory fed by omnivorous reading; he could see more parallels than other people because he knew the examples of history. Lastly, we should not forget that GKC was not regarded as a stylist for nothing. Other writers may envy how naturally it came to him, but he is a joy to read because he has a poet's ear for language, a feeling for how the sentence *sounds* in the reader's mind.

There is little doubt that Chesterton has joined the canon of major essayists. It is because he was such a great essayist that I have included so many of his works in that form in this collection, not least because most of them have been ignored since GKC's own anthologies fell out of print fifty years ago. It would be easy enough to reprint his well-known books like *Orthodoxy* or *St Thomas Aquinas*, but for me it has been a

---

1. Leaders of religious persecution under Mary Tudor and Charles II.

great pleasure to reclaim these forgotten essays and offer them for others' rediscovery. A few of the essays in this collection may benefit from further comment. There are three 'essays' in particular which demand longer discussion. I have included in this section brief extracts from two major books, *What's Wrong With the World* and *St Francis of Assisi*. Constrictions of space are the only reason why longer extracts have not been given. On the other hand, the problem of evil is central to Chesterton's thought, which leads on to the *Book of Job*.

The Mad Official is included, because it shows in a very clear way GKC's vision of how the obsession with one idea can blind us to common sense and deprive us of all humanity. To those who argue that such things could not happen now, I will merely note how in Great Britain in 1992–94 certain social workers and psychologists became convinced of organized Satanic child abuse and ritual child murder. Although the police could find no trace of any corroborating evidence whatsoever, children were removed from their families in Gestapo-style dawn raids.

In the seventeenth century Descartes invented the system of philosophic doubt: 'How can we really be sure of anything?' Since we can be mistaken in our knowledge of external things, Descartes argued that we should not trust the external world, but trust solely in our own minds, expressed in the famous formula *cogito ergo sum* – I think, therefore I am. He is thus a father figure of the school of individualism which has come to dominate Western thought ever since. Many subsequent philosophers have argued that Descartes made a basic mistake, but few can have demolished him quite so elegantly as Chesterton's *The Extraordinary Cabman*.

Two of the essays, *The New Theologian* (1912) and *The Roots of Sanity* (1929), are concerned with one individual – the Dean of St Paul's Cathedral, Dr Inge. If Chesterton ever had one permanent adversary, Inge was it. The latter may be totally forgotten now, but his position made him one of the leading figures of the Church of England in his day, and his influence was great. He was known as the 'Gloomy Dean' for his warnings about forthcoming disaster. Inge's views were somewhat strange. He described himself as a 'modern churchman', which seemed to mean that he had little time for the traditional doctrines of Christianity, being more interested in Greek philosophy, particularly neo-Platonism. He was a convinced Erastian, that is, dedicated to maintaining the position of the Church of England as a pillar of the British State, the Establishment.

From this viewpoint, Inge attacked those who appeared to be rocking the boat. In *The New Theologian* we hear Inge stating in thoroughly modern terms that global competition meant that the British workers simply had to accept lower wages and poor working conditions, although somehow this never applied to the members of the Establishment itself. GKC takes him apart with wit and precision: 'When next you hear the "liberal" Christian say we should take what is best in Oriental faiths, make quite sure what are the things that people like Dr Inge call best ... You will find the levelling of creeds quite unexpectedly close to the lowering of wages.'

Chesterton is sometimes criticized for wasting his time attacking people like Inge, but this is misguided. The latter was hugely influential at that time, and someone had to point out his errors. The Dean was most gloomy about over-population, and a keen advocate of eugenics. He repeatedly warns that the poor are overbreeding and producing defectives. In an essay published in 1917 called simply *Eugenics*, he points out that all the males in his family have won scholarships at Eton, Oxford and Cambridge, but that 'Unfortunately the birth-rate of the feeble-minded is quite 50 per cent higher than that of normal persons.' The answer was eugenics, beginning with 'the compulsory segregation of mental defectives', a policy only opposed by 'irrationalist prophets like Mr Chesterton'.

Another late Chesterton essay, called *The Erastian on the Establishment*, and addressed yet again to Dean Inge, set out why GKC fought so hard:

> a great mass, probably a majority, of our modern people are Pagans ... most of them, if they have any religion at all, have a religion of pantheism or pure ethics which most of the great Christian characters of history, Catholic or Protestant, would have instantly stamped as pagan. If you had asked Wesley or Swedenborg, or Dr Johnson, or Baxter, or Luther [all Protestant], they would have called the modern mood heathen more promptly, if possible than would Bossuet or Bellarmine [both Catholics] ... A bitter and cynical man said, 'The Church of England is our last bulwark against Christianity.' This is quite unjust as a description of the Church of England. But it is not altogether unjust as a description of Dean Inge.

The Problem of Evil

I mentioned earlier that Chesterton's 'madness' left him engrossed with the problem of evil, and with that book of the Old Testament which treats it most explicitly. References to the Book of Job crop up in all sorts of apparently unlikely places: in an essay on nonsense verse, or in his *Browning*:

> When the author of the Book of Job insists on the huge, half-witted, apparently unmeaning magnificence and might of Behemoth, he is appealing precisely to this sense of wonder provoked by the grotesque. 'Canst thou play with him as with a bird, canst thou bind him for thy maidens?' he says in an admirable passage. The notion of the hippopotamus

as a household pet is curiously in the spirit of
Browning.

Any lover of Browning will recognize the truth of that last
remark. GKC knew this because he too loved the grotesque.
A key aspect of the Book of Job is this conjunction of the
deepest reflection on the problem of evil with a delight in the
bizarre aspect of the world. Fr Ian Boyd has made the brilliant
suggestion that *The Man Who Was Thursday* is both a retelling
and a meditation on the Book of Job, and this interpretation
explains much about that novel which would otherwise be
mysterious. *The Man Who Was Thursday* is difficult to sum-
marize in a few words. At the most superficial level it is a
spy story of the sort which was popular at the time. It tells
of a poet called Gabriel Syme who becomes a temporary
policeman in order to investigate a group of anarchists plot-
ting to overthrow everything. The grand anarchist council has
seven members named after the days of the week, and Syme
becomes Thursday. An exhilarating read, it is both profound,
comic and terrifying, particularly towards the end when the
anarchist leader Sunday is revealed to be something more
than human. We might call it Kafkaesque, except that in 1908
Kafka was a humble clerk who had published nothing.

It is a pity that we know so little of Kafka's opinion on
GKC. The latter mentions Chesterton in a letter to his friend
Max Brod, but that is all. The parallels are greater than one
might think. A German scholar once told me that there is a
deadpan humour throughout most of Kafka's work which is
lost in English translation, leaving only a sense of despair and
powerlessness. In other words, 'One morning Gregor Samsa
woke up from bad dreams and found that he had turned into
a huge cockroach',[2] is meant to have absurdist humour of the

2. This is my own translation of 'Als Gregor Samsa eines Morgens aus
    unruhigen Träumen erwachte, fand er sich in seinem Bett zu einem
    ungeheren Ungezifer verwandelt'.

type popularized in Monty Python. Borges mastered English by reading Chesterton (an intriguing thought), who remained ever after his favourite author in that tongue. Borges makes the perceptive comment in *Other Inquisitions* that 'Chesterton restrained himself from being Edgar Allan Poe or Franz Kafka – but something in the make up of his personality learned to want the nightmarish, something secret, and blind and central'.

Those who want can find abundant evil in GKC's fictional writings, as he could create an atmosphere of overpowering blackness in a few lines. Discussing Gilbert's so-called 'mad period', I described several examples in the Father Brown stories: the open grave in the bleak Scottish graveyard and its apparent witchcraft in one, or the bitter cold and dark forest as a background to a story of treachery. (As Chesterton knew, Dante described the deepest level of hell, the domain of traitors, as full of bitter cold.) The counterpoint between the apparent evil of the setting and the calm sanity of the little priest is the dynamic tension that drives forward many of these stories. The critic Hugh Kingsmill wrote in the *New Statesman* of his awareness of evil things 'as a decadent quality of his imagination. One moves in an evil, oppressive twilight, swelling to a horror.' All this is true, and for years I wondered why Chesterton did not write ghost stories when he was so qualified to do so. They were fashionable and deeply popular in the Edwardian period, which produced such giants of the genre as Algernon Blackwood and M.R. James. The answer is simply that he did not want to.

Europe, and America to a lesser extent, lost the positivism of the Victorians during the First World War. Ever since then self-indulgent misery seems the dominant tone of the literary élite. In this respect GKC is the polar opposite of Samuel Beckett with his denial of meaning, or of H.P. Lovecraft in a garret feeling excited about tombs. In 1951 the distinguished literary critic Raymond Mortimer wrote: 'Happiness has almost vanished from literature. The modern writer ... feels more unhappy than his predecessors, and inclines to flaunt despair as a proof of spiritual superiority.' Chesterton alone is immune. Not through ignorance, but because he has wrestled with his own personal demons and overcome them. The essay on The Book of Job is the product of that struggle. I have included the essay, which was originally a preface to an edition of the Book itself in 1907, in its entirety. However, some background information on Job may be useful for readers who are not acquainted with it.

One of the great underlying themes of the Old Testament is the people of Israel's growing knowledge of God, and the deepening religious awareness this brought. There are certain milestones of this process of discovery, of which the Book of Job is one. From the beginning they were aware of God as creator, and as maker of the great Covenant with Moses. However, their high monotheism emphasized the huge gap between Almighty God and lowly man. God was so high that His name could not even be pronounced, but only written as YHVH. Men lived short lives, and at death were believed to go the place of shadows, Sheol, from which there was no return. It was thought that a man's goodness was reflected in the good things of this life: health, wealth, an abundant family. This 'common sense' view of life is probably not far apart from that generally held now in secular Western society.

Yet it is obvious that at times worldly success is at odds with moral worth; it is most visible when a good man is struck down. How do we account for the problem of evil in the world? The Book of Job is the first real attempt in the Old Testament to tackle this. It is in the form of a long poem, with a brief prose prologue and epilogue. It tells of a good man called Job whom God allows Satan to torment in order to test his faith. His riches are destroyed, his family killed. Finally his body is covered with a plague of stinking and painful sores. His wife urges him to curse God, but this he refuses to do. The bulk of the poem consists of a dialogue between Job and his three friends: Eliphaz, Bildad and Zophar. While Job's comforters have distinct voices, they maintain the traditional view that Job's misfortunes must be due to his own fault. In misery and pain, Job robustly defends himself, but demands an explanation from God of why this has happened to him.

In an astonishing climax, the Lord God Himself speaks to Job from the tempest. He does not answer Job directly, but poses a series of rhetorical questions which emphasize the gap of understanding between God and man. Does Job remember the creation of the world, does he understand its manifold wonders? In GKC's words:

> By a touch truly to be called inspired, when God enters, it is to ask a number more questions on His own account. In this drama of scepticism God Himself takes up the role of sceptic. He does what all the great voices defending religion have always done … He turns rationalism against itself. He seems to say that if it comes to asking questions, He can ask some questions which will fling down and flatten all conceivable human questioners … It is the root and reason of the fact that men who have religious faith have also philosophic doubt, like Cardinal Newman … These are the small streams of the delta; the Book of Job is the great cataract that creates the river.

Both Job and his comforters are rebuked for doubting God, but Job's innocence is rewarded with health and prosperity being restored to him. GKC's conclusion is:

> We see Job tormented not because he was the worst of men, but because he was the best. It is the lesson of the whole work that man is most comforted by paradoxes; and it is by all human testimony the most reassuring.

I need not suggest what a high and strange history
awaited this paradox of the best man in the worst
fortune. I need not say that in the freest and most
philosophical sense there is one Old Testament figure
who is truly a type; or say what is prefigured in the
wounds of Job.

(There is an ancient scribal note to the Book of Job which
states that he has indeed been granted the privilege of resurrection from Sheol.) Job's answer is only a partial one, but it
leads on and looks forward, like the suffering servant of the
Psalms.

In GKC's words in *The Speaker* in 1905: 'In the book of Job
is foreshadowed that better doctrine, full of a dark chivalry,
that he that bore the worst that man can suffer was the best
that wore the form of a man.' Or from those in the *Illustrated
London News* in 1906: 'From it [Job] the modern Christian
may with astonishment learn Christianity; learn, that is, that
suffering may be a strange honour and not a vulgar punishment; that the King may be conferring a decoration when he
pins the man on the cross, as much as when he pins the cross
on the man.'

The Sane Economy and the Drift to Paganism

As the twentieth century approaches its end, it increasingly
resembles its beginning. With the rise of industrialism,
the dominant political idea in Edwardian England was of
laissez-faire capitalism (laissez-faire merely being French for
'leave the market alone'). In a 'post-industrial society', our
dominant political idea is that of free market capitalism.
Recent industrialization meant that they had the problem of
widespread poverty amid an embryonic welfare state; post-
industrialization gives us the problem of widespread poverty

in a collapsing welfare state. We have the new global economy; they had the old global gold standard.

Chesterton was deeply affected by the suffering caused by industrial poverty. His views extended from individual morality to the fabric of society at large. While there is not room in this book to examine them in any detail, they were rooted in a passionate concern for the poor. He hated the way the free-market economists (the Manchester School) of the nineteenth century advocated starvation and misery for the poor as a necessary evil which also let the rich maintain their elegance. Dickens personalized it as Mr Gradgrind. The views he attributed to Dickens are his own:

> He didn't like the *mean* side of the Manchester
> philosophy: the preaching of an impossible thrift and
> an intolerable temperance ... Thus, for instance, he
> hated that Little Bethel [a workhouse] to which Kit's
> mother went: he hated it simply as Kit hated it.
> Newman could have told him it was hateful, because
> it had no root in religious history; it was not even a
> sapling sprung of the seed of some great human and
> heathen tree: it was a monstrous mushroom that grows
> in the moonshine and dies in the dawn. Dickens knew
> no more of religious history than Kit; he simply smelt
> the fungus, and it stank. *The Victorian Age in Literature*

Although GKC knew little economics, insight told him that the world had shifted from the political economy of Adam Smith, based on morality and the sense of a small community where the butcher and the baker had to face their customers anew each day. In theory it had been replaced by the idea of the iron laws of economics, essentially the mathematical calculus applying the utilitarian philosophy of Jeremy Bentham, by such as J.S. Mill and David Ricardo. In practice this meant that Big Business was given a free rein, so that the isolated individual was left facing huge industrial combines. GKC wanted to get back to the moral economics of Adam Smith, and the way to do this was to distribute as much property as possible to as many people as possible. From the mid-1920s *GK's Weekly* became a manifesto for this Distributist philosophy, which is set out in such books as *What's Wrong With the World*, and *The Outline of Sanity*. (The value of Distribution itself is a moot point; some of the members were professional wastrels. But it was an attempt to put Catholic social teaching into practical effect, and many of its ideas reappeared in the 1970s when Fritz Schumacher rediscovered that *Small is Beautiful*.)

He believed, as Catholic social teaching has always argued, that the family must be the centre of economic and social life. Chesterton suspected that both capitalists and socialists wanted to break up this unit, in order to obtain weaker, more malleable, and essentially cheaper workers. The history of the late twentieth century does not disprove him: 'a horrible suspicion that has sometimes haunted me: the suspicion that Hudge (Socialist) and Gudge (free-market Conservative) are secretly in partnership ... Gudge the plutocrat wants an anarchic industrialism; Hudge the idealist provides him with lyric praises of anarchy. Gudge wants women workers because they are cheaper; Hudge calls the woman's work "freedom to live her own life".' The above comes from *What's Wrong With the World* from which is drawn an extract I have called *The Urchin's Hair* to give the reader a brief taste of Chesterton's writing in this field.

One of the most vigorous beliefs of our own age is that of environmentalism. While at its most basic it seeks to protect the planet, there is a harder edge and 'Deep Green' which tends to blend in with 'New Age' systems of belief and approach what older generations would have called 'witch-craft'. Worship of nature seems inextricably combined with worship of the human body, and with the pursuit of sensuality. You may think that this is just the pattern of the West since the 1960s, but there was a prior great civilization based on these principles, as well as on the love of money. We have been here before.

The Roman Republic was built on the strength of the simple farmers of Latium, but following its replacement by empire the old traditional Roman values of stoicism, patriotism and pride in civic virtue slowly withered, to be replaced by the pursuit of pleasure. At the very beginning of the Empire, the Stoic philosopher and historian Seneca deplored the unrestrained pursuit of wealth and pleasure, noting that appetite grows faster than enjoyment, and that the result is world-weariness, despair, and sometimes a longing for death. Seneca may not have known the term 'Existentialism', but he was acquainted with those who 'do not want to live, and do not know how to die', who felt life to be totally meaningless and superficial. Two millennia before Freud, he spoke of unsatisfied desires leading to the '*libido moriendi*', or death instinct.

The result was debauchery and brutality. Paganism was not just veneration of the ancient civic gods of Greece and Rome, nor admiration of the beauty of nature, but rather the worship of sexuality in all its most perverse and bizarre forms, of power and lust, and the inhuman savagery of the gladiator. We may briefly remember the Empress Messalina, who shocked the hardened whores of Rome, or Nero who became so bored with ordinary orgies that he forced his mother into incest before murdering her. We may remember the 'mystery religions', and Emperor Eglabalus who had an operation to make him both male and female.

The novelist John Cowper Powys felt the evil power of paganism in 'those symbols of pure lust on the sinister brick-red walls of the scoriac streets of ancient Pompei'. This is the point and the purpose, the real value, of the return to nature as practised by St Francis. He could love the created world with a Christian purity as it had been washed clean. Chesterton sets the scene for *St Francis*:

> In the Roman Empire, long before the end, we find nature worship inevitably producing things against nature. Cases like that of Nero have passed into proverb, when Sadism sat on a throne brazen in the broad daylight. But the truth I mean is something much more subtle and universal than a conventional catalogue of atrocities. What had happened to the human imagination, as a whole, was that the whole world was coloured by dangerous and rapidly deteriorating passions. Thus the effect of treating sex as only one innocent natural thing was that every other innocent natural thing became soaked and sodden with sex. For sex cannot be admitted to a mere equality among elementary emotions or experiences like eating and sleeping. The moment sex ceases to be a servant it becomes a tyrant.

In *The Four Loves* C.S. Lewis tackles the danger that love of nature may turn into nature worship in a way which owes much to Chesterton's *St Francis*. Here is Chesterton: 'St Francis was not a lover of nature. Properly understood, a lover of nature was precisely what he was not.' And now Lewis warning us of the temptation to worship nature:

> The path peters out almost at once. Terrors and mysteries, the whole depth of God's counsels and the whole tangle of the history of the universe choke it ... The love of nature is beginning to turn into a nature religion. And then, even if it does not lead us to the Dark Gods, it will lead us to a great deal of nonsense.

The Roots of Insanity ...

In the previous chapter I described Chesterton's 'insane period' of 1892–96, and how he recovered due to the framework provided by love and hard work. Yet for a mind like his this could not be enough, and he needed to rebuild the intellectual and moral foundations of his life which had been undermined by the poison of the Decadence. As the nineteenth century ended he tried a number of fashionable philosophies such as Theosophy or Ethical Societies, but without great success. GKC came to the conclusion that the problem of all these groups was their insistence on truth as a single thing, whereas it became obvious to him that it was manifestly complex. He became increasingly sceptical of all the fashionable ideas of the time: Kipling's imperialism; Shaw and Wells' socialism; Ibsen's pessimism, or the overwhelming and all pervasive conjunction of free-market economics, materialism and Darwinian triumph of the fittest.

GKC's first great book was *Orthodoxy* (1908), but this work can be best understood in relation to its predecessor, *Heretics* (1905). During 1903–4 Chesterton was engaged in public debate with the atheist Blatchford in the pages of the *Clarion* magazine, which forced him to publish and develop his views. 'What I was defending seemed to me a plain matter of ordinary human morals. Indeed it seemed to me to raise the question of the very possibility of morals ... It was not that I began by believing in supernatural things. It was that the unbelievers began by disbelieving even in normal things.' These articles were later revised and published in book form as *Heretics*. The latter contains the negative, critical side of GKC's arguments, whereas in *Orthodoxy* he sets out his own distinctive world-view.

While *Heretics* is important as a prologue and illustrative complement to *Orthodoxy*, it is also important in its own right. I have therefore included three extracts from the earlier book on pages 223–36. GKC starts off with one of his favourite devices, looking at modern society as a man from Mars might do. He makes the valid point that all previous revolutions claimed to be restoring truth, to be orthodox, and that it was the previous authorities who were heretics. It was the unique achievement of the twentieth century to boast that it was heretical; to claim in fact that it does not matter what men believe, or as Shaw proclaimed: 'The golden rule is that there is no golden rule.' Thirty years before Professor Leavis noticed the same phenomenon, GKC saw that literature without any pretence at meaning becomes mere fiction, little more than a series of technical devices to divert and entertain.

GKC also noticed the worship of efficiency and progress, the idea that we may not know where we are going, but that we should get there as quickly and easily as possible. The parable of the monk and the lamp post, to which I have referred earlier, is on page 227 and is one of his most distinctive images. *Heretics* also showed the author's instinctive vision. To take one example at random: in the 1960s critics began to wonder whether some dark secret lay behind Kipling's manly vision. Angus Wilson wrote *The Strange Ride of Rudyard Kipling*. But Chesterton was there sixty years before them, daring to criticize the imperialist hero at the height of his popularity. He noted that Kipling did not love England, only the Empire, and more particularly the mass of men organized together for that purpose, in other words, what we might call proto-fascism.

> He admires England because she is strong, not because she is English … In a very interesting poem he says that 'If England was what England seems' – that is, weak and inefficient; if England were not what (as he believes) she is – that is powerful and practical – 'How quick we'd chuck 'er! But she ain't!'

Likewise, Chesterton saw through the call for the 'Superman' to emerge who could ignore the morality of Christianity, who felt himself above such a creed of weaklings:

> Nietzsche has a description somewhere of the disgust and disdain which consume him at the sight of the common people with their common faces and their common minds ... when Nietzsche has the incredible lack of humour and imagination to ask us to believe that his aristocracy ... is an aristocracy of strong wills, it is necessary to point out the truth. It is an aristocracy of weak nerves.

Perhaps the most profound chapter in the book is 'On Certain Writers and the Institution of the Family'. It is a fact that many of the men who have most advocated liberty as the basis of society, such as Bentham and Mill and their successors, did so because they were social failures who were unable to cope with marriage and normal family life. A man may lead a life of isolation in a great city, but this is not possible in a small village whose inhabitants are forced to learn to live with their fellows. 'In a small community our companions are chosen for us.' If this is true of towns and villages, it is doubly true of the basic building block of all human society – the family. Chesterton was writing at a time when fashionable writers were attacking the family as restrictive and confining; ninety years later we know better. It is in the inner cities, where the family has most disappeared, that we are most obviously confronted with people who seem persistently unemployable, as well as increasing crime, drug taking, and general anarchy. GKC points out that:

> The best way that a man could test his readiness to encounter the common variety of mankind would be to climb down a chimney at random, and get on as

quickly as possible with the people inside. And that is essentially what each of us did on the day when he was born.

... *And How to Restore It*

Chesterton's comprehensive and positive answer to these questions was given in *Orthodoxy*, published in 1908. He described it as a kind of intellectual autobiography: 'A series of mental pictures rather than a series of deductions, to state the philosophy in which I have come to believe ... I did not make it. God and humanity made it, and it made me.' The book commences with the typical Chestertonian device of a voyage, with the idea of a man sailing round the world, and thinking that he had landed in the South Seas, only to find that he was in fact back in England. (We may remember *The Ball and the Cross*, where the perpetual duellists land on a desert island which turns out to adjoin Margate.)

Yet as well as a physical journey there is a mental one. Whereas the traveller had made a physical journey to the East, GKC recounts how he had mentally explored Eastern religions, but found the answer waiting for him at home. Before Kakfa wrote, and before Kierkegaard became famous, Chesterton had had personal experience of the existentialist *Angst* which has gripped the twentieth century. Sanity has been described as a sense of being at ease with the universe. Gilbert put the question this way: 'How do we continue to be at once astonished at the world, and yet at home in it?' The answer was quietly waiting for him at home:

> If this book is a joke, it is a joke against me ... I only succeeded in inventing by myself an inferior copy of the existing tradition of civilized religion ... the word 'orthodoxy' used here means the Apostles Creed.

As we have noticed, the need, the quest, for sanity was always with Chesterton. *Orthodoxy's* second and third chapters, entitled 'The Maniac' and 'The Suicide of Thought', are concerned with madness, and how to resist it. Indeed, he starts off by considering the lunatic, and he illustrates the folly of one of the favourite nostrums of practical men, that to succeed you need to believe in yourself. 'The only men who really and fully believe in themselves are lunatics.' His point is that the average lunatic is someone possessed by one idea, for example that everyone is out to persecute him. Yet this is true also of the intellectual life:

> Poets do not go mad, but chess players do … poetry is sane because it floats easily in an infinite sea, reason seeks to cross the infinite sea, and so make it infinite. The result is mental exhaustion.

(The passage also illustrates again Chesterton's intuitive vision. He merely cites the chess-player as an example of pure reason, and I doubt if he knew anything of the history of chess. Yet the point is true. The first World Chess Champion, Wilhelm Steinitz, died in Ward's Island lunatic asylum in New York. The greatest player of the mid-nineteenth century, Paul Morphy, was obviously insane for the last twenty-five years of his life, but as a rich man he was merely forcibly restrained at home in New Orleans. Other leading chess players who went mad included Rubinstein, Neumann and Carlos Torre.)

GKC's point is that the world is vast, hugely complex. If we approach it humbly, we may indeed gain true knowledge. Humility is not, however, a common characteristic of twentieth-century man, whose arrogance and anger at his inability to grasp everything led him to fall into temptation – the temptation of forcing the facts to fit a single theory or ideology, and ignoring them when they do not. (The ancient Greeks believed that such overweening pride, *hubris*, led inevitably to disaster, *nemesis*.) The artist or poet normally depends upon the world for their inspiration, and so approaches it with reverence and sometimes joy. (Think of Turner, for example, lashed to a mast in order to experience fully a tempest at sea.) The reverse is most apparent in the reductionism of the scientist materialist, but such reductionism is doomed to failure as contradictory to reality. Like the lunatic, the materialist wears himself out defending his mental creation. Such endless repetition is the mark of madness. Reductionism covers some things well, but leaves out much more, and the usual tendency is to insist, like the lunatic, on the correctness of the theory.

> A man cannot think himself out of mental evil, for it is actually the organ of thought that has become diseased, ungovernable, and, as it were, independent. He can only be saved by faith or will. The moment his mere reason moves, it moves in the old circular rut.

This is a powerful evocation of the experience of madness which has the ring of truth of one who has suffered from it. Chesterton saw that this was not just true of obvious lunatics, but also those in positions of power who were obsessed with an ideology and thereby became the prisoner of one idea. (When Stalin was told that the introduction of collective farming had reduced the Soviet harvest, he merely ordered more collectivization.) It is easy to laugh at Communism now, but the same criticisms could be made about the over-arching claims of the neo-conservative or libertarian right, with their strident claim that the 'free market' is a universal panacea. More and more areas of society are being forcibly based on the profit motive, as if everything could be bought or sold. GKC's argument is like that developed sixty years later by the philosopher Karl Popper, who distinguished between 'open societies', which were open to the truth, and 'closed societies' ruled by dogmas.

Chesterton also argued, at a time when it was just beginning, that the reductionist materialism advocated by most intellectuals of the day led inevitably to spiritual poverty, not just in religion, but also in art, music — and literature — much that makes life worth living. (Is there anybody who seriously thinks that the future will describe the art, architecture and music produced between 1914 and 1990 as the height of human civilization?) He goes on:

> Our case against the exhaustive and logical theory
> of the lunatic [is that] it gradually destroyed his
> humanity. Now it is the charge against the main
> deduction of the materialist that, rightly or wrongly,
> they gradually destroyed his humanity. I do not only
> mean kindness. I mean hope, courage, poetry,
> initiative, all that is human.

This is part of the answer to the question posed at the beginning of the chapter. Twentieth-century man is miserable because he has metaphysically insisted that everything is painted grey, and then he wonders why the world appears so dull and drab. I am struck by the closeness of the line of thought in this passage to that of Hans Urs von Balthasar, a distinguished Swiss theologian known to have been close to Pope John Paul II. As Balthasar wrote in his 1982 book *The Glory of the Lord*:

> Our situation today shows that beauty demands for
> itself at least as much courage and decision as do truth
> and goodness, and she will not allow herself to be
> separated and banned from her two sisters without
> taking them along in an act of mysterious vengeance.
> We can be sure that whoever sneers at her name as if
> she were the ornament of a bourgeois past — whether
> he admits it or not — can no longer pray and soon will
> no longer be able to love.

Chesterton describes the creeping relativism of his time as 'the suicide of thought'. Relativism may seem driven by honest enquiry, but we may suspect that its motive power derives from an attack on religion in order to overthrow the traditional concept of morals. It is hysterically triumphant now – you can believe and say anything you like, except that some things are good and some bad, for that is 'élitist'! In the 1920s the Satanist Aleister Crowley advocated 'do what thou wilt shall be the whole of the law', but I doubt if even he thought that this would become conventional wisdom.

Essentially thought, logic, argument all rest on an act of faith that the mind can know the reality beyond itself in some way, and that logic will always give valid answers from true premises. But this cannot be proved. There is a pessimism which stops thought, and a need for a teaching authority to prevent the mind from destroying itself in the depths of solipsism and pessimism:

> The peril is that the human intellect is free to destroy itself ... it is idle to talk always of the alternative of faith and reason. Reason is itself a matter of faith. It is an act of faith that our thoughts have any relation to reality at all ... the young sceptic says, 'I have a right to think for myself.' But the old sceptic, the complete sceptic, says, 'I have no right to think for myself. I have no right to think at all.' There is a thought that stops thought.

It is at this point that the three great central chapters which lie at the heart of *Orthodoxy* commence. They are 'The Ethics of Elfland', 'The Flag of the World', and 'The Paradoxes of Christianity'. I have given the last of these in full, as well as the key parts of the other two.

The Everlasting Philosophy

Graham Greene once remarked that Chesterton produced three of the greatest books of the age; although I don't quite agree with his list of *Orthodoxy*, *The Everlasting Man* and *The Thing*. *The Thing* has some good writing, but it is hard to call it a masterpiece. Whereas his book on *St Thomas Aquinas* most certainly is, *St Francis* is one of Chesterton's most enjoyable works, and full of powerful insight, but nobody else has ever managed to write a popular work on the subject of the profound medieval philosopher, as GKC did in *St Thomas*. He had an enormous influence on securing the faith of the ordinary Catholic in an age which had nothing but contempt for religious belief. Fr Ronald Knox once said:

> that if every other line he wrote should disappear from circulation, Catholic posterity would still owe him an imperishable debt of gratitude so long as a copy of *The Everlasting Man* enriched its libraries ... whenever I ask an inquirer whether he has read any Catholic books his answer regularly begins, 'I've read some Chesterton, of course.'

In fact, as Father Knox perceived, of all Chesterton's religious works *The Everlasting Man* is probably the greatest. Whilst uneven, it goes beyond the vision shown in *Orthodoxy* and *St Thomas Aquinas*. They are great writing. At its best, *The Everlasting Man* is a spiritual classic. In it, particularly in the second half, which is concerned with Jesus of Nazareth, 'The Everlasting Man', Chesterton reaches a sustained level of profundity and insight of the highest level. The book was immensely popular and influential in the period before the Second World War, but like so many good things fell out of use after it.

The book is in two parts. The first part, which takes up about two-thirds of the text, is an account of history leading up to the birth of Christ. It was written as a rebuttal to H.G. Wells' *Outline of History*, an atheistic and Freudian view of society beginning in prehistoric terms with an 'Old Man' who terrorized a tribe into obedience, dragged compliant females around by the hair, etc. Chesterton points out that this nonsense is wish-fulfilment on Wells' part. There is no evidence whatsoever that this was the case, either from contemporary accounts of primitive peoples, or from what we know of prehistory. Indeed, from the cave paintings of Lascaux onwards, all societies seem to band around a religious reverence for the world.

Much of this argument now seems of historic interest only, a reply to an outdated argument of little contemporary interest. There is, however, one outstanding theme of major importance at a time like the present, when the very concept of Western civilization is under question. In a chapter called 'The End of The World', Chesterton points out that the dominant culture of the world is based on the values arising from Europe. This is often described as the Graeco-Roman philosophic tradition. (Until recently Latin and Greek were obligatory at all the great schools of England, so that pupils could be in direct contact with their cultural roots.)

However, GKC reminds us that the great pagan civic culture died around the time of Christ; all civilizations are based on an idea, and by the time of Augustus nobody believed any more either in the pagan gods, or the patriotic values on which the Republic/Empire had been built. In other words, the tree of Graeco-Roman civilization died. All the achievements of that civilization, such as Roman law and engineering, Greek philosophy and science, would have been as remote to us as the forgotten knowledge of Egypt or Babylon, except for the fact that such learning was grafted on to the living tree of the Christian faith. The Roman Empire fell, but the Church kept the tradition alive, although only because it refused to become one faith among many:

> It was the refusal of the Christians that was the
> turning point of history ... If the Christians had
> accepted ... they would have boiled down to one
> lukewarm liquid in that great pot of cosmopolitan
> corruption in which all the other myths and
> mysteries were melting ... the whole world once
> nearly died of broad-mindedness.

The loss of the living force of pagan civic tradition also meant an increasing slide to tyranny as force was the only means to bind the state together. The process was accelerated as the stern morality of the Roman Republic gave way to sensuality, divorce, perversion. As the historian Christopher Dawson (an admirer of Chesterton) wrote in 1933, when he forecast that contemporary society's attack on traditional morality and marriage would lead to a collapse of the family:

> As Leo XII pointed out, the alteration of the
> fundamental laws that govern marriage and family
> will ultimately lead to the ruin of society itself. No
> doubt the state will gain in power and prestige as the
> family declines, but state and society are not identical.
> In fact, the state is often most omnipotent and
> universal in its claims at the moment when society is
> dying, as we see in the last age of the Roman Empire.
> *Enquiries into Religion and Culture*

By the fourth century this was to lead to economic depression and near-communist state-slavery as communities were legally bound to the land to pay taxes. In Rome, as the civic spirit declined, the claims of the state became more and more oppressive, but the demands of the citizens of Rome to be fed for nothing, and to be entertained, grew steadily up to the moment of abyss. In the last century of this bureaucratic tyranny, very similar in its methods and claims to modern

Communism, the only centre of independent life was the Christian Bishop. In Dawson's words:

> He alone stood between the people and the oppression
> of the bureaucracy ... On one occasion a praetorian
> prefect was so offended that he declared that he had
> never been spoken to in such a manner. 'No doubt,'
> replied St Basil, 'you have never met a Bishop.'

Chesterton continues the theme with fascinating insights on Europe's beginning, rather than its collapse into the Dark Ages. We take it for granted that Europe, and hence the modern world, are based on the philosophic ideas of the Greeks and the organizational genius of the Romans; it need not have been so. In a chapter called 'The War of the Gods and Demons', he points out that Europe in the centuries before Christ meant the lands bordering the Mediterranean. A visitor from China after the death of Alexander the Great would have noted that Rome had a great rival:

> There was established on the opposite coast of the
> inland seas a city that bore the name of the New Town.
> It was already much older, much more powerful, and
> more prosperous than the Italian town ... It had been
> called new because it was a colony like New York or
> New Zealand. It was an outpost or settlement of the
> energy and expansion of the great commercial cities of
> Tyre and Sidon. There was a note of the new countries
> and colonies about it; a confident and commercial
> outlook. It was fond of saying things that rang with a
> certain metallic assurance; as that nobody could wash his
> hands in the seas without the leave of the New Town.

The new town was called Carthage, it was based on a dark practice as well as on keen commercial expertise: the worship of a god called Moloch. Moloch was a great brass idol with a huge open mouth; in Phoenicia where he originated he was also known as Baal, Belial or Beelzebub. This brass idol was heated until it was red hot, when living babies and young children were thrown into it. As Chesterton says:

> The worshippers of Moloch were not gross or primitive. They were probably more refined than the Romans ... These highly civilized people really met together to invoke the blessing of heaven on their empire by throwing hundreds of their infants into a large furnace.

Critics have sometimes suggested that these things did not happen, that they were Roman propaganda. About the same time as *The Everlasting Man* was being written, archaeological excavations at Carthage uncovered the charred bones of thousands of young children – perhaps Heaven guided the spade! Rome fought Carthage to the death, and nearly died herself in the struggle. When the simple farmers of Latium approved Cato's dictum, *Carthago delenda est* (Carthage must be destroyed), they were expressing the kind of moral loathing which many people felt about the regime of Adolf Hitler. We may note that if Carthage, rather than Rome, had been the victor in their great wars, furnace-statues of Moloch might have been scattered across Europe to this day.

Having set the scene, Chesterton tells the story of Jesus Christ in eighty pages and four chapters of genius. I have included the bulk of three of them on pages 287–323. I will not discuss them further here – like the best malt whisky they should be taken neat – but for two points. The first chapter in this section, 'The God in the Cave', deals with the birth of Jesus. Chesterton reminds us that after the Magi visited him looking for the newborn Messiah, King Herod ordered the massacre of all male babies born at that time:

Every one knows the story; but not every one has perhaps noted its place in the story of the strange religions of men … Only, as the purpose in his dark spirit began to show and shine in the eyes of the Idumean, a seer might perhaps have seen something like a great grey ghost that looked over his shoulder; have seen behind him, filling the dome of night and hovering for the last time over history, that vast and fearful face that was Moloch of the Carthaginians; awaiting his last tribute from a ruler of the races of Shem. The demons also, in that first festival of Christmas, feasted after their own fashion.

I have mentioned GKC's 'horrible suspicion that has sometimes haunted me: the suspicion that Hudge and Gudge were secretly in partnership.' When Chesterton wrote *The Everlasting Man*, Moloch had indeed been dead for twenty-one centuries. Yet a 'horrible suspicion' assails me also. Carthage was a great commercial empire, of the like not seen again until our day. Is it mere coincidence that our modern capitalist society is the only one in history to encourage abortion? Is it a coincidence that a ghastly replication of the sacrifice to Moloch goes on behind the closed doors and white tiles of the abortion clinics? (See also 'By the Babe Unborn', page 101.)

It has become commonplace in our relativistic age for the liberal theologian to abandon the explicit teachings of the gospels on the grounds that they are 'culturally conditioned'. In other words, we can drop Jesus' prohibition on divorce as it reflects the beliefs common to first-century Jewry living under the Roman Empire, and the argument goes, the world has moved on since then. The same thesis was used in GKC's time, although normally then by atheists rather than churchmen. But Jesus of Nazareth, Chesterton claims, is nothing like an orthodox Jew of the first century:

The freethinker frequently says that Jesus of Nazareth was a man of his time, even if he was in advance of his time; and that we cannot accept his ethics as final for humanity ... When Muhammed allowed a man four wives he was really doing something suited to the circumstances ... It is a practical compromise carrying with it the character of a particular society ... But Jesus in his view of marriage does not in the least suggest the conditions of Palestine in the first century. He does not suggest anything at all, except the sacramental view of marriage as developed long afterwards by the Catholic Church. It was quite as difficult for people then as for now.

In the previous chapter I described Chesterton's unique feat of writing an interesting and approachable book about a major philosopher. He does so not by focusing on Aquinas' sex life – to the best of our knowledge there wasn't any – but by explaining why he is so important. Chesterton begins by looking at Aquinas' first major victory, which prepared the way for the scientific method on which modern civilization depends. Ancient Greek philosophy was polarized between the idealism of Plato, who was interested in exploring the ideas people have in their minds, and of Aristotle, who was a pragmatist. The latter sought for truth in the lessons of the senses, and as such can be described as the father of the scientific method. Secular intellectual life died long before the final collapse of the Roman Empire, and life was too precarious in the Dark Ages for it to revive, with a few noble exceptions such as Alfred the Great. It was only in the thirteenth century that Europe became both prosperous and politically stable enough for it to resume. This is the period when the great universities were founded: Paris first, followed by Oxford. However, the new learning was nearly strangled at birth.

We should remember that in this period all teaching was by and for the Christian Church, and many conservative churchmen were worried by such developments. Plato they could just about accept since his idealism was close to the *logos* of St John's Gospel, but Aristotle was felt to be suspect, particularly since his works had been rediscovered and developed by Arab thinkers such as Avicenna and Averoes. Aquinas' achievement was to reconcile Aristotelian philosophy and the teachings of the Church in one great synthesis. By doing so he convinced the clerical authorities to let his teacher Albertus Magnus carry out scientific experiments such as his pioneering work in chemistry. Across the Channel a similar new freedom allowed Friar Roger Bacon to investigate optics at Oxford. Note that Aquinas *did not* fall into the trap of stating that these were different truths, but rather only different paths to truth itself. Chesterton gives a gripping account of Thomas' debate with Stiger of Brabant on this very point.

If St Francis had saved us from nature worship, St Thomas saved us from an otherworldly 'Platonic' view of God. In GKC's words:'It is best to say the truth in the simplest form – they both re-affirmed the Incarnation by bringing God back to earth.' St Thomas convinced the world that knowledge could be gained by what he called the 'five lamps of the senses', and thus by so doing reconciled science and religion:

> It seems to be strangely forgotten that both these
> saints were in actual fact imitating a Master, who was
> not Aristotle let alone Ovid, when they sanctified the
> senses or the simple things of nature; when St Francis
> walked humbly among the beasts, or St Thomas
> debated courteously among the Gentiles.

One of the greatest threats to young Christianity was the devastating heresy produced by Mani around AD 250, which mixed in the old Persian dualist beliefs with Christianity. Mani based his creed on an edited version of the New Testament, although the Old Testament was rejected. According to Mani, Jesus, a supernatural being, could not really have died, so the crucifixion was merely symbolic. The Manicheans believed that while the world may have been created by the good god Jehovah, he was inept if well-meaning, so it was effectively in the charge of the evil god, Lucifer. In effect, the world was evil, and the task of the 'elect' *Perfecti* was to deny the body and put themselves above the world. The bringing of new life into the world was especially hated by Manicheans, who hated fruitfulness and loved sterility. Homosexuality was a preferred option, a pregnant women an object of loathing. They were obliged to be vegetarian in order not to eat the product of sexual intercourse, which included eggs, while alcohol was forbidden. For them the essence of religion consisted in freeing the 'higher' spiritual body from this filthy material prison.

Manicheism seemed more or less to die out with the Roman Empire, but mysteriously reappeared in eleventh-century Bulgaria, whence it spread to northern Italy and southern France, where it was known as the Albigensian heresy (The medieval French word for Bulgarian was *Bougre* which became synonymous with unnatural practices; it was naturalized into English as 'bugger'.) Simon de Montfort led a military crusade against the Albigensians, but the Church needed an intellectual answer to the challenge, which Aquinas supplied. Chesterton points out that while crooked argument may question whether there is any difference between the Christian monk and the Manichean elect, both of them alleged to hate the body, the reverse is in fact true. The monk knows that the world is good, and that sexual love is a great joy within it, but he willingly surrenders it for the greater love of God. Compared to the Manicheans, who hated the world, who hated life, Aquinas knew the world as incarnational:

When Religion would have maddened men,
Theology kept them sane. In this sense St Thomas
simply stands up as the great orthodox theologian,
who reminded men of the creed of the creation, when
many of them were in the mood of mere destruction
... there is a general tone and temper of Aquinas
which it is as difficult to avoid as daylight in a great
house of windows. It is that *positive* position of his
mind, which is filled and soaked as with sunshine,
with the warmth of the wonder of created things.

Poet of Orthodoxy

With the exception of a few stock pieces such as *Lepanto* and *The Donkey*, Chesterton's poetry is little remembered today. Yet he was capable of examining original themes over a very strong metric rhythm. For example, in *Joseph* he looks at the subject of St Joseph's erotic feelings towards his wife, feelings which can never be consummated. A poet considered worthy of critical appraisal by Kipling, Auden and Eliot is clearly no lightweight. GKC cannot be considered as a great poet; his output is too uneven for that, but he could write great poems. When you think that poetry was his fourth or fifth occupation after journalist, critic, novelist and theologian, it is astonishing that he managed to write anything of real value at all.

The original purpose of poetry was probably as a mechanism for an illiterate culture to transmit a people's sense of itself and its values down over the centuries. We see this in Homer, and in the unnamed bards of Anglo-Saxon England. Chesterton revived this tradition in his greatest poetic work, *The Ballad of the White Horse*. Significantly, it is the one poem that he spent years polishing and revising. I venture to suggest that it is also one of the greatest Christian poems of the century.

To understand it, we need to know a little history. During the ninth century a wave of pagan Norse invaders over-whelmed the scattered kingdoms of Anglo-Saxon England. Northumbria fell first, then Mercia, as well as the smaller realms of East Anglia and Kent. The glories of the monasteries were scattered; the abbots sacrificed to Odin in the horrors of the 'blood eagle'. Located in the south-west of the country, around modern Somerset, Dorset, Wiltshire and Hampshire, Wessex was the last of the Christian kingdoms to feel the storm, but by 875 it did. Its armies were destroyed in battle, its king died soon after. The young prince Alfred inherited a kingdom without an army; to avoid capture he had to hide in the Isle of Athelney in the Somerset marshes. The situation must have seemed hopeless, everything he loved on the brink of destruction: Christianity; Civilization, England itself. Alfred's response was to pray for intercession to Our Lady (the traditional Catholic term for the Virgin Mary). In the poem he sees her in a vision, but her words are not reassuring.

In the summer of 1941 England again stood alone, against the might of Nazi Germany, her armies beaten again in the fall of Greece. *The Times* abandoned its normal leader column and merely printed part of this section of the poem.

> I tell you naught for your comfort
> Yea, naught for your desire,
> Save that the sky grows darker yet
> And the sea rises higher.
>
> Night shall be thrice over you,
> And heaven an iron cope.
> Do you have joy without a cause,
> Yea, faith without a hope?

At the end of 1941, when Russia entered the war, and Winston Churchill talked of the 'end of the beginning', *The Times* again quoted the poem:

> The high tide King Alfred cried.
> The high tide and the turn!

In reality, Alfred *was* inspired by a vision, rallied his scattered followers, and won an unexpected victory at Ethadune in 878. Further victories followed, leading to the capture of London, and the establishment of the secure Christian kingdom of Wessex. By the treaty of Wedmore the Danish chief Guthrum and his people agreed to withdraw to the North and Midlands into 'The Danelaw', and, more importantly, they were baptized as Christians. In thanksgiving Alfred founded the great Abbey of St Mary at Shaftesbury, the one great monastic foundation of the reign, and gave his daughter Ethel as the first Abbess. In the Middle Ages English devotion to Mary was such as to make the country known as 'Our Lady's Dower', but this may well date back to Alfred.

I have quoted the Dedication of the poem on pages 109–112, and it is a great shame that lack of space does not allow it to be included as a whole. I am sure that Chesterton saw parallels between Alfred defending Christian England with his sword, and his own attempts to do so with the pen. In the poem he uses the legend that Alfred spied on the Northmen as a harper, and engaged in debate with them while the arms of the North seemed triumphant.

> I will even answer the mighty earl
> That asked of Wessex men
> Why they be meek and monkish folk
> And bow to the White Lord's broken yoke;
> What sign have we save blood and smoke?
> Here is my answer then

That on you is fallen the shadow,
And not upon the Name;
That although we scatter and though we fly,
And you hang over us like the sky,
You are more tired of victory,
Than we are tired of shame.

That though you hunt the Christian man
Like a hare on the hill-side,
the hare has still more to run
Than you have heart to ride.

* * * * * * * * * * * * * * * *

Therefore your end is on you,
Is on you and your kings,
Not for a fire in Ely fen,
Not that your gods are nine or ten,
But because it is only Christian men
Guard even heathen things.

For our God hath blessed creation,
calling it good. I know
What spirit with whom you blindly band
Hath blessed destruction with his hand;
Yet by God's death the stars shall stand
And the small apples grow.

As GKC says in *Orthodoxy*, Christianity has been blamed
for all the century's evils, even though those evils have clearly
got worse as religious belief and practice have declined. Stalin
and Mao were atheists, and Hitler wanted to abolish this
'delusion of the weak' in favour of the old Nordic gods.
It is resented by the politically correct who demand that
crosses be removed from public places on the grounds

that they give offence. Yet it was not atheist liberals who abolished slavery, but Evangelical Christians following the example of John Wesley.

C.S. Lewis has written how in the dark days of 1940–41 he and friends went about reciting passages from *The Ballad of the White Horse* as the only thing which seemed to lighten that darkness. Surely now it is time for Christians to be more assertive about the good we have done and the sanity which we have to offer. Chesterton, then, can be our poet and guide for this endeavour.

Prophet of Orthodoxy / Prophet of Sanity

Boswell once told Johnson of Berkeley's theory that we know nothing directly, that we only have ideas of things in our minds. He challenged the Doctor to refute it. 'Johnson, striking his foot with mighty force against a large stone, till he rebounded from it, answered "I refute it thus".' As Chesterton saw it, Dr Johnson was great because he was a realist, and the same could also be applied to himself:

> It is this gigantic realism in Johnson's kindness, the
> directness of his emotionalism, when he is emotional,
> that gives him his hold upon generations of living
> men. There is nothing elaborate about his ethics; he
> wants to know whether a man, as a fact, is happy or
> unhappy, is lying or telling the truth. He may seem to
> be hammering at the brain through long nights of
> noise and thunder, but he can walk into the heart
> without knocking. *The Real Dr Johnson*

In the 1920s and 1930s Etienne Gilson was the most distinguished scholar of the works of St Thomas Aquinas. His reverence for Chesterton's work on the great Dominican has already been noted, but he also saw beyond the work to the sheer breadth and kindness of the man:

> Chesterton was one of the deepest thinkers who ever existed; he was deep because he was right, and he could not help being right; but he could not help being modest and charitable, so he left it to others who could understand him to know that he was right and deep; to others, he apologized for being right, and he made up for being deep by being witty. That is all they can see of him.

I want to end this introduction by briefly illustrating another aspect of GKC: the warmth of his personal advice to some of the many young people who came to him with problems or questions. (This tired, busy and hopelessly overworked man wrote hundreds of letters to such enquirers.) The first is to a young woman about to get married; the second to a girl hesitating about joining a convent:

> Dear Felicity, Your romantic puppet-play is one that *must* be performed. It must be performed because the old performance in which you and I have always believed, is coming back. Whatever you do, don't give up: or listen to cynicism which is dead – least of all to young cynics, who were born dead. Men have at last grown weary of weariness: and there is a limit to the patience of God ...

> Dear ... If you are really for It (I use, not without justice, the jovial phrase commonly used about people going to be jailed or flogged or hanged). If you are for It, it is the grandest and most glorious and deific thing that any human being can be For. It is far beyond my imagination. But never, for one instant, among all my

sins, have I ever doubted that it was *above* my imagination. I have no more doubt that a man like Fr McNabb is walking on a crystal floor over my head than I have that Quoodle [a dog] has a larger equipment of legs than I have ... But – there is still one worrying thought left in the dregs of what I call my mind ... If you must rush, this is a place you must rush to and cannot rush from ... If you have one of those black reactions *after* this, it may do you spiritual harm. It doesn't matter if you get tired of working for the Middlesex Mummies Exploration Fund and rush to the East Ealing Ethical Dance Movement – because we all live in that world and laugh at it and earn our living in it. But if you have a reaction from this greater thing – you will feel quite differently. You may be in danger of religious melancholia: for you will say 'I have had the Best and it did not help.' Anyhow you may be hurt ... and I hate your being hurt.

Like Dr Johnson, Chesterton 'can walk into the heart without knocking'.

Part One

---·---

Selected Poems

The Donkey

When fishes flew and forests walked
   And figs grew upon thorn,
Some moment when the moon was blood
   Then surely I was born.

With monstrous head and sickening cry
   And ears like errant wings,
The devil's walking parody
   On all four-footed things.

The tattered outlaw of the earth,
   Of ancient crooked will;
Starve, scourge, deride me: I am dumb,
   I keep my secret still.

Fools! For I also had my hour;
   One far fierce hour and sweet:
There was a shout about my ears,
   And palms before my feet.

The Praise of Dust

'What of vile dust?' the preacher said.
   Methought the whole world woke,

The dead stone lived beneath my foot,
   And my whole body spoke.

'You, that play tyrant to the dust,
    And stamp its wrinkled face,
This patient star that flings you not
    Far into homeless space.

'Come down out of your dusty shrine
    The living dust to see,
The flowers that at your sermon's end
    Stand blazing silently.

'Rich white and blood-red blossom; stones,
    Lichens like fire encrust;
A gleam of blue, a glare of gold,
    The vision of the dust.

'Pass them all by: till, as you come
    Where, at the city's edge,
Under a tree – I know it well –
    Under a lattice ledge,

'The sunshine falls on one brown head.
    You, too, O cold of clay,
Eater of stones, may haply hear
    The trumpets of that day,

'When God to all His paladins
    By His own splendour swore
To make a fairer face than heaven,
    Of dust and nothing more.'

By the Babe Unborn

If trees were tall and grasses short,
    As in some crazy tale,
If here and there a sea were blue
    Beyond the breaking pale,

If a fixed fire hung in the air
    To warm me one day through,
If deep green hair grew on great hills,
    I know what I should do.

In dark I lie: dreaming that there
    Are great eyes cold or kind,
And twisted streets and silent doors,
    And living men behind.

Let storm clouds come: better an hour,
    And leave to weep and fight,
Than all the ages I have ruled
    The empires of the night.

I think that if they gave me leave
    Within the world to stand,
I would be good through all the day
    I spent in fairyland.

They should not hear a word from me
    Of selfishness or scorn,
If only I could find the door,
    If only I were born.

Joseph

If the stars fell; night's nameless dreams
    Of bliss and blasphemy came true,
If skies were green and snow were gold,
    And you loved me as I loved you;

O long light hands and curled brown hair,
    And eyes where sits a naked soul;
Dare I even then draw near and burn
    My fingers in the aureole?

Yes, in the one wise foolish hour
    God gives this strange strength to a man.
He can demand, though not deserve,
    Where ask he cannot, seize he can.

But once the blood's wild wedding o'er,
    Were not dread his, half-dark desire,
To see the Christ-child in the cot,
    The Virgin Mary by the fire?

Who Goes Home?

In the city set upon slime and loam
They cry in their parliament 'Who goes home?'
And there comes no answer in arch or dome,
For none in the city of graves goes home.
Yet these shall perish and understand,
For God has pity on this great land.

Men that are men again; who goes home?
Tocsin and trumpeter! Who goes home?
For there's blood on the field and blood on the foam

And blood on the body when Man goes home.
And a voice valedictory ...Who is for Victory?
Who is for Liberty? Who goes home?

A Hymn

O God of earth and altar,
   Bow down and hear our cry,
Our earthly rulers falter,
   Our people drift and die;
The walls of gold entomb us,
   The swords of scorn divide,
Take not thy thunder from us,
   But take away our pride.

From all that terror teaches,
   From lies of tongue and pen,
From all the easy speeches
   That comfort cruel men,
From sale and profanation
   Of honour and the sword,
From sleep and from damnation,
   Deliver us, good Lord.

Tie in a living tether
   The prince and priest and thrall,
Bind all our lives together,
   Smite us and save us all;
In ire and exultation
   Aflame with faith, and free,
Lift up a living nation,
   A single sword to thee.

The House of Christmas

There fared a mother driven forth
Out of an inn to roam;
In the place where she was homeless
All men are at home.
The crazy stable close at hand,
With shaking timber and shifting sand,
Grew a stronger thing to abide and stand
Than the square stones of Rome.

For men are homesick in their homes,
And strangers under the sun,
And they lay their heads in a foreign land
Whenever the day is done.
Here we have battle and blazing eyes,
And chance and honour and high surprise,
But our homes are under miraculous skies
Where the yule tale was begun.

A Child in a foul stable,
Where the beasts feed and foam;
Only where He was homeless
Are you and I at home;
We have hands that fashion and heads that know,
But our hearts we lost – how long ago!
In a place no chart nor ship can show
Under the sky's dome.

This world is wild as an old wives' tale,
And strange the plain things are,
The earth is enough and the air is enough
For our wonder and our war;
But our rest is as far as the fire-drake swings
And our peace is put in impossible things

Where clashed and thundered unthinkable wings
Round an incredible star.

To an open house in the evening
Home shall men come,
To an older place than Eden
And a taller town than Rome.
To the end of the way of the wandering star,
To the things that cannot be and that are,
To the place where God was homeless
And all men are at home.

A Cloud Was On the Mind of Men
Dedication of 'The Man Who Was Thursday', to Edmund Clerihew Bentley

A cloud was on the mind of men, and wailing went the
    weather,
Yea, a sick cloud upon the soul when we were boys together.
Science announced nonentity and art admired decay;
The world was old and ended: but you and I were gay.
Round us in antic order their crippled vices came –
Lust that had lost its laughter, fear that had lost its shame.
Like the white lock of Whistler, that lit our aimless gloom,
Men showed their own white feather as proudly as a plume.
Life was a fly that faded, and death a drone that stung;
The world was very old indeed when you and I were young.
They twisted even decent sin to shapes not to be named:
Men were ashamed of honour; but we were not ashamed.
Weak if we were and foolish, not thus we failed, not thus;
When that black Baal blocked the heavens he had no hymns
    from us.
Children we were – our forts of sand were even as weak as
    we,
High as they went we piled them up to break that bitter sea.

Fools as we were in motley, all jangling and absurd,
When all church bells were silent our cap and bells were
    heard.
Not all unhelped we held the fort, our tiny flags unfurled;
Some giants laboured in that cloud to lift it from the world.
I find again the book we found, I feel the hour that flings
Far out of fish-shaped Paumanok¹ some cry of cleaner
    things;
And the Green Carnation² withered, as in forest fires that
    pass,
Roared in the wind of all the world ten million leaves of
    grass;
Or sane and sweet and sudden as a bird sings in the rain –
Truth out of Tusitala³ spoke and pleasure out of pain.
Yea, cool and clear and sudden as a bird sings in the grey,
Dunedin to Samoa spoke, and darkness unto day.
But we were young; we lived to see God break their bitter
    charms,
God and the good Republic come riding back in arms:
We have seen the city of Mansoul, even as it rocked, relieved –
Blessed are they who did not see, but being blind, believed.

This is a tale of those old fears, even of those emptied hells,
And none but you shall understand the true thing that it
    tells –
Of what colossal gods of shame could cow men and yet
    crash,
Of what huge devils hid the stars, yet fell at a pistol flash.
The doubts that were so plain to chase, so dreadful to
    withstand –
Oh, who shall understand but you; yea, who shall
    understand?
The doubts that drove us through the night as we two talked
    amain,

And day had broken on the streets e'er it broke upon the
    brain.
Between us, by the peace of God, such truth can now be
    told;
Yea, there is strength in striking root, and good in growing
    old.
We have found common things at last, and marriage and a
    creed,
And I may safely write it now, and you may safely read.

1. *Paumanok* is the Indian name for Long Island, where Walt Whitman
   was born in 1818.
2. *The Green Carnation* refers to Oscar Wilde.
3. *Tusitala* 'Chief Teller of Stories' was the Samoan name given to
   R. L. Stevenson.

A Second Childhood

When all my days are ending
And I have no song to sing,
I think I shall not be too old
To stare at everything;
As I stared once at a nursery door
Or a tall tree and a swing.

Wherein God's ponderous mercy hangs
On all my sins and me,
Because He does not take away
The terror from the tree
And stones still shine along the road
That are and cannot be.

Men grow too old for love, my love,
Men grow too old for wine,
But I shall not grow too old to see
Unearthly daylight shine,
Changing my chamber's dust to snow
Till I doubt if it be mine.

Behold, the crowning mercies melt,
The first surprises stay;
And in my dross is dropped a gift
For which I dare not pray:
That a man grow used to grief and joy
But not to night and day.

Men grow too old for love, my love,
Men grow too old for lies,
But I shall not grow too old to see
Enormous night arise,
A cloud that is larger than the world
And a monster made of eyes.

Nor am I worthy to unloose
The latchet of my shoe;
Or shake the dust from off my feet
Or the staff that bears me through
On ground that is too good to last,
Too solid to be true.

Men grow too old to woo, my love,
Men grow too old to wed:
But I shall not grow too old to see
Hung crazily overhead
Incredible rafters when I wake
And find I am not dead.

A thrill of thunder in my hair:
Though blackening clouds be plain,
Still I am stung and startled
By the first drop of the rain:
Romance and pride and passion pass
And these are what remain.

Strange crawling carpets of the grass,
Wide windows of the sky:
So in this perilous grace of God
With all my sins go I:
And things grow new though I grow old,
Though I grow old and die.

The Ballad of the White Horse
Dedication

Of great limbs gone to chaos,
    A great face turned to night –
Why bend above a shapeless shroud
Seeking in such archaic cloud
    Sight of strong lords and light?

Where seven sunken Englands[1]
    Lie buried one by one,
Why should one idle spade, I wonder,
Shake up the dust of thanes like thunder
    To smoke and choke the sun?

In cloud of clay so cast to heaven
    What shape shall man discern?
These lords may light the mystery
Of mastery or victory,
And these ride high in history,
    But these shall not return.

Gored on the Norman gonfalon
   The Golden Dragon died:[2]
We shall not wake with ballad strings
The good time of the smaller things,
We shall not see the holy kings
   Ride down by Severn side.

Stiff, strange, and quaintly coloured
   As the broidery of Bayeux
The England of that dawn remains,
And this of Alfred and the Danes
Seems like the tales a whole tribe feigns
   Too English to be true.

Of a good king on an island
   That ruled once on a time;
And as he walked by an apple tree
There came green devils out of the sea
With sea-plants trailing heavily
   And tracks of opal slime.

Yet Alfred is no fairy tale;
   His days as our days ran,
He also looked forth for an hour
On peopled plains and skies that lower,
From those few windows in the tower
   That is the head of a man.

But who shall look from Alfred's hood
   Or breathe his breath alive?
His century like a small dark cloud
Drifts far; it is an eyeless crowd,
Where the tortured trumpets scream aloud
   And the dense arrows drive.

Lady, by one light only
   We look from Alfred's eyes,
We know he saw athwart the wreck
The sign that hangs about your neck,
Where One more than Melchizedek
   Is dead and never dies.

Therefore I bring these rhymes to you.
   Who brought the cross to me,
Since on you flaming without flaw
I saw the sign that Guthrum saw
When he let break his ships of awe,
   And laid peace on the sea.

Do you remember when we went
   Under a dragon moon,
And 'mid volcanic tints of night
Walked where they fought the unknown fight
And saw black trees on the battle-height,
   Black thorn on Ethandune?

And I thought, 'I will go with you,
   As man with God has gone,
And wander with a wandering star,
The wandering heart of things that are,
The fiery cross of love and war
   That like yourself, goes on.'

O go you onward; where you are
   Shall honour and laughter be,
Past purpled forest and pearlèd foam,
God's winged pavilion free to roam,
Your face, that is a wandering home,
   A flying home for me.

Ride through the silent earthquake lands,
   Wide as a waste is wide,
Across these days like deserts, when
Pride and a little scratching pen
Have dried and split the hearts of men,
   Heart of the heroes, ride.

Up through an empty house of stars,
   Being what heart you are,
Up the inhuman steps of space
As on a staircase go in grace,
Carrying the firelight on your face
   Beyond the loneliest star.

Take these; in memory of the hour
   We strayed a space from home
And saw the smoke-hued hamlets, quaint
With Westland king and Westland saint,
And watched the western glory faint
   Along the road to Frome.

1. Anglo-Saxon England originally consisted of seven kingdoms.
2. The Golden Dragon was the symbol of the Kingdom of Wessex; the reference is to the Norman Conquest in 1066.

Preface to the Ballad of St Barbara. To F.C.
In Memoriam Palestine, 1919

Do you remember one immortal
Lost moment out of time and space,
What time we thought, who passed the portal
Of that divine disastrous place
Where Life was slain and Truth was slandered
On that one holier hill than Rome,

How far abroad our bodies wandered
That evening when our souls came home?

The mystic city many-gated,
With monstrous columns, was your own:
Herodian stones fell down and waited
Two thousand years to be your throne.
In the grey rocks the burning blossom
Glowed terrible as the sacred blood:
It was no stranger to your bosom
Than bluebells of an English wood.

Do you remember a road that follows
The way of unforgotten feet,
Where from the waste of rocks and hollows
Climb up the crawling crooked street
The stages of one towering drama
Always ahead and out of sight ...
Do you remember Aceldama
And the jackal barking in the night?

Life is not void or stuff for scorners:
We have laughed loud and kept our love,
We have heard singers in tavern corners
And not forgotten the birds above:
We have known smiters and sons of thunder
And not unworthily walked with them,
We have grown wiser and lost not wonder;
And we have seen Jerusalem.

The Convert[1]

After one moment when I bowed my head
And the whole world turned over and came upright,
And I came out where the old road shone white,
I walked the ways and heard what all men said,
Forests of tongues, like autumn leaves unshed,
    Being not unlovable but strange and light;
    Old riddles and new creeds, not in despite
    But softly, as men smile about the dead.

The sages have a hundred maps to give
That trace their crawling cosmos like a tree,
They rattle reason out through many a sieve
That stores the sand and lets the gold go free:
And all these things are less than dust to me
Because my name is Lazarus and I live.

1. This poem was written on 30 July 1922 – the day of Chesterton's
   reception into the Catholic Church.

Part Two

Selected Essays

Tom Jones and Morality

There seems to be an extraordinary idea abroad that Fielding was in some way an immoral or offensive writer. I have been astounded by the number of the leading articles, literary articles, and other articles written about him just now in which there is a curious tone of apologizing for the man. One critic says that after all he couldn't help it, because he lived in the eighteenth century; another says that we must allow for the change of manners and ideas; another says that he was not altogether without generous and humane feelings; another suggests that he clung feebly, after all, to a few of the less important virtues. What on earth does all this mean? Fielding described Tom Jones as going on in a certain way, in which, most unfortunately, a very large number of young men do go on. It is unnecessary to say that Henry Fielding knew that it was an unfortunate way of going on. Even Tom Jones knew that. He said in so many words that it was a very unfortunate way of going on; he said, one may almost say, that it had ruined his life; the passage is there for the benefit of anyone who may take the trouble to read the book. There is ample evidence (though even this is of a mystical and indirect kind), there is ample evidence that Fielding probably thought that it was better to be Tom Jones than to be an utter coward and sneak. There is simply not one rag or thread or speck of evidence to show that Fielding thought that it was better to be Tom Jones than to be a good man. All that he is concerned with is the description of a definite and very real type of young man; the young man whose passions and whose selfish necessities sometimes seemed to be stronger than anything else in him.

The practical morality of Tom Jones is bad, though not so bad, *spiritually* speaking, as the practical morality of Arthur Pendennis or the practical morality of Pip, and certainly nothing like so bad as the profound practical immorality of Daniel Deronda. The practical morality of Tom Jones is bad; but I cannot see any proof that his theoretical morality was particularly bad. There is no need to tell the majority of modern young men even to live up to the theoretical ethics of Henry Fielding. They would suddenly spring into the stature of archangels if they lived up to the theoretic ethics of poor Tom Jones. Tom Jones is still alive, with all his good and all his evil; he is walking about the streets; we meet him every day. We meet with him, we drink with him, we smoke with him, we talk with him, we talk about him. The only difference is that we have no longer the intellectual courage to write about him. We split up the supreme and central human being, Tom Jones, into a number of separate aspects. We let Mr J.M. Barrie write about him in his good moments, and make him out better than he is. We let Zola write about him in his bad moments, and make him out much worse that he is. We let Maeterlinck celebrate those moments of spiritual panic which he knows to be cowardly; we let Mr Rudyard Kipling celebrate those moments of brutality which he knows to be far more cowardly. We let obscene writers write about the obscenities of this ordinary man. We let puritan writers write about the purities of this ordinary man. We look through one peephole that makes men out as devils, and we call it the new art. We look through another peephole that makes men out as angels, and we call it the New Theology. But if we pull down some dusty old books from the bookshelf, if we turn over some old mildewed leaves, and if in that obscurity and decay we find some faint traces of a tale about a complete man, such a man as is walking on the pavement outside, we suddenly pull a long face, and we call it the coarse morals of a bygone age.

The truth is that all these things mark a certain change in the general view of morals; not, I think, a change for the better. We have grown to associate morality in a book with a kind of optimism and prettiness; according to us, a moral book is a book about moral people. But the old idea was almost exactly the opposite; a moral book was a book about immoral people. A moral book was full of pictures like Hogarth's 'Gin Lane' or 'Stages of Cruelty', or it recorded, like the popular broadsheet, 'God's dreadful judgement' against some blasphemer or murderer. There is philosophical reason for this change. The homeless scepticism of our time has reached a subconscious feeling that morality is somehow merely a matter of human taste — an accident of psychology. And if goodness only exists in certain human minds, a man wishing to praise goodness will naturally exaggerate the amount of it that there is in human minds or the number of human minds in which it is supreme. Every confession that man is vicious is a confession that virtue is visionary. Every book which admits that evil is real is felt in some vague way to be admitting that good is unreal. The modern instinct is that if the heart of man is evil, there is nothing that remains good. But the older feeling was that if the heart of man was ever so evil, there was something that remained good — goodness remained good. An actual avenging virtue existed outside the human race; to that men rose, or from that men fell away. Therefore, of course, this law itself was as much demonstrated in the breach as in the observance. If Tom Jones violated morality, so much the worse for Tom Jones. Fielding did not feel, as a melancholy modern would have done, that every sin of Tom Jones was in some way breaking the spell, or we may even say destroying the fiction of morality. Men spoke of the sinner breaking the law; but it was rather the law that broke him. And what modern people call the foulness and freedom of Fielding is generally the severity and moral stringency of Fielding. He would not have thought that he was serving morality at all if he had written a book all about nice people. Fielding would have considered Mr Ian Maclaren extremely immoral; and there is something to be said for that view. Telling the truth about the terrible struggle of the human soul is surely a very elementary part of the ethics of honesty. If the characters are not wicked, the book is.

This older and firmer conception of right as existing outside human weakness and without reference to human error can be felt in the very lightest and loosest of the works of old English literature. It is commonly unmeaning enough to call Shakespeare a great moralist; but in this particular way Shakespeare is a very typical moralist. Whenever he alludes to right and wrong it is always with this old implication. Right is right, even if nobody does it. Wrong is wrong, even if everybody is wrong about it.

All Things Considered, 1908

Humanitarianism and Strength

Somebody writes complaining of something I said about progress. I have forgotten what I said, but I am quite certain that it was (like a certain Mr Douglas in a poem which I have also forgotten) tender and true. In any case, what I say now is this. Human history is so rich and complicated that you can make out a case for any course of improvement or retrogression. I could make out that the world has been growing more democratic, for the English franchise has certainly grown more democratic. I could also make out that the world has been growing more aristocratic, for the English Public Schools have certainly grown more aristocratic. I could prove the decline of militarism by the decline of flogging; I could prove the increase of militarism by the increase of standing armies and conscription. But I can prove anything in this way. I can prove that the world has always been growing greener. Only lately men have invented absinthe and the *Westminster Gazette*. I could prove the world has grown less green. There are no more Robin Hood foresters, and fields are being covered with houses. I could show that the world was less red with khaki or more red with the new penny stamps. But in all cases progress means progress only in some particular thing. Have you ever noticed that strange line of Tennyson, in which he confesses, half consciously, how very *conventional* progress is? –

Let the great world spin for ever down the ringing grooves of change.

Even in praising change, he takes for a simile the most unchanging thing. He calls our modern change a groove. And it is a groove; perhaps there was never anything so groovy.

Nothing would induce me in so idle a monologue as this to discuss adequately a great political matter like the question of the military punishments in Egypt. But I may suggest one broad reality to be observed by both sides, and which is, generally speaking, observed by neither. Whatever else is right, it is utterly wrong to employ the argument that we Europeans must do to savages and Asiatics whatever savages and Asiatics do to us. I have even seen some controversialists use the metaphor, 'We must fight them with their own weapons.' Very well; let those controversialists take their metaphor, and take it literally. Let us fight the Sudanese with their own weapons. Their own weapons are large, very clumsy knives, with an occasional old-fashioned gun. Their own weapons are also torture and slavery. If we fight them with torture and slavery, we shall be fighting badly, precisely as if we fought them with clumsy knives and old guns. That is the whole strength of our Christian civilization, that it does fight with its own weapons and not with other people's. It is not true that superiority suggests a tit for tat. It is not true that if a small hooligan puts his tongue out at the Lord Chief Justice, the Lord Chief Justice immediately realizes that his only chance of maintaining his position is to put his tongue out at the little hooligan. The hooligan may or may not have any respect at all for the Lord Chief Justice: that is a matter which we may contentedly leave as a solemn psychological mystery. But if the hooligan has any respect at all for the Lord Chief Justice, that respect is certainly extended to the Lord Chief Justice entirely because he does not put his tongue out.

Exactly in the same way the ruder or more sluggish races regard the civilization of Christendom. If they have any respect for it, it is precisely because it does not use their own coarse and cruel expedients. According to some modern moralists, whenever Zulus cut off the heads of dead Englishmen, Englishmen must cut off the heads of dead Zulus. Whenever Arabs or Egyptians constantly use the whip to their slaves, Englishmen must use the whip to their subjects. And on a similar principle (I suppose), whenever an English Admiral has to fight cannibals the English Admiral ought to eat them. However unattractive a menu consisting entirely of barbaric kings may appear to an English gentleman, he must try to sit down to it with an appetite. He must fight the Sandwich Islanders with their own weapons; and their own weapons are knives and forks. But the truth of the matter is, of course, that to do this kind of thing is to break the whole spell of our supremacy. All the mystery of the white man, all the fearful poetry of the white man, so far as it exists in the eyes of these savages, consists in the fact that we do not do such things. The Zulus point at us and say, 'Observe the advent of these inexplicable demi-gods, these magicians, who do not cut off the noses of their enemies.' The Sudanese say to each other, 'This hardy people never flogs its servants; it is superior to the simplest and most obvious human pleasures.' And the cannibals say, 'The austere and terrible race, the race that denies itself even boiled missionary, is upon us: let us flee.'

Whether or no these details are a little conjectural, the general proposition I suggest is the plainest common sense. The elements that make Europe upon the whole the most humanitarian civilization are precisely the elements that make it upon the whole the strongest. For the power which makes a man able to entertain a good impulse is the same as that which enables him to make a good gun; it is imagination. It is imagination that makes a man outwit his enemy, and it is imagination that makes him spare his enemy. It is precisely because this picturing of the other man's point of view is in the main a thing in which Christians and Europeans specialize, that Christians and Europeans, with all their faults, have carried to such perfection both the arts of peace and war.

They alone have invented machine guns, and they alone have invented ambulances; they have invented ambulances (strange as it may sound) for the same reason for which they have invented machine guns. Both involve a vivid calculation of remote events. It is precisely because the East, with all its wisdom, is cruel, that the East, with all its wisdom, is weak. And it is precisely because savages are pitiless that they are still – merely savages. If they could imagine their enemy's sufferings they could also imagine his tactics. If Zulus did cut off the Englishman's head they might really borrow it. For if you do not understand a man you cannot crush him. And if you do understand him, very probably you will not.

When I was about seven years old I used to think that the chief modern danger was a danger of over-civilization. I am inclined to think now that the chief modern danger is that of a slow return towards barbarism, just such a return towards barbarism as is indicated in the suggestions of barbaric retaliation of which I have just spoken. Civilization in the best sense merely means the full authority of the human spirit over all externals. Barbarism means the worship of those externals in their crude and unconquered state. Barbarism means the worship of Nature; and in recent poetry, science and philosophy there has been too much of the worship of Nature. Wherever men begin to talk much and with great solemnity about the forces outside man, the note of it is barbaric. When men talk much about heredity and environment they are almost barbarians. The modern men of science are many of them almost barbarians. Mr Blatchford is in great danger of becoming a barbarian. For barbarians (especially the truly squalid and unhappy barbarians) are always talking about these scientific subjects from morning till night. That is why they remain squalid and unhappy; that is why they remain barbarians. Hottentots are always talking about heredity, like Mr Blatchford. Sandwich Islanders are always talking about environment, like Mr Suthers. Savages — those that are truly stunted or depraved — dedicate nearly all their tales and sayings to the subject of physical kinship, of a curse on this or that tribe, of a taint in this or that family, of the invincible law of blood, of the unavoidable evil of places. The true savage is a slave, and is always talking about what he must do; the true civilized man is a free man and is always talking about what he may do. Hence all the Zola heredity and Ibsen heredity that has been written in our time affects me as not merely evil, but as essentially ignorant and retrogressive. This sort of science is almost the only thing that can with strict propriety be called reactionary. Scientific determinism is simply the primal twilight of all mankind; and some men seem to be returning to it.

Another savage trait of our time is the disposition to talk about material substances instead of about ideas. The old civilization talked about the sin of gluttony or excess. We talk about the Problem of Drink — as if drink could be a problem. When people have come to call the problem of human intemperance the Problem of Drink, and to talk about curing it by attacking the drink traffic, they have reached quite a dim stage of barbarism. The thing is an inverted form of fetish worship; it is no sillier to say that a bottle is a god than to say that a bottle is a devil. The people who talk about the curse of drink will probably progress down that dark hill. In a little while we shall have them calling the practice of wife-beating the Problem of Pokers; the habit of housebreaking will be called the Problem of the Skeleton-Key Trade; and for all I know they may try to prevent forgery by shutting up all the stationers' shops by Act of Parliament.

I cannot help thinking that there is some shadow of this uncivilized materialism lying at present upon a much more dignified and valuable cause. Everyone is talking just now about the desirability of ingeminating peace and averting war. But even war and peace are physical states rather than moral states, and in talking about them only we have by no means got to the bottom of the matter. How, for instance, do we as a matter of fact create peace in one single community? We do not do it by vaguely telling every one to avoid fighting and to submit to anything that is done to him. We do it by definitely defining his rights and then undertaking to avenge his wrongs. We shall never have a common peace in Europe till we have a common principle in Europe. People talk of 'The United States of Europe'; but they forget that it needed the very doctrinal 'Declaration of Independence' to make the United States of America. You cannot agree about nothing any more than you can quarrel about nothing.

All Things Considered, 1908

A Plea for Popular Philosophy

What modern people want to be made to understand is simply that all argument begins with an assumption; that is, with something that you do not doubt. You can, of course, if you like, doubt the assumption at the beginning of your argument, but in that case you are beginning a different argument with another assumption at the beginning of it. Every argument begins with an infallible dogma, and that infallible dogma can only be disputed by falling back on some other infallible dogma; you can never prove your first statement or it would not be your first. All this is the alphabet of thinking ... And it has this special and positive point about it, that it can be taught in a school, like the other alphabet. Not to start an argument without stating your postulates could be taught in philosophy as it is taught in Euclid, in a common schoolroom with a blackboard. And I think it might be taught in some simple and rational degree even to the young, before they go out into the streets and are delivered over entirely to the logic and philosophy of the *Daily Mail*.

Much of our chaos about religion and doubt arises from this — that our modern sceptics always begin by telling us what they do not believe. But even in a sceptic we want to know first what he does believe. Before arguing, we want to know what we need not argue about. And this confusion is infinitely increased by the fact that all the sceptics of our time are sceptics at different degrees of the dissolution of scepticism ...

Now you and I have, I hope, this advantage over all those clever new philosophers, that we happen not to be mad. All of us believe in St Paul's Cathedral; most of us believe in St Paul. But let us clearly realize this fact, that we do believe in a number of things which are part of our existence, but which cannot be demonstrated. Leave religion for the moment wholly out of the question. All sane men, I say, believe firmly and unalterably in a certain number of things which are unproved and unprovable. Let us state them roughly.

(1) Every sane man believes that the world around him and the people in it are real, and not his own delusion or dream. No man starts burning London in the belief that his servant will soon wake him for breakfast. But that I, at any given moment, am not in a dream, is unproved and unprovable. That anything exists except myself is unproved and unprovable.

(2) All sane men believe that this world not only exists, but matters. Every man believes there is a sort of obligation on us to interest ourselves in this vision or panorama of life. He would think a man wrong who said, 'I did not ask for this farce and it bores me. I am aware that an old lady is being murdered downstairs, but I am going to sleep.' That there is any such duty to improve the things we did not make is a thing unproved and unprovable.

(3) All sane men believe that there is such a thing as a self or ego, which is continuous. There is no inch of my brain matter the same as it was ten years ago. But if I have saved a man in battle ten years ago, I am proud; if I have run away, I am ashamed. That there is such a paramount 'I' is unproved and unprovable. But it is more than unproved and unprovable; it is definitely disputed by many metaphysicians.

(4) Lastly, most sane men believe, and all sane men in practice assume, that they have a power of choice and responsibility for action.

Surely it might be possible to establish some plain, dull statement such as the above, to make people see where they stand. And if the youth of the future must not (at present) be taught any religion, it might at least be taught, clearly and firmly, the three or four sanities and certainties of human free thought.

Daily News, 22 June 1907

No Such Thing

Educational conferences are always interesting for the simple reason that under the title of Education you can discuss anything whatever that comes into your head. This is the main fact which, in spite of all the talk on the subject of education, no one seems to notice in connection with it. The chief thing about the subject of education is that it is not a subject at all. There is no such thing as education. The thing is merely a loose phrase for the passing on to others of whatever truth or virtue we happen to have ourselves. It is typical of our time that the more doubtful we are about the value of philosophy, the more certain we are about the value of education. That is to say, the more doubtful we are about whether we have any truth, the more certain we are (apparently) that we can teach it to children. The smaller our faith in doctrine, the larger is our faith in doctors ...

Hence, I believe that the whole business of modern education is an immense imposture or convention, an excuse for grown-up people talking about large matters at large. The poor wretches are forbidden in our time to have a proper human religion; that which they ought to discuss in the form of theology they are driven to discuss under the disgusting excuse of education. Talking about serious questions is a pleasure; it is perhaps the greatest mere pleasure known to man. Even devils (as Milton truly perceived) would discuss theology. But in our time it is a secret pleasure; it is enjoyed in dark corners, like a vice.

I need hardly say that the fact that education allows of a man discussing anything is the reason why I have put it first. The actual text which caught my eye and revealed the vagaries and various possibilities of the theme was the report of the Conference of Head Teachers at which Professor Muirhead lectured on Moral Instruction. The phrase Moral Instruction is generally used, of course, with reference to such a programme as that advanced by the Moral Instruction League; it is generally used as signifying the proposal to substitute certain ethical lessons for the religious instruction (somewhat dim and dubious as it is) which is given in most schools. So far as this meaning is concerned, my own position is a simple and, I hope, an inoffensive one. I even offer a compromise or bargain, exactly as if I were a politician. I am quite prepared to promise the secularists secular education if they on their side will promise (on the tombs of their mothers) not to have moral instruction. Secular education seems to me intellectually clean and comprehensible. Moral instruction seems to me unclean, intolerable; I would destroy it with fire. Teaching the Old Testament by itself means teaching ancient Hebrew ethics which are simple, barbaric, rudimentary, and, to a Christian, unsatisfying. Teaching moral instruction means teaching modern London, Birmingham and Boston ethics which are not barbaric and rudimentary, but are corrupt, hysterical and crawling with worms and which are, to a Christian, not unsatisfying but detestable. The old Jew who says you must fight only for your tribe is inadequate; but the modern prig who says you must never fight for anything is substantially and specifically immoral. I know quite well, of course, that the non-religious ethics suggested for modern schools do not verbally assert these things; they only talk about peaceful reform, true Christianity and the importance of Count Tolstoy. It is all a matter of tone and implication; but then so is all teaching. Education is implication. It is not the things you say which children respect; when you say things, they very commonly laugh and do the opposite. It is the things you assume that really sink into them. It is the things you forget even to teach that they learn ...

Churches, philosophies, sects, social influences, all educational authorities have disagreed, have distorted each other's meaning, have destroyed each other's proposals, in this matter of education. But here I hope I offer a peaceful proposition on which all churches and all philosophies can agree. I am the bearer of the only real olive branch. All educational authorities can agree upon the simple proposition that I lay down. There is no such thing as education. Education does not exist. That will indeed be a blessed gospel to spread through the modern world, and even my feet will be beautiful upon the mountains when I proclaim it. For indeed this is the nearest statement of the truth. There is no education apart from some particular kind of education. There is no education that is not sectarian education.

Illustrated London News, 1907

The Diabolist

Every now and then I have introduced into my essays an element of truth. Things that really happened have been mentioned, such as meeting President Kruger[1] or being thrown out of a cab. What I have now to relate really happened; yet there was no element in it of practical politics or of personal danger. It was simply a quiet conversation which I had with another man. But that quiet conversation was by far the most terrible thing that has ever happened to me in my life. It happened so long ago that I cannot be certain of the exact words of the dialogue, only of its main questions and answers; but there is one sentence in it for which I can answer absolutely and word for word. It was a sentence so awful that I could not forget it if I would. It was the last sentence spoken; and it was not spoken to me.

The thing befell me in the days when I was at an art school. An art school is different from almost all other schools or colleges in this respect: that, being of new and crude creation and of lax discipline, it presents a specially strong contrast between the industrious and the idle. People at an art school either do an atrocious amount of work or do no work at all. I belonged, along with other charming people, to the latter

---

1. Paul Kruger (1825–1904): reviled leader of the Boers in South Africa.

class; and this threw me often into the society of men who were very different from myself, and who were idle for reasons very different from mine. I was idle because I was very much occupied; I was engaged about that time in discovering, to my own extreme and lasting astonishment, that I was not an atheist. But there were others also at loose ends who were engaged in discovering what Carlyle called (I think with needless delicacy) the fact that ginger is hot in the mouth.

I value that time, in short, because it made me acquainted with a good representative number of blackguards. In this connection there are two very curious things which the critic of human life may observe. The first is the fact that there is one real difference between men and women; that women prefer to talk in twos, while men prefer to talk in threes. The second is that when you find (as you often do) three young cads and idiots going about together and getting drunk together every day, you generally find that one of the three cads and idiots is (for some extraordinary reason) not a cad and not an idiot. In those small groups devoted to a drivelling dissipation there is almost always one man who seems to have condescended to his company; one man who, while he can talk a foul triviality with his fellows, can also talk politics with a Socialist, or philosophy with a Catholic.

It was just such a man whom I came to know well. It was strange, perhaps, that he liked his dirty, drunken society; it was stranger still, perhaps, that he liked my society. For hours of the day he would talk with me about Milton or Gothic architecture; for hours of the night he would go where I have no wish to follow him, even in speculation. He was a man with a long, ironical face, and close and red hair; he was by class a gentleman, and could walk like one, but preferred, for some reason, to walk like a groom carrying two pails. He looked like a sort of Super-jockey; as if some archangel had gone on the Turf. And I shall never forget the half-hour in which he and I argued about real things for the first and the last time.

Along the front of the big building of which our school was a part ran a huge slope of stone steps, higher, I think, than those that lead up to St Paul's Cathedral. On a black wintry evening he and I were wandering on these cold heights, which seemed as dreary as a pyramid under the stars. The one thing visible below us in the blackness was a burning and blowing fire; for some gardener (I suppose) was burning something in the grounds, and from time to time the red sparks went whirling past us like a swarm of scarlet insects in the dark. Above us also it was gloom; but if one stared long enough at that upper darkness, one saw vertical stripes of grey in the black and then became conscious of the colossal façade of the Doric building, phantasmal, yet filling the sky, as if Heaven were still filled with the gigantic ghost of Paganism.

The man asked me abruptly why I was becoming orthodox. Until he said it, I really had not known that I was; but the moment he had said it I knew it to be literally true. And the process had been so long and full that I answered him at once, out of existing stores of explanation.

'I am becoming orthodox,' I said, 'because I have come, rightly or wrongly, after stretching my brain till it bursts, to the old belief that heresy is worse even than sin. An error is more menacing than a crime, for an error begets crimes. An Imperialist is worse than a pirate. For an Imperialist keeps a school for pirates; he teaches piracy disinterestedly and without an adequate salary. A Free Lover is worse than a profligate. For a profligate is serious and reckless even in his shortest love; while a Free Lover is cautious and irresponsible even in his longest devotion. I hate modern doubt, because it is dangerous.'

'You mean dangerous to morality,' he said in a voice of wonderful gentleness. 'I expect you are right. But why do you care about morality?'

I glanced at his face quickly. He had thrust out his neck as he had a trick of doing; and so brought his face abruptly into the light of the bonfire from below, like a face in the footlights. His long chin and high cheekbones were lit up infernally from underneath; so that he looked like a fiend staring down into the flaming pit. I had an unmeaning sense of being tempted in a wilderness; and even as I paused a burst of red sparks broke past.

'Aren't those sparks splendid?' I said.

'Yes,' he replied.

'That is all that I ask you to admit,' I said. 'Give me those few red specks and I will deduce Christian morality. Once I thought like you, that one's pleasure in a flying spark was a thing that could come and go with that spark. Once I thought that the delight was as free as the fire. Once I thought that red star we see was alone in space. But now I know that the red star is only on the apex of an invisible pyramid of virtues. That red fire is only the flower on a stalk of living habits, which you cannot see. Only because your mother made you say "Thank you" for a bun are you now able to thank Nature or chaos for those red stars of an instant or for the white stars of all time. Only because you were humble before fireworks on the fifth of November do you now enjoy any fireworks that you chance to see. You only like them being red because you were told about the blood of the martyrs; you only like them being bright because brightness is a glory. That flame flowered out of virtues, and it will fade with virtues. Seduce a woman, and that spark will be less bright. Shed blood, and that spark will be less red. Be really bad, and they will be to you like the spots on a wallpaper.'

He had a horrible fairness of the intellect that made me despair of his soul. A common harmless atheist would have denied that religion produced humility or humility a simple joy: but he admitted both. He only said, 'But shall I not find in evil a life of its own? Granted that for every woman I ruin one of those red sparks will go out: will not the expanding pleasure of ruin …?'

'Do you see that fire?' I asked. 'If we had a real fighting democracy, someone would burn you in it; like the devil-worshipper that you are.'

'Perhaps,' he said in his tired, fair way. 'Only what you call evil I call good.'

He went down the great steps alone, and I felt as if I wanted the steps swept and cleaned. I followed later, and as I went to find my hat in the low, dark passage where it hung, I suddenly heard his voice again, but the words were inaudible. I stopped, startled: then I heard the voice of one of the vilest of his associates saying, 'Nobody can possibly know.' And then I heard those two or three words which I remember in every syllable and cannot forget. I heard the Diabolist say, 'I tell you I have done everything else. If I do that I shan't know the difference between right and wrong.' I rushed out without daring to pause; and as I passed the fire I did not know whether it was hell or the furious love of God.

I have since heard that he died: it may be said, I think, that he committed suicide; though he did it with tools of pleasure, not with tools of pain. God help him, I know the road he went; but I have never known, or even dared to think, what was that place at which he stopped and refrained.

Tremendous Trifles, 1909

The Extraordinary Cabman

———

On the day that I met the strange cabman I had been lunching in a little restaurant in Soho in company with three or four of my best friends. My best friends are all either bottomless sceptics or quite uncontrollable believers, so our discussion at luncheon turned upon the most ultimate and terrible ideas. And the whole argument worked out ultimately to this: that the question is whether a man can be certain of anything at all. I think he can be certain, for if (as I said to my friend, furiously brandishing an empty bottle) it is impossible intellectually to entertain certainty, what is this certainty which it is impossible to entertain? If I have never experienced such a thing as certainty I cannot even say that a thing is not certain. Similarly, if I have never experienced such a thing as green I cannot even say that my nose is not green. It may be as green as possible for all I know, if I have really no experience of greenness. So we shouted at each other and shook the room; because metaphysics is the only thoroughly emotional thing. And the difference between us was very deep, because it was a difference as to the object of the whole thing called broad-mindedness or the opening of the intellect. For my friend said that he opened his intellect as the sun opens the fans of a palm tree, opening for opening's sake, opening infinitely for ever. But I said that I opened my intellect as I opened my mouth, in order to shut it again on something solid. I was doing it at the moment. And as I warmly pointed out, it would look uncommonly silly if I went on opening my mouth infinitely, for ever and ever.

Now when this argument was over, or at least when it was cut short (for it will never be over), I went away with one of my companions, who in the confusion and comparative insanity of a General Election had somehow become a Member of Parliament, and I drove with him in a cab from the corner of Leicester Square to the members' entrance of the House of Commons, where the police received me with a quite unusual tolerance. Whether they thought that he was my keeper or that I was his keeper is a discussion between us which still continues.

It is necessary in this narrative to preserve the utmost exactitude of detail. After leaving my friend at the House I took the cab on a few hundred yards to an office in Victoria Street which I had to visit. I then got out and offered him more than his fare. He looked at it, but not with the surly doubt and general disposition to try it on which is not unknown among normal cabmen. But this was no normal, perhaps, no human cabman. He looked at it with a dull and infantile astonishment, clearly quite genuine. 'Do you know, sir,' he said, 'you've only given me 1s. 8d.?' I remarked, with some surprise, that I did know it. 'Now you know, sir,' said he in a kindly, appealing, reasonable way, 'you know that ain't the fare from Euston.' 'Euston,' I repeated vaguely, for the phrase at that moment sounded to me like China or Arabia. 'What on earth has Euston got to do with it?' 'You hailed me just outside Euston Station,' began the man, with astonishing precision, 'and then you said …' 'What in the name of Tartarus are you talking about?' I said, with Christian forbearance. 'I took you at the south-west corner of Leicester Square.' 'Leicester Square,' he exclaimed, loosening a kind of cataract of scorn; 'why, we ain't been near Leicester Square today. You hailed me outside Euston Station, and you said …' 'Are you mad, or am I?' I asked, with scientific calm.

I looked at the man. No ordinary dishonest cabman would think of creating so solid and colossal and creative a lie. And this man was not a dishonest cabman. If ever a human face was heavy and simple and humble, and with great big blue eyes protruding like a frog's, if ever (in short) a human face was all that a human face should be, it was the face of that resentful and respectful cabman. I looked up and down the street; an unusually dark twilight seemed to be coming on. And for one second the old nightmare of the sceptic put its finger on my nerve. What was certainty? Was anybody certain of anything? Heavens! to think of the dull rut of the sceptics who go on asking whether we possess a future life. The exciting question for real scepticism is whether we possess a past life. What is a minute ago, rationalistically considered, except a tradition and a picture? The darkness grew deeper from the road. The cabman calmly gave me the most elaborate details of the gesture, the words, the complex but consistent course of action which I had adopted since that remarkable occasion when I had hailed him outside Euston Station. How did I know (my sceptical friends would say) that I had not hailed him outside Euston? I was firm about my assertion; he was quite equally firm about his. He was obviously quite as honest a man as I, and a member of a much more respectable profession. In that moment the universe and the stars swung just a hair's breadth from their balance, and the foundations of the earth were moved. But for the same reason that I believe in drinking wine, for the same reason that I believe in free will, for the same reason that I believe in fixed character of virtue, the reason that could only be expressed by saying that I do not choose to be a lunatic, I continued to believe that this honest cabman was wrong, and I repeated to him that I had really taken him at the corner of Leicester Square. He began with the same evident and ponderous sincerity, 'You hailed me outside Euston Station, and you said ...'

And at this moment there came over his features a kind of frightful transfiguration of living astonishment, as if he had been lit up like a lamp from the inside. 'Why, I beg your pardon, sir,' he said. 'I beg your pardon. I beg your pardon. You took me from Leicester Square. I remember now. I beg your pardon.' And with that this astonishing man let out his whip with a sharp crack at his horse and went trundling away. The whole of which interview, before the banner of St George I swear, is strictly true.

I looked at the strange cabman as he lessened in the distance and the mists. I do not know whether I was right in fancying that although his face had seemed so honest there was something unearthly and demoniac about him when seen from behind. Perhaps he had been sent to tempt me from my adherence to those sanities and certainties which I had defended earlier in the day. In any case, it gave me pleasure to remember that my sense of reality, though it had rocked for an instant, had remained erect.

Tremendous Trifles, 1909

The Urchin's Hair

And now, as this book is drawing to a close, I will whisper in the reader's ear a horrible suspicion that has sometimes haunted me: the suspicion that Hudge and Gudge are secretly in partnership. That the quarrel they keep up in public is very much of a put-up job, and that the way in which they perpetually play into each other's hands is not an everlasting coincidence. Gudge, the plutocrat, wants an anarchic industrialism; Hudge, the idealist, provides him with lyric praises of anarchy. Gudge wants women workers because they are cheaper; Hudge calls the woman's work 'freedom to live her own life'. Gudge wants steady and obedient workmen; Hudge preaches teetotalism – to workmen, not to Gudge. Gudge wants a tame and timid population who will never take arms against tyranny; Hudge proves from Tolstoy that nobody must take arms against anything. Gudge is naturally a healthy and well-washed gentleman; Hudge earnestly preaches the perfection of Gudge's washing to people who can't practise it. Above all, Gudge rules by a coarse and cruel system of sacking and sweating and bi-sexual toil which is totally inconsistent with the free family and which is bound to destroy it; therefore Hudge, stretching out his arms to the universe with a prophetic smile, tells us that the family is something that we shall soon gloriously outgrow.

I do not know whether the partnership of Hudge and Gudge is conscious or unconscious. I only know that between them they still keep the common man homeless. I only know I still meet Jones walking the streets in the grey twilight, looking sadly at the poles and barriers and low red goblin lanterns which still guard the house which is none the less his because he has never been in it.

Here, it may be said, my book ends just where it ought to begin. I have said that the strong centres of modern English property must swiftly or slowly be broken up, if even the idea of property is to remain among Englishmen. There are two ways in which it could be done, a cold administration by quite detached officials, which is called Collectivism, or a personal distribution, so as to produce what is called Peasant Proprietorship. I think the latter solution the finer and more fully human, because it makes each man, as somebody blamed somebody for saying of the Pope, a sort of small god. A man on his own turf tastes eternity or, in other words, will give ten minutes more work than is required. But I believe I am justified in shutting the door on this vista of argument, instead of opening it. For this book is not designed to prove the case for Peasant Proprietorship, but to prove the case against modern sages who turn reform to a routine. The whole of this book has been a rambling and elaborate urging of one purely ethical fact. And if by any chance it should happen that there are still some who do not quite see what that point is, I will end with one plain parable, which is none the worse for being also a fact.

A little while ago certain doctors and other persons permitted by modern law to dictate to their shabbier fellow citizens, sent out an order that all little girls should have their hair cut short. I mean, of course, all little girls whose parents were poor. Many very unhealthy habits are common among rich little girls, but it will be long before any doctors interfere forcibly with them. Now, the case for this particular interference was this, that the poor are pressed down from above into such stinking and suffocating underworlds of squalor, that poor people must not be allowed to have hair, because in their case it must mean lice in the hair. Therefore, the doctors propose to abolish the hair. It never seems to have occurred to them to abolish the lice. Yet it could be done. As is common in most modern discussions the unmentionable thing is the pivot of the whole discussion. It is obvious to any Christian man (that is, to any man with a free soul), that any coercion applied to a cabman's daughter ought, if possible, to be applied to a Cabinet Minister's daughter. I will not ask why the doctors do not, as a matter of fact, apply their rule to a Cabinet Minister's daughter. I will not ask, because I know. They do not because they dare not. But what is the excuse they would urge, what is the plausible argument they would use, for thus cutting and clipping poor children and not rich? Their argument would be that the disease is more likely to be in the hair of poor people than of rich. And why? Because the poor children are forced (against all the instincts of the highly domestic working classes) to crowd together in close rooms under a wildly inefficient system of public instruction; and because in one out of the forty children there may be offence. And why? Because the poor man is so ground down by the great rents of the great ground landlords that his wife often has to work as well as he. Therefore she has no time to look after the children; therefore one in forty of them is dirty. Because the working man has these two persons on top of him, the landlord sitting (literally) on his stomach, and the schoolmaster sitting (literally) on his head, the working man must allow his little girl's hair, first to be neglected from poverty, next to be poisoned by promiscuity, and, lastly, to be abolished by hygiene. He, perhaps, was proud of his little girl's hair. But he does not count.

Upon this simple principle (or rather precedent) the sociological doctor drives gaily ahead. When a crapulous tyranny crushes men down into the dirt, so that their very hair is dirty, the scientific course is clear. It would be long and laborious to cut off the heads of the tyrants; it is easier to cut off the hair of the slaves. In the same way, if it should ever happen that poor children, screaming with toothache, disturbed any school-master or artistic gentleman, it would be easy to pull out all the teeth of the poor; if their nails were disgustingly dirty, their nails could be plucked out; if their noses were indecently blown, their noses could be cut off. The appearance of our humbler fellow citizen could be quite strikingly simplified before we had done with him. But all this is not a bit wilder than the brute fact that a doctor can walk into the house of a free man, whose daughter's hair may be as clean as spring flowers, and order him to cut it off. It never seems to strike these people that the lesson of lice in the slums is the wrongness of slums, not the wrongness of hair. Hair is, to say the least of it, a rooted thing. Its enemy (like the other insects and oriental armies of whom we have spoken) sweep upon us but seldom. In truth, it is only by eternal institutions like hair that we can test passing institutions like empires. If a house is so built as to knock a man's head off when he enters it, it is built wrong.

The mob can never rebel unless it is conservative, at least enough to have conserved some reasons for rebelling. It is the most awful thought in all our anarchy, that most of the ancient blows struck for freedom would not be struck at all today, because of the obscuration of the clean, popular customs from which they came. The insult that brought down the hammer of Wat Tyler[1] might now be called a medical examination. That which Virginius[2] loathed and avenged as foul slavery might now be praised as free love. The cruel taunt of Foulon,[3] 'Let them eat grass', might now be represented as

1. Wat Tyler was the leader of the Peasants' Revolt against the tyrannical nobles in 1381. He killed the Lord Mayor of London with a hammer.
2. Virginius killed his own daughter rather than let her become the forced concubine of a Roman official.
3. Foulon was an adviser to the court of Louis XVI just before the French Revolution of 1789. When he was told that the people were starving, he replied 'Let them eat grass!'

the dying cry of an idealistic vegetarian. Those great scissors of science that would snip off the curls of the poor little school children are ceaselessly snapping closer and closer to cut off all the corners and fringes of the arts and honours of the poor. Soon they will be twisting necks to suit clean collars, and hacking feet to fit new boots. It never seems to strike them that the body is more than raiment; that the Sabbath was made for man; that all institutions shall be judged and damned by whether they have fitted the normal flesh and spirit. It is the test of political sanity to keep your head. It is the test of artistic sanity to keep your hair on.

Now the whole parable and purpose of these last pages, and indeed of all these pages, is this: to assert that we must instantly begin all over again, and begin at the other end. I begin with a little girl's hair. That I know is a good thing at any rate. Whatever else is evil, the pride of a good mother in the beauty of her daughter is good. It is one of those adamantine tendernesses which are the touchstones of every age and race. If other things are against it, other things must go down. If landlords and laws and sciences are against it, landlords and laws and sciences must go down. With the red hair of one she-urchin in the gutter I will set fire to all modern civilization. Because a girl should have long hair, she should have clean hair; because she should have clean hair, she should not have an unclean home: because she should not have an unclean home, she should have a free and leisured mother; because she should have a free mother, she should not have an usurious landlord; because there should not be an usurious landlord, there should be a redistribution of property, because there should be a redistribution of property, there shall be a revolution. That little urchin with the gold-red hair, whom I have just watched toddling past my house, she shall not be lopped and lamed and altered; her hair shall not be cut short like a convict's; no, all the kingdoms of the earth shall be hacked about and mutilated to suit her. She is the human and sacred image; all around her the social fabric shall sway and split and fall; the pillars of society shall be shaken, and the roofs of ages come rushing down; and not one hair of her head shall be harmed.

What's Wrong With the World, 1910

The Man Who Thinks Backwards

The man who thinks backwards is a very powerful person today: indeed, if he is not omnipotent, he is at least omnipresent. It is he who writes nearly all the learned books and articles, especially of the scientific or sceptical sort; all the articles on Eugenics and Social Evolution and Prison Reform and the Higher Criticism and all the rest of it. But especially it is this strange and tortuous being who does most of the writing about female emancipation and the reconsidering of marriage. For the man who thinks backwards is very frequently a woman.

Thinking backwards is not quite easy to define abstractedly; and perhaps the simplest method is to take some object, as plain as possible, and from it illustrate the two modes of thought: the right mode in which all real results have been rooted; the wrong mode, which is confusing all our current discussions, especially our discussions about the relations of the sexes. Casting my eye round the room, I notice an object which is often mentioned in the higher and subtler of these debates about the sexes: I mean a poker. I will take a poker and think about it; first forwards and then backwards, and so, perhaps, show what I mean.

The sage desiring to think well and wisely about a poker will begin somewhat as follows. Among the live creatures that crawl about this star the queerest is the thing called Man. This plucked and plumeless bird, comic and forlorn, is the butt of all the philosophies. He is the only naked animal; and this quality, once, it is said, his glory, is now his shame. He has to go outside himself for everything that he wants. He might almost be considered as an absent-minded person who had gone bathing and left his clothes everywhere, so that he has hung his hat upon the beaver and his coat upon the sheep. The rabbit has white warmth for a waistcoat, and the glow-worm has a lantern for a head. But man has no heat in his hide, and the light in his body is darkness; and he must look for light and warmth in the wild, cold universe in which he is cast. This is equally true of his soul and of his body; he is the one creature that has lost his heart as much as he has lost his hide. In a spiritual sense he has taken leave of his senses; and even in a literal sense he has been unable to keep his hair on. And just as this external need of his has lit in his dark brain the dreadful star called religion, so it has lit in his hand the only adequate symbol of it: I mean the red flower called Fire. Fire, the most magic and startling of all material things, is a thing known only to man and is the expression of his sublime externalism. It embodies all that is human in his hearths and all that is divine on his altars. It is the most human thing in the world; seen across wastes of marsh or medleys of forest, it is veritably the purple and golden flag of the sons of Eve. But there is about this generous and rejoicing thing an alien and awful quality: the quality of torture. Its presence is life; its touch is death. Therefore, it is always necessary to have an intermediary between ourselves and this dreadful deity; to have a priest to intercede for us with the god of life and death; to send an ambassador to the fire. That priest is the poker. Made of a material more merciless and warlike than the other instruments of domesticity, hammered on the anvil and born itself in the flame, the poker is strong enough to enter the burning fiery furnace, and, like the holy children, not be consumed. In this heroic service it is often battered and twisted, but is the more honourable for it, like any other soldier who has been under fire.

Now all this may sound very fanciful and mystical, but it is the right view of pokers, and no one who takes it will ever go in for any wrong view of pokers, such as using them to beat one's wife or torture one's children, or even (though that is more excusable) to make a policeman jump, as the clown does in the pantomime. He who has thus gone back to the beginning, and seen everything as quaint and new, will always see things in their right order, the one depending on the other in degree of purpose and importance: the poker for the fire and the fire for the man and the man for the glory of God.

This is thinking forwards. Now our modern discussions about everything, Imperialism, Socialism, or Votes for Women, are all entangled in an opposite train of thought, which runs as follows.

A modern intellectual comes in and sees a poker. He is a positivist; he will not begin with any dogmas about the nature of man, or any day-dreams about the mystery of fire. He will begin with what he can see, the poker; and the first thing he sees about the poker is that it is crooked. He says, 'Poor poker; it's crooked.' Then he asks how it came to be crooked; and is told that there is a thing in the world (with which his temperament has hitherto left him unacquainted), a thing called fire. He points out, very kindly and clearly, how silly it is of people, if they want a straight poker, to put it into a chemical combustion which will very probably heat and warp it. 'Let us abolish fire,' he says, 'and then we shall have perfectly straight pokers. Why should you want a fire at all?' They explain to him that a creature called Man wants a fire, because he has no fur or feathers. He gazes dreamily at the embers for a few seconds, and then shakes his head. 'I doubt if such an animal is worth preserving,' he says. 'He must eventually go under in the cosmic struggle when pitted against well-armoured and warmly protected species, who have wings and trunks and spires and scales and horns and shaggy hair. If Man cannot live without these luxuries, you had better abolish Man.' At this point, as a rule, the crowd is convinced; it heaves up all its clubs and axes, and abolishes him. At least, one of him.

Before we begin discussing our various new plans for the people's welfare, let us make a kind of agreement that we will argue in a straightforward way, and not in a tail-foremost way. The typical modern movements may be right; but let them be defended because they are right, not because they are typical modern movements. Let us begin with the actual woman or man in the street, who is *cold*; like mankind before the finding of fire. Do not let us begin with the end of the last red-hot discussion – like the end of a red-hot poker. Imperialism may be right. But if it is right, it is right because England has some divine authority like Israel, or some human authority like Rome; not because we have saddled ourselves with South Africa, and don't know how to get rid of it. Socialism may be true. But if it is true, it is true because the tribe or the city can really declare all land to be common land, not because Harrod's Stores exist and the commonwealth must copy them. Female suffrage may be just. But if it is just, it is just because women are women, not because women are sweated workers and white slaves and all sorts of things that they ought never to have been. Let not the Imperialist accept a colony because it is there, nor the Suffragist seize a vote because it is lying about, nor the Socialist buy up an industry merely because it is for sale.

Let us ask ourselves first what we really do want, not what recent legal decisions have told us to want, or recent logical philosophies proved that we must want, or recent social prophecies predicted that we shall some day want. If there must be a British Empire, let it be British, and not, in mere panic, American or Prussian. If there ought to be female suffrage, let it be female, and not a mere imitation as coarse as the male blackguard or as dull as the male clerk. If there is to be Socialism, let it be social; that is, as different as possible from all the big commercial departments of today. The really good journeyman tailor does not cut his coat according to his cloth; he asks for more cloth. The really practical statesman does not fit himself to existing conditions; he denounces the conditions as unfit. History is like some deeply planted tree which, though gigantic in girth, tapers away at last into tiny twigs; and we are in the topmost branches. Each of us is trying to bend the tree by a twig: to alter England through a distant colony, or to capture the State through a small State department, or to destroy all voting through a vote. In all such bewilderment he is wise who resists this temptation of trivial triumph or surrender, and happy (in an echo of the Roman poet) who remembers the roots of things.

A Miscellany of Men, 1912

The Mad Official

Going mad is the slowest and dullest business in the world. I have very nearly done it more than once in my boyhood, and so have nearly all my friends, born under the general doom of mortals, but especially of moderns; I mean the doom that makes a man come almost to the end of thinking before he comes to the first chance of living.

But the process of going mad is dull, for the simple reason that a man does not know that it is going on. Routine and literalism and a certain dry-throated earnestness and mental thirst, these are the very atmosphere of morbidity. If once the man could become conscious of his madness, he would cease to be mad.[1] He studies certain texts in Daniel or cryptograms in Shakespeare through monstrously magnifying spectacles, which are on his nose night and day. If once he could take off the spectacles he would smash them. He deduces all his fantasies about the Sixth Seal or the Anglo-Saxon Race from one unexamined and invisible first principle. If he could once see the first principle, he would see that it is not there.

This slow and awful self-hypnotism of error is a process

1. Editor's note: All the published versions of this essay have the line as 'If once the man could become conscious of his madness, he would cease to be man.' This seems an obvious misprint which I have corrected.

that can occur not only with individuals, but also with whole societies. It is hard to pick out and prove; that is why it is hard to cure. But this mental degeneration may be brought to one test, which I truly believe to be a real test. A nation is not going mad when it does extravagant things, so long as it does them in an extravagant spirit. Crusaders not cutting their beards till they found Jerusalem, Jacobins calling each other Harmodius and Epaminondas when their names were Jacques and Jules: these are wild things, but they were done in wild spirits at a wild moment.

But whenever we see things done wildly, but taken tamely, then the State is growing insane. For instance, I have a gun licence. For all I know, this would logically allow me to fire off fifty-nine enormous field-guns day and night in my back garden. I should not be surprised at a man doing it; for it would be great fun. But I should be surprised at the neighbours putting up with it, and regarding it as an ordinary thing merely because it might happen to fulfil the letter of my licence.

Or, again, I have a dog licence; and I may have the right (for all I know) to turn ten thousand wild dogs loose in Buckinghamshire. I should not be surprised if the law were like that; because in modern England there is practically no law to be surprised at. I should not be surprised even at the man who did it; for a certain kind of man, if he lived long under the English landlord system, might do anything. But I should be surprised at the people who consented to stand it. I should, in other words, think the world a little mad if the incident were received in silence.

Now things every bit as wild as this are being received in silence every day. All strokes slip on the smoothness of a polished wall. All blows fall soundless on the softness of a padded cell. For madness is a passive as well as an active state: it is a paralysis, a refusal of the nerves to respond to the normal stimuli, as well as an unnatural stimulation. There are commonwealths, plainly to be distinguished here and there in history, which pass from prosperity to squalor, or from glory to insignificance, or from freedom to slavery, not only in silence, but with serenity. The face still smiles while the limbs, literally and loathsomely, are dropping from the body. These are peoples that have lost the power of astonishment at their own actions. When they give birth to a fantastic fashion or a foolish law, they do not start or stare at the monster they have brought forth. They have grown used to their own unreason; chaos is their cosmos; and the whirlwind is the breath of their nostrils. These nations are really in danger of going off their heads *en masse*; of becoming one vast vision of imbecility, with toppling cities and crazy countrysides, all dotted with industrious lunatics. One of these countries is modern England.

Now here is an actual instance, a small case of how our social conscience really works: tame in spirit, wild in result, blank in realization; a thing without the light of mind in it. I take this paragraph from a daily paper:

> At Epping, yesterday, Thomas Woolbourne, a Lambourne labourer, and his wife were summoned for neglecting their five children. Dr Alpin said he was invited by the inspector of the NSPCC to visit defendants' cottage. Both the cottage and the children were dirty. The children looked exceedingly well in health, but the conditions would be serious in case of illness. Defendants were stated to be sober. The man was discharged. The woman, who said she was hampered by the cottage having no water supply and that she was ill, was sentenced to six weeks' imprisonment. The sentence caused surprise, and the woman was removed crying, 'Lord, save me!'

I know no name for this but Chinese. It calls up the mental picture of some archaic and changeless Eastern Court, in which men with dried faces and stiff ceremonial costumes perform some atrocious cruelty to the accompaniment of formal proverbs and sentences of which the very meaning has been forgotten. In both cases the only thing in the whole farrago that can be called real is the wrong. If we apply the lightest touch of reason to the whole Epping prosecution it dissolves into nothing.

I here challenge any person in his five wits to tell me what that woman was sent to prison for. Either it was for being poor, or it was for being ill. Nobody could suggest, nobody will suggest, nobody, as a matter of fact, did suggest, that she had committed any other crime. The doctor was called in by a Society for the Prevention of Cruelty to Children. Was this woman guilty of cruelty to children? Not in the least. Did the doctor say she was guilty of cruelty to children? Not in the least. Was there any evidence even remotely bearing on the sin of cruelty? Not a rap. The worst that the doctor could work himself up to saying was that though the children were 'exceedingly' well, the conditions would be serious in case of illness. If the doctor will tell me any conditions that would be comic in case of illness, I shall attach more weight to his argument.

Now this is the worst effect of modern worry. The mad doctor has gone mad. He is literally and practically mad; and still he is quite literally and practically a doctor. The only question is the old one, *Quis docebit ipsum doctorem?*[2] Now cruelty to children is an utterly unnatural thing; instinctively accursed of earth and heaven. But neglect of children is a

---

2. Chesterton here is playing with Juvenal's old motto: *quis custodiet ipsos custodes*? ('Who is to guard the guards themselves?') GKC's version means 'Who will teach the teacher himself', as well as being a typical Chestertonian pun on the word 'doctor'.

natural thing; like neglect of any other duty. It is a mere difference of degree that divides extending arms and legs in calisthenics and extending them on the rack. It is a mere difference of degree that separates any operation from any torture. The thumb-screw can easily be called manicure. Being pulled about by wild horses can easily be called massage. The modern problem is not so much what people will endure as what they will not endure. But I fear I interrupt ... The boiling oil is boiling; and the Tenth Mandarin is already reciting the 'Seventeen Serious Principles and the Fifty-three Virtues of the Sacred Emperor'.

A Miscellany of Men, 1912

The New Theologian

It is an old story that names do not fit things; it is an old story
that the oldest forest is called the New Forest, and that Irish
stew is almost peculiar to England. But these are traditional
titles that tend, of their nature, to stiffen; it is the tragedy of
today that even phrases invented for today do not fit it. The
forest has remained new while it is nearly a thousand years
old; but our fashions have grown old while they were still
new.

The extreme example of this is that when modern wrongs
are attacked, they are almost always attacked wrongly. People
seem to have a positive inspiration for finding the inappropriate phrase to apply to an offender; they are always accusing
a man of theft when he has been convicted of murder. They
must accuse Sir Edward Carson of outrageous rebellion,
when his offence has really been a sleek submission to the
powers that be. They must describe Mr Lloyd George as using
his eloquence to rouse the mob, whereas he has really shown
considerable cleverness in damping it down. It was probably
under the same impulse towards a mysterious misfit of names
that people denounced Dr Inge as 'the Gloomy Dean'.

Now there is nothing whatever wrong about being a
Dean; nor is there anything wrong about being gloomy. The
only question is what dark but sincere motives have made you
gloomy. What dark but sincere motives have made you a

Dean. Now the address of Dr Inge which gained him this erroneous title was mostly concerned with a defence of the modern capitalists against the modern strikers, from whose protest he appeared to anticipate appalling results. Now if we look at the facts about that gentleman's depression and also about his Deanery, we shall find a very curious state of things.

When Dr Inge was called 'the Gloomy Dean' a great injustice was done him. He had appeared as the champion of our capitalist community against the forces of revolt; and anyone who does that exceeds in optimism rather than pessimism. A man who really thinks that strikers have suffered no wrong, or that employers have done no wrong – such a man is not a Gloomy Dean, but a quite wildly and dangerously happy Dean. A man who can feel satisfied with modern industrialism must be a man with a mysterious fountain of high spirits. And the actual occasion is not less curious; because, as far as I can make out, his title to gloom reposes on his having said that our workers demand high wages, while the placid people of the Far East will quite cheerfully work for less.

This is true enough, of course, and there does not seem to be much difficulty about the matter. Men of the Far East will submit to very low wages for the same reason that they will submit to 'the punishment known as Li, or Slicing'; for the same reason that they will praise polygamy and suicide; for the same reason that they subject the wife utterly to the husband or his parents; for the same reason that they serve their temples with prostitutes for priests; for the same reason that they sometimes seem to make no distinction between sexual passion and sexual perversion. They do it, that is, because they are Heathens; men with traditions different from ours about the limits of endurance and the gestures of self-respect. They may be very much better than we are in hundreds of other ways; and I can quite understand a man (though hardly a Dean) really preferring their historic virtues to those of Christendom. A man may perhaps feel more comfortable among his Asiatic coolies than among his European comrades: and as we are to allow the Broadest Thought in the Church, Dr Inge has as much right to his heresy as anybody else. It is true that, as Dr Inge says, there are numberless Orientals who will do a great deal of work for very little money; and it is most undoubtedly true that there are several high-placed and prosperous Europeans who like to get work done and pay as little as possible for it.

But I cannot make out why, with his enthusiasm for heathen habits and traditions, the Dean should wish to spread in the East the ideas which he has found so dreadfully unsettling in the West. If some thousands of years of paganism have produced the patience and industry that Dean Inge admires, and if some thousand years of Christianity have produced the sentimentality and sensationalism which he regrets, the obvious deduction is that Dean Inge would be much happier if he were a heathen Chinese. Instead of supporting Christian missions to Korea or Japan, he ought to be at the head of a great mission in London for converting the English to Taoism or Buddhism. There his passion for the moral beauties of paganism would have free and natural play; his style would improve; his mind would begin slowly to clear; and he would be free from all sorts of little irritating scrupulosities which must hamper even the most conservative Christian in his full praise of sweating and the sack.

In Christendom he will never find rest. The perpetual public criticism and public change which is the note of all our history springs from a certain spirit far too deep to be defined. It is deeper than democracy; nay, it may often appear to be non-democratic; for it may often be the special defence of a minority or an individual. It will often leave the ninety-and-nine in the wilderness and go after that which is lost. It will often risk the State itself to right a single wrong; and do justice though the heavens fall. Its highest expression is not even in the formula of the great gentlemen of the French

Revolution who said that all men were free and equal. Its highest expression is rather in the formula of the peasant[1] who said that a man's a man for a' that. If there were but one slave in England, and he did all the work while the rest of us made merry, this spirit that is in us would still cry aloud to God night and day. Whether or no this spirit was produced by, it clearly works with, a creed which postulates a humanized God and a vividly personal immortality. Men must not be busy merely like a swarm, or even happy merely like a herd; for it is not a question of men, but of a man. A man's meals may be poor, but they must not be bestial; there must always be that about the meal which permits of its comparison to the sacrament. A man's bed may be hard, but it must not be abject or unclean: there must always be about the bed something of the decency of the death-bed.

This is the spirit which makes the Christian poor begin their terrible murmur whenever there is a turn of prices or a deadlock of toil that threatens them with vagabondage or pauperization; and we cannot encourage the Dean with any hope that this spirit can be cast out. Christendom will continue to suffer all the disadvantages of being Christian: it is the Dean who must be gently but firmly altered. He had absent-mindedly strayed into the wrong continent and the wrong creed. I advise him to chuck it.

But the case is more curious still. To connect the Dean with Confucian temples or traditions may have appeared fantastic; but it is not. Dr Inge is not a stupid old Tory Rector, strict both on Church and State. Such a man might talk nonsense about the Christian Socialists being 'court chaplains of King Demos' or about his own superb valour in defying the democracy that rages in the front pews of Anglican churches. We should not expect a mere old-fashioned country clergyman to know that Demos has never been king in England and

1. Robert Burns: 'For a 'that and a 'that.'

precious seldom anywhere else; we should not expect him to realize that if King Demos had any chaplains they would be uncommonly poorly paid. But Dr Inge is not old-fashioned; he considers himself highly progressive and advanced. He is a New Theologian; that is, he is liberal in theology – and nothing else. He is apparently in sober fact, and not as in any fantasy, in sympathy with those who would soften the superior claim of our creed by urging the rival creeds of the East; with those who would absorb the virtues of Buddhism or of Islam. He holds a high seat in that modern Parliament of Religions where all believers respect each other's unbelief.

Now this has a very sharp moral for modern religious reformers. When next you hear the 'liberal' Christian say that we should take what is best in oriental faiths, make quite sure what are the things that people like Dr Inge call best; what are the things that people like Dr Inge propose to take. You will not find them imitating the military valour of the Muslim. You will not find them imitating the miraculous ecstasy of the Hindu. The more you study the 'broad' movement of today, the more you will find that these people want something much less like Chinese metaphysics, and something much more like Chinese labour. You will find the levelling of creeds quite unexpectedly close to the lowering of wages. Dr Inge is the typical latitudinarian of today; and was never more so than when he appeared not as the apostle of the blacks, but as the apostle of the blacklegs. Preached, as it is, almost entirely among the prosperous and polite, our brotherhood with Buddhism or Mohammedanism practically means this – that the poor must be as meek as Buddhists, while the rich may be as ruthless as Mohammedans. That is what they call the reunion of all religions.

A Miscellany of Men, 1912

The Sentimentalism of Divorce

Divorce is a thing which the newspapers now not only advertise, but advocate, almost as if it were a pleasure in itself. It may be, indeed, that all the flowers and festivities will now be transferred from the fashionable wedding to the fashionable divorce. A superb iced and frosted divorce cake will be provided for the feast, and in military circles will be cut with the co-respondent's sword. A dazzling display of divorce presents will be laid out for the inspection of the company, watched by a detective dressed as an ordinary divorce guest. Perhaps the old divorce breakfast will be revived; anyhow, toasts will be drunk, the guests will assemble on the doorstep to see the husband and wife go off in opposite directions; and all will go merry as a divorce court bell. All this, though to some it might seem a little fanciful, would really be far less fantastic than the sort of things that are really said on the subject. I am not going to discuss the depth and substance of that subject. I myself hold a mystical view of marriage; but I am not going to debate it here. But merely in the interests of light and logic I would protest against the way in which it is frequently debated. The process cannot rationally be called a debate at all. It is a sort of chorus of sentimentalists in the sensational newspapers, perpetually intoning some such formula as this: 'We respect marriage, we reverence marriage, holy, sacred, ineffably exquisite and ideal marriage. True marriage is love, and when love alters, marriage alters, and when love stops or begins again, marriage does the same; wonderful, beautiful, beatific marriage.'

Now, with all reasonable sympathy with everything sentimental, I may remark that all that talk is tosh. Marriage is an institution like any other, set up deliberately to have certain functions and limitations; it is an institution like private property or conscription, or the legal liberties of the subject. To talk as if it were made or melted with certain changing moods is a mere waste of words. The object of private property is that as many citizens as possible should have a certain dignity and pleasure in being masters of material things. But suppose a dog-stealer were to say that as soon as a man was bored with his dog it ceased to be his dog, and he ceased to be responsible for it. Suppose he were to say that by merely coveting the dog, he could immediately morally possess the dog. The answer would be that the only way to make men responsible for dogs was to make the relation a legal one, apart from the likes and dislikes of the moment. Suppose a burglar were to say: 'Private property I venerate, private property I revere; but I am convinced that Mr Brown does not truly value his silver Apostle spoons as such sacred objects should be valued – they have therefore ceased to be his property; in reality they have already become my property for I appreciate their precious character as nobody else can do.' Suppose a murderer were to say: 'What can be more amiable and admirable than human life lived with a due sense of its priceless opportunity! But I regret to observe that Mr Robinson has lately been looking decidedly tired and melancholy; life accepted in this depressing and demoralizing spirit can no longer truly be called life; it is rather my own exuberant and perhaps exaggerated joy of life which I must gratify by cutting his throat with a carving knife.'

It is obvious that these philosophers would fail to understand what we mean by a rule, quite apart from the problem of its exceptions. They would fail to grasp what we mean by an institution, whether it be the institution of law, of property, or of marriage. A reasonable person will certainly reply to the burglar: 'You will hardly soothe us by merely poetical praises of property; because your case would be much more convincing if you denied, as the Communists do, that property ought to exist at all. There may be, there certainly are, gross abuses in private property; but, so long as it is an institution at all, it cannot alter merely with moods and emotions. A farm cannot simply float away from a farmer, in proportion as his interest in it grows fainter than it was. A house cannot shift away by inches from a householder, by certain fine shades of feeling that he happens to have about it. A dog cannot drift away like a dream, and begin to belong to somebody else who happens just then to be dreaming of him. And neither can the serious social relation of husband and wife, of mother and father, or even of man and woman, be resolved in all its relations by passions and reactions of sentiment.' This question is quite apart from the question of whether there are exceptions to the rule of loyalty, or what they are. The primary point is that there is an institution to which to be loyal. If the new sentimentalists mean what they say, when they say they venerate that institution, they must not suggest that an institution can be actually identical with an emotion. And that is what their rhetoric does suggest, so far as it can be said to suggest anything.

These writers are always explaining to us why they believe in divorce. I think I can easily understand why they believe in divorce. What I do not understand is why they believe in marriage. Just as the philosophical burglar would be more philosophical if he were a Bolshevist, so this sort of divorce advocate would be more philosophical if he were a Free Lover. For his arguments never seem to touch on marriage as an institution, or anything more than an individual experience. The real explanation of this strange indifference to the institutional idea is, I fancy, something not only deeper, but wider; something affecting all the institutions of the modern world. The truth is that these sociologists are not at all interested in promoting the sort of social life that marriage does promote. The sort of society of which marriage has always been the strongest pillar is what is sometimes called the distributive society; the society in which most of the citizens have a tolerable share of property, especially property in land. Everywhere, all over the world, the farm goes with the family and the family with the farm. Unless the whole domestic group hold together with a sort of loyalty or local patriotism, unless the inheritance of property is logical and legitimate, unless the family quarrels are kept out of the courts of officialism, the tradition of family ownership cannot be handed on unimpaired. On the other hand, the Servile State, which is the opposite of the distributive state, has always been rather embarrassed by the institution of marriage. It is an old story that the negro slavery of *Uncle Tom's Cabin* did its worst work in the breaking-up of families. But, curiously enough, the same story is told from both sides. For the apologists of the Slave States, or, at least, of the Southern States, made the same admission even in their own defence. If they denied breaking up the slave family, it was because they denied that there was any slave family to break up.

Free Love is the direct enemy of freedom. It is the most obvious of all the bribes that can be offered by slavery. In servile societies a vast amount of sexual laxity can go on in practice, and even in theory, save when now and then some cranky speculator or crazy squire has a fad for some special breed of slaves like a breed of cattle. And even that lunacy would not last long; for lunatics are the minority among slave owners. Slavery has a much more sane and a much more subtle appeal to human nature than that. It is much more likely that, after a few such fads and freaks, the new Servile State would settle down into the sleepy resignation of the old

Servile State; the old pagan repose in slavery, as it was before Christianity came to trouble and perplex the world with ideals of liberty and chivalry. One of the conveniences of that pagan world is that, below a certain level of society, nobody really need bother about pedigree or paternity at all. A new world began when slaves began to stand on their dignity as virgin martyrs. Christendom is the civilization that such martyrs made; and slavery is its returning enemy. But of all the bribes that the old pagan slavery can offer, this luxury and laxity is the strongest; nor do I deny that the influences desiring the degradation of human dignity have here chosen their instrument well.

Fancies vs Fads, 1923

The World St Francis Found

In the course of random reading a man comes across a pagan custom that strikes him as picturesque or a Christian action that strikes him as cruel; but he does not enlarge his mind sufficiently to see the main truth about pagan custom or the Christian reaction against it. Until we understand, not necessarily in detail, but in their big bulk and proportion that pagan progress and that Christian reaction, we cannot really understand the point of history at which St Francis appears or what his great popular mission was all about.

Now everybody knows, I imagine, that the twelfth and thirteenth centuries were an awakening of the world. They were a fresh flowering of culture and the creative arts after a long spell of much sterner and even more sterile experience which we call the Dark Ages. They may be called an emancipation; they were certainly an end; an end of what may at least seem a harsher and more inhuman time. But what was it that was ended? From what was it that men were emancipated? That is where there is a real collision and point at issue between the different philosophies of history. On the merely external and secular side, it has been truly said that men awoke from a sleep; but there had been dreams in that sleep of a mystical and sometimes of a monstrous kind. In that rationalistic routine into which most modern historians have fallen, it is considered enough to say that they were emancipated from mere savage superstition and advanced towards mere civilized enlightenment. Now this is the big blunder that stands as a stumbling-block at the very beginning of our story. Anybody who supposes that the Dark Ages were plain darkness and nothing else, and that the dawn of the thirteenth century was plain daylight and nothing else, will not be able to make head or tail of the human story of St Francis of Assisi. The truth is that the joy of St Francis and his Jongleurs de Dieu was not merely an awakening. It was something which cannot be understood without understanding their own mystical creed. The end of the Dark Ages was not merely the end of a sleep. It was certainly not merely the end of a superstitious enslavement. It was the end of something belonging to a quite definite but quite different order of ideas.

It was the end of a penance; or, if it be preferred, a purgation. It marked the moment when a certain spiritual expiation had been finally worked out and certain spiritual diseases had been finally expelled from the system. They had been expelled by an era of asceticism, which was the only thing that could have expelled them. Christianity had entered the world to cure the world; and she had cured it in the only way in which it could be cured.

Viewed merely in an external and experimental fashion, the whole of the high civilization of antiquity had ended in the learning of a certain lesson; that is, in its conversion to Christianity. But that lesson was a psychological fact as well as a theological faith. That pagan civilization had indeed been a very high civilization. It would not weaken our thesis, it might even strengthen it, to say that it was the highest that humanity ever reached. It had discovered its still unrivalled arts of poetry and plastic representation; it had discovered its own permanent political ideals; it had discovered its own clear system of logic and of language. But above all, it had discovered its own mistake.

That mistake was too deep to be ideally defined; the shorthand of it is to call it the mistake of nature worship. It might almost as truly be called the mistake of being natural; and it was a very natural mistake. The Greeks, the great guides and pioneers of pagan antiquity, started out with the idea of something splendidly obvious and direct; the idea that if man walked straight ahead on the high road of reason and nature, he could come to no harm; especially if he was, as the Greek was, eminently enlightened and intelligent. We might be so flippant as to say that man was simply to follow his nose, so long as it was a Greek nose. And the case of the Greeks themselves is alone enough to illustrate the strange but certain fatality that attends upon this fallacy. No sooner did the Greeks themselves begin to follow their own noses and their own notion of being natural, than the queerest thing in history seems to have happened to them. It was much too queer to be an easy matter to discuss. It may be remarked that our more repulsive realists never give us the benefit of their realism. Their studies of unsavoury subjects never take note of the testimony which they bear to the truths of a traditional morality. But if we had the taste for such things, we could cite thousands of such things as part of the case for Christian morals. And an instance of this is found in the fact that nobody has written, in this sense, a real moral history of the Greeks. Nobody has seen the scale or the strangeness of the story. The wisest men in the world set out to be natural; and the most unnatural thing in the world was the very first thing they did. The immediate effect of saluting the sun and the sunny sanity of nature was a perversion spreading like a pestilence. The greatest and even the purest philosophers could not apparently avoid this low sort of lunacy. Why? It would seem simple enough for the people whose poets had conceived Helen of Troy, whose sculptors had carved the Venus of Milo, to remain healthy on the point. The truth is that people who worship health cannot remain healthy. When

Man goes straight he goes crooked. When he follows his nose he manages somehow to put his nose out of joint, or even to cut off his nose to spite his face; and that in accordance with something much deeper in human nature than nature worshippers could ever understand. It was the discovery of that deeper thing, humanly speaking, that constituted the conversion to Christianity. There is a bias in man like the bias in the bowl; and Christianity was the discovery of how to correct the bias and therefore hit the mark. There are many who will smile at the saying; but it is profoundly true to say that the glad good news brought by the Gospel was the news of original sin.

Rome rose at the expense of her Greek teachers largely because she did not entirely consent to be taught these tricks. She had a much more decent domestic tradition; but she ultimately suffered from the same fallacy in her religious tradition; which was necessarily in no small degree the heathen tradition of nature worship. What was the matter with the whole heathen civilization was that there was nothing for the mass of men in the way of mysticism, except that concerned with the mystery of the nameless forces of nature, such as sex and growth and death. In the Roman Empire also, long before the end, we find nature worship inevitably producing things that are against nature. Cases like that of Nero have passed into a proverb, when sadism sat on a throne brazen in the broad daylight. But the truth I mean is something much more subtle and universal than a conventional catalogue of atrocities. What had happened to the human imagination, as a whole, was that the whole world was coloured by dangerous and rapidly deteriorating passions; by natural passions becoming unnatural passions. Thus the effect of treating sex as only one innocent natural thing was that every other innocent natural thing became soaked and sodden with sex. For sex cannot be admitted to a mere equality among elementary emotions or experiences like eating and sleeping. The moment sex ceases to be a servant it becomes a tyrant. There is something dangerous and disproportionate in its place in human nature, for whatever reason; and it does really need a special purification and dedication. The modern talk about sex being free like any other sense, about the body being beautiful like any tree or flower, is either a description of the Garden of Eden or a piece of thoroughly bad psychology, of which the world grew weary two thousand years ago.

This is not to be confused with mere self-righteous sensationalism about the wickedness of the pagan world. It was not so much that the pagan world was wicked as that it was good enough to realize that its paganism was becoming wicked, or rather was on the logical high road to wickedness. I mean that there was no future for 'natural magic'; to deepen it was only to darken it into black magic. There was no future for it; because in the past it had only been innocent because it was young. We might say it had only been innocent because it was shallow. Pagans were wiser than paganism; that is why the pagans became Christians. Thousands of them had philosophy and family virtues and military honour to hold them up; but by this time the purely popular thing called religion was certainly dragging them down. When this reaction against the evil is allowed for, it is true to repeat that it was an evil that was everywhere. In another and more literal sense its name was Pan.

It was no metaphor to say that these people needed a new heaven and a new earth; for they had really defiled their own earth and even their own heaven. How could their case be met by looking at the sky, when erotic legends were scrawled in stars across it?; how could they learn anything from the love of birds and flowers after the sort of love stories that were told of them? It is impossible here to multiply evidences, and one small example may stand for the rest. We know what sort of sentimental associations are called up to us by the phrase 'a garden'; and how we think mostly of the memory of melancholy and innocent romances, or quite as often of some gracious maiden lady or kindly old parson pottering under a yew hedge, perhaps in sight of a village spire. Then, let anyone who knows a little Latin poetry recall suddenly what would once have stood in place of the sundial or the fountain, obscene and monstrous in the sun; and of what sort was the god of their gardens.

Nothing could purge this obsession but a religion that was literally unearthly. It was no good telling such people to have a natural religion full of stars and flowers; there was not a flower or even a star that had not been stained. They had to go into the desert where they could find no flowers or even into the cavern where they could see no stars. Into that desert and that cavern the highest human intellect entered for some four centuries; and it was the very wisest thing it could do. Nothing but the stark supernatural stood up for its salvation; if God could not save it, certainly the gods could not. The early Church called the gods of paganism devils; and the early Church was perfectly right. Whatever natural religion may have had to do with their beginnings, nothing but fiends now inhabited those hollow shrines. Pan was nothing but panic. Venus was nothing but venereal vice. I do not mean for a moment, of course, that all the individual pagans were of this character even to the end; but it was as individuals that they differed from it. Nothing distinguishes paganism from Christianity so clearly as the fact that the individual thing called philosophy had little or nothing to do with the social thing called religion. Anyhow it was no good to preach natural religion to people to whom nature had grown as unnatural as any religion. They knew much better than we do what was the matter with them and what sort of demons at once tempted and tormented them; and they wrote across that great space of history the text: 'This sort goeth not out but by prayer and fasting.'

Now the historic importance of St Francis and the transition from the twelfth to the thirteenth century, lies in the fact that they marked the end of this expiation. Men at the close of the Dark Ages may have been rude and unlettered and unlearned in everything but wars with heathen tribes, more barbarous than themselves, but they were clean. They were like children; the first beginnings of their rude arts have all the clean pleasure of children.

Now I have taken these two or three examples of the earlier medieval movements in order to note about them one general character, which refers back to the penance that followed paganism. There is something in all these movements that is bracing even while it is still bleak, like a wind blowing between the clefts of the mountains. That wind, austere and pure, of which the poet speaks, is really the spirit of the time, for it is the wind of a world that has at last been purified. To anyone who can appreciate atmospheres there is something clear and clean about the atmosphere of this crude and often harsh society. Its very lusts are clean; for they have no longer any smell of perversion. Its very cruelties are clean; they are not the luxurious cruelties of the amphitheatre. They come either of a very simple horror at blasphemy or a very simple fury at insult. Gradually against this grey background beauty begins to appear, as something really fresh and delicate and above all surprising. Love returning is no longer what was once called platonic but what is still called chivalric love. The flowers and stars have recovered their first innocence. Fire and water are felt to be worthy to be the brother and sister of a saint. The purge of paganism is complete at last.

For water itself has been washed. Fire itself has been purified as by fire. Water is no longer that water into which slaves were flung to feed the fishes. Fire is no longer that fire through which children were passed to Moloch. Flowers smell no more of the forgotten garlands gathered in the garden of Priapus; stars stand no more as signs of the far frigidity of gods as cold as those cold fires. They are all like things newly made and awaiting new names, from one who shall come to name them. Neither the universe nor the earth have now any longer the old sinister significance of the world. They await a new reconciliation with man, but they are already capable of being reconciled. Man has stripped from his soul the last rag of nature worship, and can return to nature.

While it was yet twilight a figure appeared silently and suddenly on a little hill above the city, dark against the fading darkness. For it was the end of a long and stern night, a night of vigil, not unvisited by stars. He stood with his hands lifted, as in so many statues and pictures, and about him was a burst of birds singing; and behind him was the break of day.

St Francis of Assisi, 1923

St Francis and 'The Love of Nature'

From that cavern, that was a furnace of glowing gratitude and humility, there came forth one of the strongest and strangest and most original personalities that human history has known. He was, among other things, emphatically what we call a character; almost as we speak of a character in a good novel or play. He was not only a humanist but a humorist; a humorist especially in the old English sense of a man always in his humour, going his own way and doing what nobody else would have done. The anecdotes about him have a certain biographical quality of which the most familiar example is Dr Johnson; which belongs in another way to William Blake or to Charles Lamb. The atmosphere can only be defined by a sort of antithesis; the act is always unexpected and never inappropriate. Before the thing is said or done it cannot even be conjectured; but after it is said or done it is felt to be merely characteristic. It is surprisingly and yet inevitably individual. This quality of abrupt fitness and bewildering consistency belongs to St Francis in a way that marks him out from most men of his time. Men are learning more and more of the solid social virtues of medieval civilization; but those impressions are still social rather than individual. The medieval world was far ahead of the modern world in its sense of the things in which all men are at one: death and the daylight of reason and the common conscience that holds communities together. Its generalizations were saner and sounder than the mad materialistic theories of today; nobody would have tolerated a Schopenhauer scorning life or a Nietzsche living only for scorn. But the modern world is more subtle in its sense of the things in which men are not at one; in the temperamental varieties and differentiations that make up the personal problems of life. All men who can think themselves now realize that the great schoolmen had a type of thought that was wonderfully clear; but it was as it were deliberately colourless. All are now agreed that the greatest art of the age was the art of public buildings; the popular and communal art of architecture. But it was not an age for the art of portrait painting. Yet the friends of St Francis have really contrived to leave behind a portrait; something almost resembling a devout and affectionate caricature. There are lines and colours in it that are personal almost to the extent of being perverse, if one can use the word perversity of an inversion that was also a conversion. Even among the saints he has the air of a sort of eccentric, if one may use the word of one whose eccentricity consisted in always turning towards the centre.

Before resuming the narrative of his first adventures, and the building of the great brotherhood which was the beginning of so merciful a revolution, I think it well to complete this imperfect personal portrait here; and having attempted in the last chapter a tentative description of the process, to add in this chapter a few touches to describe the result. I mean by the result the real man as he was after his first formative experiences; the man whom men met walking about on the Italian roads in his brown tunic tied with a rope. For that man, saving the grace of God, is the explanation of all that followed; men acted quite differently according to whether they had met him or not. If we see afterwards a vast tumult, an appeal to the Pope, mobs of men in brown habits besieging the seats of authority, papal pronouncements, heretical sessions, trial and triumphant survival, the world full of a new movement, the friar a household word in every corner of Europe, and if we ask *why* all this happened, we can only approximate to any answer to our own question if we can, in some faint and indirect imaginative fashion, hear one human voice or see one human face under a hood. There is no answer except that Francis Bernardone had happened; and we must try in some sense to see what we should have seen if he had happened to us. In other words, after some groping suggestions about his life from the inside, we must again consider it from the outside; as if he were a stranger coming up the road towards us, along the hills of Umbria, between the olives or the vines.

Francis of Assisi was one of the founders of the medieval drama, and therefore of the modern drama. He was the very reverse of a theatrical person in the selfish sense; but for all that he was pre-eminently a dramatic person. This side of him can best be suggested by taking what is commonly regarded as a reposeful quality; what is commonly described as a love of nature. We are compelled to use the term; and it is entirely the wrong term.

St Francis was not a lover of nature. Properly understood, a lover of nature was precisely what he was not. The phrase implies accepting the material universe as a vague environment, a sort of sentimental pantheism. In the romantic period of literature, in the age of Byron and Scott, it was easy enough to imagine that a hermit in the ruins of a chapel (preferably by moonlight) might find peace and a mild pleasure in the harmony of solemn forests and silent stars, while he pondered over some scroll or illuminated volume, about the liturgical nature of which the author was a little vague. In short, the hermit might love nature as a background. Now for St Francis nothing was ever in the background. We might say that his mind had no background, except perhaps that divine darkness out of which the divine love had called up every coloured creature one by one. He saw everything as dramatic, distinct from its setting, not all of a piece like a picture but in action like a play. A bird went by him like an arrow; something with a story and a purpose, though it was a purpose of life and not a purpose of death. A bush could stop him like a brigand; and indeed he was as ready to welcome the brigand as the bush.

In a word, we talk about a man who cannot see the wood for the trees. St Francis was a man who did not want to see the wood for the trees. He wanted to see each tree as a separate and almost a sacred thing, being a child of God and therefore a brother or sister of man. But he did not want to stand against a piece of stage scenery used merely as a background, and inscribed in a general fashion: 'Scene: a wood.' In this sense we might say that he was too dramatic for the drama. The scenery would have come to life in his comedies; the walls would really have spoken like Snout the Tinker, and the trees would really have come walking to Dunsinane. Everything would have been in the foreground; and in that sense in the footlights. Everything would be in every sense a character. This is the quality in which, as a poet, he is the very opposite of a pantheist. He did not call nature his mother; he called a particular donkey his brother or a particular sparrow his sister. If he had called a pelican his aunt or an elephant his uncle, as he might possibly have done, he would still have meant that they were particular creatures assigned by their Creator to particular places; not mere expressions of the evolutionary energy of things. That is where his mysticism is so close to the common sense of the child. A child has no difficulty about understanding that God made the dog and the cat; though he is well aware that the making of dogs and cats out of nothing is a mysterious process beyond his own imagination. But no child would understand what you meant if you mixed up the dog and the cat and everything else into one monster with a myriad legs and called it nature. The child would resolutely refuse to make head or tail of any such animal. St Francis was a mystic, but he believed in mysticism and not in mystification.

As a mystic he was the mortal enemy of all those mystics who melt away the edges of things and dissolve an entity into its environment. He was a mystic of the daylight and the darkness; but not a mystic of the twilight. He was the very contrary of that sort of oriental visionary who is only a mystic because he is too much of a sceptic to be a materialist. St Francis was emphatically a realist, using the word realist in its much more real medieval sense. In this matter he really was akin to the best spirit of his age, which had just won its victory over the nominalism of the twelfth century. In this indeed there was something symbolic in the contemporary art and decoration of his period; as in the art of heraldry. The Franciscan birds and beasts were really rather like heraldic birds and beasts; not in the sense of being fabulous animals but in the sense of being treated as if they were facts, clear and positive and unaffected by the illusions of atmosphere and perspective. In that sense he did see a bird sable on a field azure or a sheep argent on a field vert. But the heraldry of humility was richer than the heraldry of pride; for it saw all these things that God had given as something more precious and unique than the blazonry that princes and peers had only given to themselves. Indeed out of the depths of that surrender it rose higher than the highest titles of the feudal age; than the laurel of Caesar or the Iron Crown of Lombardy. It is an example of extremes that meet, that the Little Poor Man, who had stripped himself of everything and named himself as nothing, took the same title that has been the wild vaunt of the vanity of the gorgeous Asiatic autocrat, and called himself the Brother of the Sun and Moon.

The phrase about his brotherhood with the sun and moon, and with the water and the fire, occurs of course in his famous poem called 'The Canticle of the Creatures' or 'The Canticle of the Sun'. He sang it wandering in the meadows in the sunnier season of his own career, when he was pouring upwards into the sky all the passions of a poet. It is a supremely characteristic work, and much of St Francis could be reconstructed from that work alone. Though in some ways the thing is as simple and straightforward as a ballad, there is a delicate instinct of differentiation in it. Notice, for instance, the sense of sex in inanimate things, which goes far beyond the arbitrary genders of a grammar. It was not for nothing that he called fire his brother, fierce and gay and strong, and water his sister, pure and clear and inviolate. Remember that St Francis was neither encumbered nor assisted by all that Greek and Roman polytheism turned into allegory, which has been to European poetry often an inspiration, too often a convention.

St Francis of Assisi, 1923

The Book of Job

The Book of Job is among the other Old Testament books both a philosophical riddle and a historical riddle. It is the philosophical riddle that concerns us in such an introduction as this; so we may dismiss first the few words of general explanation or warning which should be said about the historical aspect. Controversy has long raged about which parts of this epic belong to its original scheme and which are interpolations of considerably later date. The doctors disagree, as it is the business of doctors to do; but upon the whole, [the] trend of investigation has always been in the direction of maintaining that the parts interpolated, if any, were the prose prologue and epilogue and possibly the speech of the young man who comes in with an apology at the end. I do not profess to be competent to decide such questions. But whatever decision the reader may come to concerning them, there is a general truth to be remembered in this connection. When you deal with any ancient artistic creation do not suppose that it is anything against it that it grew gradually. The Book of Job may have grown gradually just as Westminster Abbey grew gradually. But the people who made the old folk poetry, like the people who made Westminster Abbey, did not attach that importance to the actual date and the actual author, that importance which is entirely the creation of the almost insane individualism of modern times. We may put aside the case of

Job, as one complicated with religious difficulties, and take any other, say the case of the *Iliad*. Many people have maintained the characteristic formula of modern scepticism, that Homer was not written by Homer, but by another person of the same name. Just in the same way many have maintained that Moses was not Moses but another person called Moses. But the thing really to be remembered in the matter of the *Iliad* is that if other people did interpolate the passages, the thing did not create the same sense of shock as would be created by such proceedings in these individualistic times. The creation of the tribal epic was to some extent regarded as a tribal work, like the building of the tribal temple. Believe then, if you will, that the prologue of Job and the epilogue and the speech of Elihu are things inserted after the original work was composed. But do not suppose that such insertions have that obvious and spurious character which would belong to any insertions in a modern individualistic book. Do not regard the insertions as you would regard a chapter in George Meredith which you afterwards found had not been written by George Meredith, or half a scene in Ibsen which you found had been cunningly sneaked in by Mr William Archer. Remember that this old world which made these old poems like the *Iliad* and Job, always kept the tradition of what it was making. A man could almost leave a poem to his son to be finished as he would have finished it, just as a man could leave a field to his son, to be reaped as he would have reaped it. What is called Homeric unity may be a fact or not. The *Iliad* may have been written by one man. It may have been written by a hundred men. But let us remember that there was more unity in those times in a hundred men than there is unity now in one man. Then a city was like one man. Now one man is like a city in civil war.

Without going, therefore, into questions of unity as understood by the scholars, we may say of the scholarly riddle that the book has unity in the sense that all great traditional creations have unity; in the sense that Canterbury Cathedral has unity. And the same is broadly true of what I have called the philosophical riddle. There is a real sense in which the Book of Job stands apart from most of the books included in the canon of the Old Testament. But here again those are wrong who insist on the entire absence of unity. Those are wrong who maintain that the Old Testament is a mere loose library; that it has no consistency or aim. Whether the result was achieved by some supernal spiritual truth, or by a steady national tradition, or merely by an ingenious selection in after times, the books of the Old Testament have a quite perceptible unity. To attempt to understand the Old Testament without realizing this main idea is as absurd as it would be to study one of Shakespeare's plays without realizing that the author of them had any philosophical object at all. It is as if a man were to read the history of Hamlet, Prince of Denmark, thinking all the time that he was reading what really purported to be the history of an old Danish pirate prince. Such a reader would not realize at all that Hamlet's procrastination was on the part of the poet intentional. He would merely say, 'How long Shakespeare's hero does take to kill his enemy.' So speak the Bible smashers, who are unfortunately always at bottom Bible worshippers. They do not understand the special tone and intention of the Old Testament; they do not understand its main idea, which is the idea of all men being merely the instruments of a higher power.

Those, for instance, who complain of the atrocities and treacheries of the judges and prophets of Israel have really got a notion in their head that has nothing to do with the subject. They are too Christian. They are reading back into the pre-Christian scriptures a purely Christian idea – the idea of saints, the idea that the chief instruments of God are very particularly good men. There is a deeper, a more daring, and a more interesting idea than the old Jewish one. It is the idea that innocence has about it something terrible which in the long run makes and re-makes empires and the world. But the Old Testament idea was much more what may be called the common sense idea, that strength is strength, that cunning is cunning, that worldly success is worldly success, and that Jehovah uses these things for His own ultimate purpose, just as He uses natural forces or physical elements. He uses the strength of a hero as He uses that of a Mammoth – without any particular respect for the Mammoth. I cannot comprehend how it is that so many simple-minded sceptics have read such stories as the fraud of Jacob and supposed that the man who wrote it (whoever he was) did not know that Jacob was a sneak just as well as we do. The primeval human sense of honour does not change so much as that. But these simple-minded sceptics are, like the majority of modern sceptics, Christians. They fancy that the patriarchs must be meant for patterns; they fancy that Jacob was being set up as some kind of saint; and in that case I do not wonder that they are a little startled. That is not the atmosphere of the Old Testament at all. The heroes of the Old Testament are not the sons of God, but the slaves of God, gigantic and terrible slaves, like the genii, who were the slaves of Aladdin.

The central idea of the great part of the Old Testament may be called the idea of the loneliness of God. God is not only the chief character of the Old Testament; God is properly the only character in the Old Testament. Compared with His clearness of purpose all the other wills are heavy and automatic, like those of animals; compared with His actuality all the sons of flesh are shadows. Again and again the note is struck, 'With whom hath he taken counsel?' 'I have trodden the wine press alone, and of the peoples there was no man with me.' All the patriarchs and prophets are merely His tools of weapons; for the Lord is a man of war. He uses Joshua like an axe or Moses like a measuring rod. For Him Samson is only a sword and Isaiah a trumpet. The saints of Christianity are supposed to be like God, to be, as it were, little statuettes of

Him. The Old Testament hero is no more supposed to be of the same nature as God than a saw or a hammer is supposed to be of the same shape as the carpenter. This is the main key and characteristic of the Hebrew scriptures as a whole. There are, indeed, in those scriptures innumerable instances of the sort of rugged humour, keen emotion, and powerful individuality which is never wanting in great primitive prose and poetry. Nevertheless the main characteristic remains; the sense not merely that God is stronger than man, not merely that God is more secret than man, but that He means more, that He knows better what He is doing, that compared with Him we have something of the vagueness, the unreason, and the vagrancy of the beasts that perish. 'It is He that sitteth above the earth, and the inhabitants thereof are as grasshoppers.' We might almost put it thus. The book is so intent upon asserting the personality of God that it almost asserts the impersonality of man. Unless this gigantic cosmic brain has conceived a thing, that thing is insecure and void; man has not enough tenacity to ensure its continuance. 'Except the Lord build the house their labour is but lost that build it. Except the Lord keep the city the watchman watcheth but in vain.'

Everywhere else, then, the Old Testament positively rejoices in the obliteration of man in comparison with the divine purpose. The Book of Job stands definitely alone because the Book of Job definitely asks, 'But what is the purpose of God?' Is it worth the sacrifice even of our miserable humanity? Of course it is easy enough to wipe out our own paltry wills for the sake of a will that is grander and kinder. Let God use His tools; let God break His tools. But what is He doing and what are they being broken for? It is because of this question that we have to attack as a philosophical riddle the riddle of the Book of Job.

The present importance of the Book of Job cannot be expressed adequately even by saying that it is the most interesting of ancient books. We may almost say of the Book of Job that it is the most interesting of modern books. In truth, of course, neither of the two phrases covers the matter, because fundamental human religion and fundamental human ir-religion are both at once old and new; philosophy is either eternal or it is not philosophy. The modern habit of saying, 'This is my opinion, but I may be wrong,' is entirely irrational. If I say that it may be wrong I say that it is not my opinion. The modern habit of saying, 'Every man has a different philosophy; this is my philosophy and it suits me' – the habit of saying this is mere weak mindedness. A cosmic philosophy is not constructed to fit a man; a cosmic philosophy is constructed to fit a cosmos. A man can no more possess a private religion than he can possess a private sun and moon.

The first of the intellectual beauties of the Book of Job is that it is all concerned with this desire to know the actuality; the desire to know what is, and not merely what seems. If moderns were writing the book we should probably find that Job and his comforters got on quite well together by the simple operation of referring their differences to what is called the temperament, saying that the comforters were by nature 'optimists' and Job by nature a 'pessimist'. And they would be quite comfortable, as people can often be, for some time at least, by agreeing to say what is obviously untrue. For if the word 'pessimist' means anything at all, then emphatically Job is not a pessimist. His case alone is sufficient to refute the modern absurdity of referring everything to physical temperament. Job does not in any sense look at life in a gloomy way. If wishing to be happy and being quite ready to be happy constitute an optimist, Job is an optimist; he is an outraged and insulted optimist. He wishes the universe to justify itself, not because he wishes it to be caught out, but because he really wishes it to be justified. He demands an explanation from God, but he does not do it at all in the spirit in which Hampden might demand an explanation from Charles I. He does it in the spirit in which a wife might demand an explanation from her husband whom she really respected. He remonstrates with his Maker because he is proud of his Maker. He even speaks of the Almighty as his enemy, but he never doubts, at the back of his mind, that his enemy has some kind of a case which he does not understand. In a fine and famous blasphemy he says, 'Oh, that mine adversary had written a book!' It never really occurs to him that it could possibly be a bad book. He is anxious to be convinced, that is, he thinks that God could convince him. In short, we may say again that if the word optimist means anything (which I doubt) Job is an optimist. He shakes the pillars of the world and strikes insanely at the heavens; he lashes the stars, but it is not to silence them; it is to make them speak.

In the same way we may speak of the official optimists, the comforters of Job. Again, if the word pessimist means anything (which I doubt) the comforters of Job may be called pessimists rather than optimists. All that they really believe is not that God is good but that God is so strong that it is much more judicious to call Him good. It would be the exaggeration of censure to call them evolutionists; but they have something of the vital error of the evolutionary optimist. They will keep on saying that everything in the universe fits into everything else: as if there were anything comforting about a number of nasty things all fitting into each other. We shall see later how God in the great climax of the poem turns this particular argument upside down.

When, at the end of the poem, God enters (somewhat abruptly), is struck the sudden and splendid note which makes the thing as great as it is. All the human beings through the story, and Job especially, have been asking questions of God. A more trivial poet would have made God enter in some sense or other in order to answer the questions. By a touch truly to be called inspired, when God enters, it is to ask a number more questions on His own account. In this drama of scepticism God Himself takes up the role of sceptic. He does what all the great voices defending religion have always done. He does, for instance, what Socrates did. He turns rationalism against itself. He seems to say that if it comes to asking questions, He can ask some questions which will fling down and flatten out all conceivable human questioners. The poet by an exquisite intuition has made God ironically accept a kind of controversial equality with His accusers. He is willing to regard it as if it were a fair intellectual duel: 'Gird up now thy loins like a man; for I will demand of thee, and answer thou Me.' The Everlasting adopts an enormous and sardonic humility. He is quite willing to be prosecuted. He only asks for the right which every prosecuted person possesses; He asks to be allowed to cross-examine the witness for the prosecution. And He carries yet further the correctness of the legal parallel. For the first question, essentially speaking, which He asks of Job is the question that any criminal accused by Job would be most entitled to ask. He asks Job who he is. And Job, being a man of candid intellect, takes a little time to consider, and comes to the conclusion that he does not know.

This is the first great fact to notice about the speech of God, which is the culmination of the enquiry. It represents all human sceptics routed by a higher scepticism. It is this method, used sometimes by supreme and sometimes by mediocre minds, that has ever since been the logical weapon of the true mystic. Socrates, as I have said, used it when he showed that if you only allowed him enough sophistry he could destroy all the sophists. Jesus Christ used it when He reminded the Sadducees, who could not imagine the nature of marriage in heaven, that if it came to that they had not really imagined the nature of marriage at all. In the break up of Christian theology in the eighteenth century, Butler[1] used

1. Bishop Joseph Butler (1692–1752) is recognized as one of the leading Anglican theologians of the eighteenth century. His best known work is *The Analogy of Religion*.

it, when he pointed out that rationalistic arguments could be used as much against vague religion as against doctrinal religion, as much against rationalistic ethics as against Christian ethics. It is the root and reason of the fact that men who have religious faith have also philosophic doubt, like Cardinal Newman,[2] Mr Balfour[3] or Mr Mallock. These are the small streams of the delta; the Book of Job is the first great cataract that creates the river. In dealing with the arrogant asserter of doubt, it is not the right method to tell him to stop doubting. It is rather the right method to tell him to go on doubting, to doubt a little more, to doubt every day newer and wilder things in the universe, until at last, by some strange enlightenment, he may begin to doubt himself.

This, I say, is the first fact touching the speech; the fine inspiration by which God comes in at the end, not to answer riddles, but to propound them. The other great fact which, taken together with this one, makes the whole work religious instead of merely philosophical, is that other great surprise which makes Job suddenly satisfied with the mere presentation of something impenetrable. Verbally speaking the enigmas of Jehovah seem darker and more desolate than the enigmas of Job; yet Job was comfortless before the speech of Jehovah and is comforted after it. He has been told nothing, but he feels the terrible and tingling atmosphere of something which is too good to be told. The refusal of God to explain His design is itself a burning hint of His design. The riddles of God are more satisfying than the solutions of man.

Thirdly, of course, it is one of the splendid strokes that God rebukes alike the man who accused, and the men who

---

2. John Henry Newman (1801–90): a leading Anglican clergyman who converted to Catholicism in 1845. His book, *Apologia Pro Vita Sua*, is regarded as a spiritual classic.
3. Arthur Balfour was Prime Minister from 1902 to 1906. In 1879 he wrote *In Defence of Philosophic Doubt*.

defended Him; that He knocks down pessimists and optimists with the same hammer.

And it is in connection with the mechanical and supercilious comforters of Job that there occurs the still deeper imagery, sudden and splendid suggestions that the secret of God is a bright and not a sad one — semi-accidental suggestions, like light seen for an instant through the cracks of a closed door. It would be difficult to praise too highly, in a purely poetical sense, the instinctive exactitude and ease with which these more optimistic insinuations are let fall in other connections, as if the Almighty Himself were scarcely aware that He was letting them out. For instance, there is that famous passage where Jehovah with devastating sarcasm asks Job where he was when the foundations of the world were laid, and then (as if merely fixing a date) mentions the time when the sons of God shouted for joy. One cannot help feeling, even upon this meagre information, that they must have had something to shout about. Or again, when God is speaking of snow and hail in the mere catalogue of the physical cosmos, He speaks of them as a treasury that He has laid up against the day of battle — a hint of some huge Armageddon in which evil shall be at last overthrown.

Nothing could be better, artistically speaking, than this optimism breaking through agnosticism like fiery gold round the edges of a black cloud. Those who look superficially at the barbaric origin of the epic may think it fanciful to read so much artistic significance into its casual similes or accidental phrases. But no one who is well acquainted with great examples of semi-barbaric poetry, as in the 'Song of Roland' or the old ballads, will fall into this mistake. No one who knows what primitive poetry is, can fail to realize that while its conscious form is simple some of its finer effects are subtle. The *Iliad* contrives to express the idea that Hector and Sarpedon have a certain tone or tint of sad and chivalrous resignation, not bitter enough to be called pessimism and not jovial enough to be called optimism; Homer could never have said this in elaborate words. But somehow he contrives to say it in simple words. The 'Song of Roland' contrives to express the idea that Christianity imposes upon its heroes a paradox; a paradox of great humility in the matter of their sins combined with great ferocity in the matter of their ideas. Of course the 'Song of Roland' could not say this; but it conveys this. In the same way the Book of Job must be credited with many subtle effects which were in the author's soul without being, perhaps, in the author's mind. And of these by far the most important remains even yet to be stated. I do not know, and I doubt whether even scholars know, if the Book of Job had a great effect or had any effect upon the after development of Jewish thought. But if it did have any effect it may have saved them from an enormous collapse and decay. Here in this book the question is really asked whether God invariably punishes vice with terrestrial punishment and rewards virtue with terrestrial prosperity. If the Jews had answered that question wrong they might have lost all their influence in human history. They might have sunk even down to the level of modern well-educated society. For when once people have begun to believe that prosperity is the reward of virtue their next calamity is obvious. If prosperity is regarded as the reward of virtue it will be regarded as the symptom of virtue. Men will leave off the heavy task of making good men successful. They will adopt the easier task of making our successful men good. This, which has happened throughout modern commerce and journalism, is the ultimate Nemesis of the wicked optimism of the comforters of Job. If the Jews could be saved from it, the Book of Job saved them. The Book of Job is chiefly remarkable, as I have insisted throughout, for the fact that it does not end in a way that is conventionally satisfactory. Job is not told that his misfortunes were due to his sins or a part of any plan for his improvement. But in the prologue we see Job tormented not because he was the worst of men, but because he was the best. It is the lesson of the whole work that man is most comforted by paradoxes; and it is by all human testimony the most reassuring. I need not suggest what a high and strange history awaited this paradox of the best man in the worst fortune. I need not say that in the freest and most philosophical sense there is one Old Testament figure who is truly a type; or say what is prefigured in the wounds of Job.

GKC as MC, 1929[4]

---

4. Originally written in 1907 as a foreword to an edition of the Book of Job.

Obstinate Orthodoxy

I have been asked to explain something about myself which seems to be regarded as very extraordinary. The problem has been presented to me in the form of a cutting from a very flattering American article, which yet contained a certain suggestion of wonder. So far as I can understand, it is thought extraordinary that a man should be ordinary. I am ordinary in the correct sense of the term; which means the acceptance of an order; a Creator and the Creation, the common sense of gratitude for Creation, life and love as gifts permanently good, marriage and chivalry as laws rightly controlling them, and the rest of the normal traditions of our race and religion. It is also thought a little odd that I regard the grass as green, even after some newly-discovered Slovak artist has painted it grey; that I think daylight very tolerable in spite of thirteen Lithuanian philosophers sitting in a row and cursing the light of day; and that, in matters more polemical, I actually prefer weddings to divorces and babies to birth control. These eccentric views, which I share with the overwhelming majority of mankind, past and present, I should not attempt to defend here one by one. And I only give a general reply for a particular reason. I wish to make it unmistakably plain that my defence of these sentiments is not sentimental. It would be easy to gush about these things; but I defy the reader, after reading this, to find the faintest trace of the tear of sensibility.

I hold this view not because it is sensibility, but because it is sense.

On the contrary, it is the sceptics who are the sentimentalists. More than half the 'revolt' and the talk of being advanced and progressive is simply a weak sort of snobbishness which takes the form of a worship of Youth. Some men of my generation delight in declaring that they are of the Party of the Young and defending every detail of the latest fashions or freaks. If I do not do that, it is for the same reason that I do not dye my hair or wear stays. But even when it is less despicable than that, the current phrase that everything must be done for youth, that the rising generation is all that matters, is in sober fact a piece of pure sentimentalism. It is also, within reason, a perfectly natural piece of sentiment. All healthy people like to see the young enjoying themselves; but if we turn that pleasure into a principle, we are sentimentalists. If we desire the greatest happiness of the greatest number, it will be obvious that the greatest number, at any given moment, are rather more likely to be between twenty-five and seventy than to be between seventeen and twenty-five. Sacrificing everything to the young will be like working only for the rich. They will be a privileged class and the rest will be snobs or slaves. Moreover, the young will always have a fair amount of fun under the worst conditions; if we really wish to console the world, it will be much more rational to console the old. This is what I call facing facts; and I have continued to believe in most of these traditions because they are facts. I could give a great many other examples; for instance, chivalry. Chivalry is not the romantic, but the realistic, view of the sexes. It is so realistic that the real reasons for it cannot always be given in print.

If those called free thinkers are sentimentalists, those called free lovers are open and obvious sentimentalists. We can always convict such people of sentimentalism by their weakness for euphemism. The phrase they use is always softened and suited for journalistic appeals. They talk of free love when they mean something quite different, better defined as free lust. But being sentimentalists they feel bound to simper and coo over the word 'love'. They insist on talking about birth control when they mean less birth and no control. We could smash them to atoms, if we could be as indecent in our language as they are immoral in their conclusions. And as it is with morals, so it is with religion. The general notion that science establishes agnosticism is a sort of mystification produced by talking Latin and Greek instead of plain English. Science is the Latin for knowledge. Agnosticism is the Greek for ignorance. It is not self-evident that ignorance is the goal of knowledge. It is the ignorance and not the knowledge that produces the current notion that free thought weakens theism. It is the real world, that we see with our own eyes, that obviously unfolds a plan of things that fit into each other. It is only a remote and misty legend that ever pretended to explain it by the automatic advantage of the 'fit'. As a fact, modern evolutionists, even when they are still Darwinians, do not pretend that the theory explains all varieties and adaptations. Those who know are rather rescuing Darwin at the expense of Darwinism. But it is those who do not know who doubt or deny; it is typical that their myth is actually called the Missing Link. They actually know nothing of their own argument except that it breaks down somewhere. But it is worthwhile to ask why this loose legend has such power over many; and I will proceed to my suggestion. I have not changed my mind; nor, indeed, have they changed their mind. They have only changed their mood.

What we call the intellectual world is divided into two types of people – those who worship the intellect and those who use it. There are exceptions; but, broadly speaking, they are never the same people. Those who use the intellect never worship it; they know too much about it. Those who worship the intellect never use it; as you can see by the things they say about it. Hence there has arisen a confusion about intellect and intellectualism; and, as the supreme expression of that confusion, something that is called in many countries the Intelligentsia, and in France more especially, the Intellectuals. It is found in practice to consist of clubs and coteries of people talking mostly about books and pictures, but especially new books and new pictures; and about music, so long as it is very modern music; or what some would call very unmusical music. The first fact to record about it is that what Carlyle said of the world is very specially true of the intellectual world – that it is mostly fools.

Indeed, it has a curious attraction for complete fools, as a warm fire has for cats. I have frequently visited such societies, in the capacity of a common or normal fool, and I have almost always found there a few fools who were more foolish that I had imagined to be possible to man born of woman; people who had hardly enough brains to be called half-witted. But it gave them a glow within to be in what they imagined to be the atmosphere of intellect; for they worshipped it like an unknown god. I could tell many stories of that world. I remember a venerable man with a very long beard who seemed to live at one of these clubs. At intervals he would hold up his hand as if for silence and preface his remarks by saying, 'A Thought.' And then he would say something that sounded as if a cow had suddenly spoken in a drawing-room. I remember once a silent and much-enduring man (I rather think it was my friend Mr Edgar Jepson, the novelist) who could bear it no longer and cried with a sort of expiring gasp, 'But, Good God, man, you don't call that a *thought*, do you?' But that was pretty much the quality of the thought of such thinkers, especially of the freethinkers. Out of this social situation arises one sort of exception to the rule. Intelligence does exist even in the Intelligentsia. It does sometimes happen that a man of real talent has a weakness for flattery, even the flattery of fools. He would rather say something that silly people think clever than something which only clever people could perceive to be true. Oscar Wilde was a man of this type. When he said somewhere that an immoral woman is the sort of woman a man never gets tired of, he used a phrase so baseless as to be perfectly pointless. Everybody knows that a man may get tired of a whole procession of immoral women, especially if he is an immoral man. That was 'a Thought'; otherwise something to be uttered, with uplifted hand, to people who could not think at all. In their poor muddled minds there was some vague connection between wit and cynicism; so they never applauded him so warmly as a wit, as when he was cynical without being witty. But when he said, 'A cynic is a man who knows the price of everything and the value of nothing,' he made a statement (in excellent epigrammatic form) which really meant something. But it would have meant his own immediate dethronement if it could have been understood by those who only enthroned him for being cynical.

Anyhow, it is in this intellectual world, with its many fools and few wits and fewer wise men, that there goes on perpetually a sort of ferment of fashionable revolt and negation. From this comes all that is called destructive criticism; though, as a matter of fact, the new critic is generally destroyed by the next critic long before he has had any chance of destroying anything else. When people say solemnly that the world is in revolt against religion or private property or patriotism or marriage, they mean that *this* world is in revolt against them; or rather, is in permanent revolt against everything. Now, as a matter of fact, this world has a certain excuse for being always in that state of excitement, apart from mere fuss and mere folly. The reason is rather an important one; and I would ask anyone who really does want to think, and especially to think freely, to pause upon it seriously for a moment. It arises from the fact that these people are so much concerned with the study of Art. It collapses into mere drivelling and despair, because they try to transfer their treatment of art to the treatment of morals and philosophy. In this they make a bad blunder in reasoning. But then, as I have explained, intellectuals are not very intellectual.

The Arts exist, as we should put it in our primeval fashion, to show forth the glory of God; or, to translate the same thing in terms of our psychology, to awaken and keep alive the sense of wonder in man. The success of any work of art is achieved when we say of any subject, a tree or a cloud or a human character, 'I have seen that a thousand times and I never saw it before.' Now for this purpose a certain variation of venue is natural and even necessary. Artists change what they call their attack; for it is to some extent their business to make it a surprise attack. They have to throw a new light on things; and it is not surprising if it is sometimes an invisible ultra-violet ray or one rather resembling a black ray of madness or death. But when the artist extends the eccentric experience from art to real life, it is quite different. He is like an absent-minded sculptor turning his chisel from chipping at the bust to chipping at the bald head of the distinguished sitter. And these anarchic artists do suffer a little from absence of Mind.

Let us take a practical case for the sake of simplicity Many moderns will be heard scoffing at what they would call 'chocolate-box art'; meaning an insipid and sickly art. And it is easy to call up the sort of picture that might well make anybody ill. I will suppose, for the sake of argument, that we are looking sadly at the outside of a chocolate box (now, I need hardly say, empty) and that we see painted on it in rather pallid colours a young woman with golden ringlets gazing from a balcony and holding a rose in the spotlight caused by a convenient ray of moonlight. Any similar touches may be added to the taste or distaste of the critic; she may be convulsively clasping a letter or conspicuously wearing an engagement ring or languidly waving farewell to a distant gentleman in a gondola; or anything else I can think of, calculated to cause pain to the sensitive critic. I sympathize with the critic's feeling; but I think he goes quite wrong in his thinking.

Now, what do we mean when we say that this is a silly picture, or a stale subject, or something very difficult to bear, even when we are fortified by chocolates to endure it? We mean it is possible to have too much of a good thing; to have too many chocolate boxes, as to have too many chocolates. We mean that it is not a picture, but a picture of a picture. Ultimately it is a picture of innumerable pictures; not a real picture of a rose or a girl or a beam of moonlight. In other words, artists have copied artists, right away back to the first sentimental pictures of the Romantic Movement.

But roses have not copied roses. Moonbeams have not imitated each other. And though a woman can copy women in externals, it is only in externals and not in existence; her womanhood was not copied from any other woman. Considered as realities, the rose and the moon and the woman are simply themselves. Suppose that scene to be a real one, and there is nothing particularly imitative about it. The flower is unquestionably fresh as the young woman is unquestionably young. The rose is a real object, which would smell as sweet by any other name, or by no name. The girl is a particular person, whose personality is entirely new to the world and whose experiences are entirely new to herself. If she does indeed choose to stand in that attitude on that balcony holding that botanical specimen (which seems improbable), we have no right to doubt that she has her own reasons for doing so. In short, when once we conceive the thing as reality, we have no reason whatever to dismiss it as mere repetition. So long as we are thinking of the thing as copied mechanically and for money, as a piece of monotonous and mercenary ornament, we naturally feel that the flower is in a special sense an artificial flower and that the moonlight is all moonshine.

We feel inclined to welcome even wild variations in the decorative style; and to admire the new artist who will paint the rose black, lest we should forget that it is a deep red, or the moonshine green, that we may realize it is something more subtle than white. But the moon is the moon and the rose is the rose; and we do not expect the real things to alter. Nor is there any reason to expect the rules about them to alter. Nor is there any reason, so far as this question is concerned, to expect the woman to alter her attitude either about the beauty of the rose or the obligations of the engagement ring. These things, considered as real things, are quite unaffected by the variation of artistic attack in fictitious things. The moon will continue to affect the tides, whether we paint it blue or green or pink with purple spots. And the man who imagines that artistic revolutions must always affect morals is like a man who should say, 'I am so bored with seeing pink roses painted on chocolate boxes that I refuse to believe that roses grow well in a clay soil.'

In short, what the critics would call romanticism is in fact the only form of realism. It is also the only form of rationalism. The more a man uses his reason upon realities, the more he will see that the realities remain much the same, though the representations are very different. And it is only the representations that are repetitions. The sensations are always sincere; the individuals are always individual. If the real girl is experiencing a real romance, she is experiencing something old, but not something stale. If she has plucked something from a real rose tree, she is holding a very ancient symbol, but a very recent rose. And it is exactly in so far as a man *can* clear his head, so as to see actual things as they are, that he will see these things as permanently important as they are. Exactly in so far as his head is confused with current fashions and aesthetic modes of the moment, he will see nothing about it except that it is like a picture on a chocolate box, and not like a picture at the Post-Futurist Gallery. Exactly in so far as he is thinking about real people, he will see that they are really romantic. Exactly in so far as he is thinking only about pictures and poems and decorative styles, he will think that romance is a false or old-fashioned style. He can only see people as imitating pictures; whereas the real people are not imitating anything. They are only being themselves – as they will always be. Roses remain radiant and mysterious, however many pink rosebuds are sprinkled like pips over cheap wallpapers. Falling in love remains radiant and mysterious, however threadbare be the thousandth repetition of a rhyme as a valentine or a cracker motto. To see this fact is to live in a world of facts. To be always thinking of the banality of bad wallpapers and valentines is to live in a world of fictions.

Now the main truth about all this sceptical revolt, and all the rest of it, is that it was born in a world of fictions. It came from the Intelligentsia, who were perpetually discussing novels and plays and pictures instead of people. They insisted on putting 'real life' on the stage and never saw it in the street. They professed to be putting realism into their novels when there was less and less of it in their conversation, as compared with the conversation of the common people. And that perpetual experiment, and shifting of the standpoint, which was natural enough in an artist seeking for certain effects (as it is natural in a photographer hovering around and focusing and fussing with his camera), was wholly inapplicable to any study of the permanent rules and relations of society. When these people began to play about with morals and meta-physics, they simply produced a series of mad worlds where they might have been harmlessly producing a series of mad pictures. Pictures are always meant to catch a certain aspect, at a certain angle, in a certain light; sometimes in light that is almost as brief as lightning. But when the artists became anarchists and began to exhibit the community and the cosmos by these flashes of lightning, the result was not realism but simply nightmare. Because a particular painter, for a particular purpose, might paint the red rose black, the pessimist deduced that the red rose of love and life was really as black as it was painted. Because one artist, from one angle, seized a momentary impression of moonlight as green, the philosopher solemnly put on a pair of green spectacles and declared that is was now a solid scientific certainty that the moon must be crawling with maggots, because it was made of green cheese.

In short, there might have been some value in the old cry of art for the artists; if it had meant that the artists would confine themselves to the medium of art. As a fact, they were always meddling with the medium of morals and religion; and they imported into them the unrest, the changing moods and the merely experimental tricks of their own trade. But a man with a solid sense of reality can see that this is utterly unreal. Whatever the laws of life and love and human relations may be, it is monstrously improbable that they ought to be changed with every fashion in poetry any more than with every fashion in pantaloons. It is insane that there should be a new pattern of hearts or heads whenever there is a new pattern of hats. These things are realities, like a high tide or a clay soil; and you do not get rid of high tides and clay soils by calling roses and moonlight old-fashioned and sentimental. I will venture to say, therefore, and I trust without undue vanity, that I have remained rooted in certain relations and traditions, not because I am a sentimentalist or even a romanticist; but because I am a realist. And I realize that morals must not change with moods, as Cubism must not mean chopping up real houses into cubes, or Vorticism swallowing real ships in whirlpools.

I have not changed my views on these things because there has never been any reason to change them. For anybody impelled by reason and not by running with a crowd will, for instance, perceive that there are always the same arguments for a Purpose and therefore a Personality in things, if he is a thinking person. Only it is now made easy for him to admit vaguely that there may be a Purpose, while denying that there is a Personality, so long as he happens to be a very unthinking person. It is quite as certain as it ever was that life is a gift of God immensely valuable and immensely valued; and anybody can prove it by putting a pistol to the head of a pessimist. Only a certain sort of modern does not like any problem presented to his head; and would dislike a plain question almost as much as a pistol. It is obvious common sense, and obviously consonant to real life, that romantic love is normal to youth and has its natural development in marriage and parenthood as the corresponding conditions of age. None of the nonsense talked about this, that or the other individual irritation or licence has ever made any difference to that solid social truth, for anyone who cares whether things are true, apart from whether they are trite. It is the man who cannot see that a thing is true, although it is trite, who is very truly a victim of mere words and verbal associations. He is the fool who has grown so furious with paper roses that he will not believe that the real rose has a root; nor (till he discovers it with an abrupt and profane ejaculation) that it has a thorn.

The truth is that the modern world has had a mental breakdown; much more than a moral breakdown. Things are being settled by mere associations because there is a reluctance to settle them by arguments. Nearly all the talk about what is advanced and what is antiquated has become a sort of giggling excitement about fashions. The most modern of the moderns stare at a picture of a man making love to a lady in a crinoline with exactly the same sort of vacant grin with which yokels stare at a stranger in an outlandish sort of hat. They regard their fathers of another age exactly as the most insular would regard the foreigners from another country. They seem mentally incapable of getting any further than the statement that our girls are shingled and short-skirted while their silly old great-grandmothers wore ringlets and hoops. That seems to satisfy all their appetite for satire; they are a simple race, a little like savages. They are exactly like the sort of cockney tripper who would roar with laughter because French soldiers wore red trousers and blue coats, while English soldiers were dressed properly in blue trousers and red coats. I have not altered my lines of thought for people who think in this fashion. Why should I?

The Thing, 1929

The Roots of Sanity

———

The Dean of St Paul's, when he is right, is very right. He is right with all that ringing emphasis that makes him in other matters so rashly and disastrously wrong. And I cannot but hail with gratitude the scorn with which he spoke lately of all the newspaper nonsense about using monkey glands to turn old men into young men; or into young monkeys, if that is to be the next step towards the Superman. Not unnaturally, he tried to balance his denunciation of that very experimental materialism which he is always accusing us of denouncing, by saying that this materialism is one evil extreme and that Catholicism is the other. In that connection he said some of the usual things which he commonly finds it easy to say, and we generally find it tolerably easy to answer.

For instance, it is a good example of the contradictory charges brought against Rome that the Dean apparently classes us with those who leave children entirely 'unwarned' about the moral dangers of the body. Considering that we have been abused for decades on the ground that we forced on the young the infamous suggestions of the confessional, this is rather funny.

Only the other day I noted that Sir Arthur Conan Doyle revived this charge of an insult to innocence; and I will leave Dean Inge and Sir Arthur to fight it out. And when he charges us with indifference to eugenics and the breeding of criminals and lunatics, it is enough that he has himself to denounce the perversion of science manifested in the monkey business. He might permit others to resent equally the schemes by which men are to act like lunatics and criminals in order to avoid lunacy and crime.

There is, however, another aspect of this matter of being right or wrong, which is not so often associated with us, but which is equally consistent with our philosophy. And it has a notable bearing on the sort of questions here raised by Dean Inge. It concerns not only the matters in which the world is wrong, but rather especially the matters in which the world is right. The world, especially the modern world, has reached a curious condition of ritual or routine; in which we might almost say that it is wrong even when it is right. It continues to a great extent to do the sensible things. It is rapidly ceasing to have any of the sensible reasons for doing them. It is always lecturing us on the deadness of tradition; and it is living entirely on the life of tradition. It is always denouncing us for superstition; and its own principal virtues are now almost entirely superstitions.

I mean that when we are right, we are right by principle; and when they are right, they are right by prejudice. We can say, if they prefer it so, that they are right by instinct. But anyhow, they are still restrained by healthy prejudice from many things into which they might be hurried by their own unhealthy logic. It it easiest to take very simple and even extreme examples; and some of the extremes are nearer to us than some may fancy.

Thus, most of our friends and acquaintances continue to entertain a healthy prejudice against cannibalism. The time when this next step in ethical evolution will be taken seems as yet far distant. But the notion that there is not very much difference between the bodies of men and animals — that is not by any means far distant, but exceedingly near. It is expressed in a hundred ways, as a sort of cosmic communism.

We might almost say that it is expressed in every other way except cannibalism.

It is expressed, as in the Voronoff notion, in putting pieces of animals into men. It is expressed, as in the vegetarian notion, in not putting pieces of animals into men. It is expressed in letting a man die as a dog dies or in thinking it more pathetic that a dog should die than a man. Some are fussy about what happens to the bodies of animals, as if they were quite certain that a rabbit resented being cooked, or that an oyster demanded to be cremated. Some are ostentatiously indifferent to what happens to the bodies of men; and deny all dignity to the dead and all affectionate gesture to the living. But all these have obviously one thing in common; and that is that they regard the human and bestial body as common things. They think of them under a common generalization; or under conditions at best comparative. Among people who have reached this position, the *reason* for disapproving of cannibalism has already become very vague. It remains as a tradition and an instinct. Fortunately, thank God, though it is now very vague, it is still very strong. But though the number of earnest ethical pioneers who are likely to begin to eat boiled missionary is very small, the number of those among them who could explain their own real reason for not doing so is still smaller.

The real reason is that all such social sanities are now the traditions of old Catholic dogmas. Like many other Catholic dogmas, they are felt in some vague way even by heathens, so long as they are healthy heathens. But when it is a question of their not being merely felt but formulated, it will be found to be a formula of the Faith. In this case it is all those ideas that Modernists most dislike, about 'special creation' and that divine image that does not come merely by evolution, and the chasm between man and the other creatures. In short, it is those very doctrines with which men like Dean Inge are perpetually reproaching us, as things that forbid us a complete confidence in science or a complete unity with animals. It is these that stand between men and cannibalism – or possibly monkey glands. They have the prejudice; and long may they retain it! We have the principle, and they are welcome to it when they want it.

If Euclid were demonstrating with diagrams for the first time, and used the argument of the *reductio ad absurdum*, he would now only produce the impression that his own argument was absurd. I am well aware that I expose myself to this peril by extending my opponent's argument to an extreme, which may be considered an extravagance. The question is, why is it an extravagance? I know that in this case it will be answered that the social feature of cannibalism is rare in our culture. So far as I know, there are no cannibal restaurants threatening to become fashionable in London like Chinese restaurants. Anthropophagy[1] is not like anthroposophy, a subject of society lectures; and, varied as are the religions and moralities among us, the cooking of missionaries is not yet a mission. But if anyone has so little of logic as to miss the meaning of an extreme example, I should have no difficulty in giving a much more practical and even pressing example. A few years ago, all sane people would have said that Adamitism[2] was quite as mad as anthropophagy. A banker walking down the streets with no clothes on would have been quite as nonsensical as a butcher selling man instead of mutton. Both would be the outbreak of a lunatic under the delusion that he was a savage. But we have seen the New Adamite or No Clothes Movement start quite seriously in Germany; start indeed with a seriousness of which only Germans are capable. Englishmen probably are still English enough to laugh at it and dislike it. But they laugh by instinct; and they only dislike by instinct. Most of them, with their present

1. 'man-eating'.
2. Now known as 'naturism'.

muddled moral philosophy, would probably have great diffi-culty in refuting the Prussian professor of nakedness, however heartily they might desire to kick him. For if we examine the current controversies, we shall find the same negative and defenceless condition as in the case of the theory of canni-balism. All the fashionable arguments used against Puritanism do in fact lead to Adamitism. I do not mean, of course, that they are not often practically healthy as against Puritanism; still less do I mean that there are no better arguments against Puritanism. But I mean that in pure logic the civilized man has laid open his guard; and is, as it were, naked against the inroads of nakedness. So long as he is content merely to argue that the body is beautiful or that what is natural is right, he has surrendered to the Adamite in theory, though it may be, please God, a long time before he surrenders in practice. Here again the modern theorist will have to defend his own sanity with a prejudice. It is the medieval theologian who can defend it with a reason. I need not go into that reason at length; it is enough to say that it is founded on the Fall of Man, just as the other instinct against cannibalism is founded on the Divinity of Man. The Catholic argument can be put shortly by saying that there is nothing the matter with the human body; what is the matter is with the human soul.

In other words, if man were completely a god, it might be true that all aspects of his bodily being were godlike; just as if he were completely a beast, we could hardly blame him for any diet, however beastly. But we say that experience confirms our theory of his human complexity. It has nothing to do with the natural things themselves. If red roses mysteri-ously maddened men to commit murder, we should make rules to cover them up; but red roses would be quite as pure as white ones.

In most modern people there is a battle between the new opinions, which they do not follow out to their end, and the old traditions, which they do not trace back to their beginning. If they followed the new notions forward, it would lead them to Bedlam. If they followed the better instincts backward, it would lead them to Rome. At the best they remain suspended between two logical alternatives, trying to tell themselves, as does Dean Inge, that they are merely avoiding two extremes. But there is this great difference in his case, that the question on which he is wrong is, in however perverted a form, a matter of science, whereas the matter in which he is right is by this time simply a matter of sentiment. I need not say that I do not use the word here in a contemptuous sense, for in these things there is a very close kinship between sentiment and sense. But the fact remains that all the people in his position can only go on being sensible. It is left for us to be also reasonable.

The Thing, 1929

On Evil Euphemisms

Somebody has sent me a book on Companionate Marriage;
so called because the people involved are not married and
will very rapidly cease to be companions. I have no intention
of discussing here that somewhat crude colonial project. I
will merely say that it is here accompanied with subtitles and
other statements about the rising generation and the revolt of
youth. And it seems to me exceedingly funny that, just when
the rising generation boasts of not being sentimental, when it
talks of being very scientific and sociological – at that very
moment everybody seems to have forgotten altogether what
was the social use of marriage and to be thinking wholly and
solely of the sentimental. The practical purposes mentioned as
the first two reasons for marriage, in the Anglican marriage
service, seem to have gone completely out of sight for some
people, who talk as if there were nothing but a rather wild
version of the third, which may relatively be called romantic.
And this, if you please, is supposed to be an emancipation
from Victorian sentiment and romance.

But I only mention this matter as one of many, and one
which illustrates a still more curious contradiction in this
modern claim. We are perpetually being told that this rising
generation is very frank and free, and that its whole social
ideal is frankness and freedom. Now I am not at all afraid of
frankness. What I am afraid of is fickleness. And there is a truth

in the old proverbial connection between what is fickle and what is false. There is in the very titles and terminology of all this sort of thing a pervading element of falsehood. Everything is to be called something that it is not; as in the characteristic example of Companionate Marriage. Everything is to be recommended to the public by some sort of synonym which is really a pseudonym. It is a talent that goes with the time of electioneering and advertisement and newspaper headlines; but whatever else such a time may be, it certainly is not specially a time of truth.

In short, these friends of frankness depend almost entirely on euphemism. They introduce their horrible heresies under new and carefully complimentary names; as the Furies were called the Eumenides. The names are always flattery; the names are also nonsense. The name of birth control, for instance, is sheer nonsense. Everybody has always exercised birth control; even when they were so paradoxical as to permit the process to end in a birth. Everybody has always known about birth control, even if it took the wild and unthinkable form of self-control. The question at issue concerns different forms of birth prevention; and I am not going to debate it here. But if I did debate it, I would call it by its name. The same is true of an older piece of sentiment indulged in by the frank and free: the expression 'Free Love'. That also is a euphemism; that is, it is a refusal of people to say what they mean. In that sense, it is impossible to prevent *love* being free, but the moral problem challenged concerns not the passions, but the will. There are a great many other examples of this sort of polite fiction; these respectable disguises adopted by those who are always railing against respectability. In the immediate future there will probably be more still. There really seems no necessary limit to the process; and however far the anarchy of ethics may go, it may always be accompanied with this curious and pompous ceremonial. The sensitive youth of the future will never be called upon to accept forgery as Forgery. It will be easy enough to call it Homoeography or Script-Assimilation or something else that would suggest, to the simple or the superficial, that nothing was involved by a sort of socializing or unification of individual handwriting. We should not, like the more honest Mr Fagin, teach little boys to pick pockets; for Mr Fagin becomes far less honest when he becomes Professor Faginski, the great sociologist, of the University of Jena. But we should call it by some name implying the transference of something; I cannot at the moment remember the Greek either for pocket or pocket handkerchief. As for the social justification of murder, that has already begun; and earnest thinkers had better begin at once to think about a nice inoffensive name for it. The case for murder, on modern relative and evolutionary ethics, is quite overwhelming. There is hardly one of us who does not, in looking round his or her social circle, recognize some chatty person or energetic social character whose disappearance, without undue fuss or farewell, would be a bright event for us all. Nor is it true that such a person is dangerous only because he wields unjust legal or social powers. The problem is often purely psychological, and not in the least legal; and no legal emancipations would solve it. Nothing would solve it but the introduction of that new form of liberty which we may agree to call, perhaps, the practice of Social Subtraction. Or, if we like, we can model the new name on the other names I have mentioned. We may call it Life Control or Free Death; or anything else that has as little to do with the point of it as Companionate Marriage has to do with either marriage or companionship.

Anyhow, I respectfully refuse to be impressed by the claim to candour and realism put forward just now for men, women and movements. It seems to me obvious that this is not really the age of audacity, but merely of advertisement; which may rather be described as caution kicking up a fuss. Much of the mistake arises from the double sense of the word publicity.

For publicity also is a thoroughly typical euphemism or evasive term. Publicity does not mean revealing public life in the interests of public spirit. It means merely flattering private enterprises in the interests of private persons. It means paying compliments in public; but not offering criticisms in public. We should all be very much surprised if we walked out of our front door one morning and saw a hoarding on one side of the road saying, 'Use Miggle's Milk; It Is All Cream', and a hoarding on the other side of the road inscribed, 'Don't Use Miggle's Milk; It's Nearly All Water'. The modern world would be much upset if I were allowed to set up a flaming sky sign proclaiming my precise opinion of the Colonial Port Wine praised in the flaming sign opposite. All this advertisement may have something to do with the freedom of trade; but it has nothing to do with the freedom of truth. Publicity must be praise and praise must to some extent be euphemism. It must put the matter in a milder and more inoffensive form than it might be put, however much that mildness may seem to shout through megaphones or flare in headlines. And just as this sort of loud evasion is used in favour of bad wine and bad milk, so it is used in favour of bad morals. When some body wishes to wage a social war against what all normal people have regarded as a social decency, the very first thing he does is to find some artificial term that shall sound relatively decent. He has no more of the real courage that would pit vice against virtue than the ordinary advertiser has the courage to advertise ale as arsenic. His intelligence, such as it is, is entirely a commercial intelligence, and to that extent entirely conventional. He is a shopkeeper who dresses the shop window; he is certainly the very reverse of a rebel or a rioter who breaks the shop window. If only for this reason, I remain cold and decline the due reverence to Companionate Marriage and the book which speaks so reverentially about the Revolt of Youth. For this sort of revolt strikes me as nothing except revolting; and certainly not particularly realistic. With the passions which are natural to youth we all sympathize; with the pain that often arises from loyalty and duty we all sympathize still more; but nobody need sympathize with publicity experts picking pleasant expressions for unpleasant things; and I for one prefer the coarse language of our fathers.

Come to Think of It, 1930

The Spice of Life

I am more and more convinced that neither in your special spices nor in mine, neither in honeypots nor quartpots, neither in mustard nor in music, nor in any other distraction from life, is the secret we are all seeking, the secret of enjoying life. I am perfectly certain that all our world will end in despair, unless there is some way of making the mind itself, the ordinary thought we have at ordinary times, more healthy and more happy than they seem to be just now, to judge by most modern novels and poems. You have to be happy in those quiet moments when you remember that you are alive; not in those noisy moments when you forget. Unless we can learn again to enjoy life, we shall not long enjoy the spices of life. I once read a French fairy tale that expressed exactly what I mean. Never believe that French wit is shallow; it is the shining surface of French irony, which is unfathomable. It was about a pessimist poet who decided to drown himself; and as he went down to the river, he gave away his eyes to a blind man, his ears to a deaf man, his legs to a lame man, and so on, up to the moment when the reader was waiting for the splash of his suicide; but the author wrote that this senseless trunk settled itself on the shore and began to experience the joy of living: *la joie de vie*.

When we consider what he (modern man) receives, it is indeed a most magnificent wonder and wealth and concentration of amusement. He can travel in a racing car almost as quick as a cannon-ball; and still have his car fitted up with wireless from all the ends of the earth. He can get Vienna and Moscow; he can hear Cairo and Warsaw; and if he cannot see England, through which he happens to be travelling, that is after all a small matter. In a century, no doubt, his car will travel like a comet, and his wireless will hear the noises in the moon. But all this does not help him when the car stops; and he has to stand stamping about in a line, with nothing to think about. All this does not help him even when the wireless stops and he has to sit still in a silent car with nothing to talk about. If you consider what are the things poured into him, what are the things he receives, then indeed they are colossal cataracts of things, cosmic Niagaras that have never before poured into any human being are pouring into him. But if you consider what comes out of him, as a result of all this absorption, the result we have to record is rather serious. In the vast majority of cases, nothing. Not even conversation, as it used to be. He does not conduct long arguments, as young men did when I was young. The first and startling effect of all this noise is silence. Second, when he does have the itch to write or say something, it is always an itch in the sense of an irritation.

Everything has its better and baser form; and there is irritation and irritation. There is a great deal of difference between the irritation of Aldous Huxley and the irritation of some nasty little degenerate in a novel by Aldous Huxley. But honestly I do not think I am unfair to the whole trend of the time, if I say that it is intellectually irritated; and therefore without that sort of rich repose in the mind which I mean, when I say that a man when he is alone can be happy because he is alive. For instance, a man of genius of the same generation, for whom I have a very special admiration, is Mr T. S. Eliot. But nobody will deny that there was a sense in which, originally, even his inspiration was irritation. He began with pure pessimism; he has since found much finer and more subtle things; but I hardly think he has found repose. And it is just here that I will have the effrontery to distinguish between his generation and mine. It used to be thought impudent for a boy to criticize an old gentleman, it now requires far more sublime impudence for an older man to criticize a younger. Yet I defend my own idea of the spiritual spice of life against even the spirituality that finds this ordinary life entirely without spice. I know very well that Mr Eliot described the desolation he found more than the desolation he felt. But I think that *The Waste Land* was at least a world in which he had wandered. And as I am describing the recent world, I may as well describe it as he described it, in *The Hollow Men* – though nobody would describe him as a hollow man. This is the impression of many impressions.

> This is the way the world ends
> This is the way the world ends
> This is the way the world ends
> Not with a bang but a whimper.

Now forgive me if I say, in my old-world fashion, that I'm damned if I ever felt like that. I recognize the great realities Mr Eliot has revealed; but I do not admit that this is the deepest reality. I am ready to admit that our generation made too much of romance and comfort, but even when I was uncomfortable I was more comfortable than that. I was more comfortable on the iron seat. I was more happy in the cold waiting room. I knew the world was perishable and would end, but I did not think it would end with a whimper, but if anything with a trump of doom. It is doubtless a grotesque spectacle that the great-grandfathers should still be dancing with indecent gaiety, when the young are so grave and sad; but in this matter of the spice of life, I will defend the spiritual appetite of my own age. I will even be so indecently frivolous as to break into song, and say to the young pessimists:-

> Some sneer; some snigger; some simper;
> In the youth where we laughed and sang,
> And *they* may end with a whimper
> But *we* will end with a bang.

BBC, 1936[1]

---

1. 'The Spice of Life' was Chesterton's last radio broadcast for the BBC, and one of the last things he wrote.

Part Three

Major Writings

Introductory Remarks on the Importance of Orthodoxy

Nothing more strangely indicates an enormous and silent evil of modern society than the extraordinary use which is made nowadays of the word 'orthodox'. In former days the heretic was proud of not being a heretic. It was the kingdoms of the world and the police and the judges who were heretics. He was orthodox. He had no pride in having rebelled against them; they had rebelled against him. The armies with their cruel security, the kings with their cold faces, the decorous processes of State, the reasonable processes of law – all these like sheep had gone astray. The man was proud of being orthodox, was proud of being right. If he stood alone in a howling wilderness he was more than a man; he was a church. He was the centre of the universe; it was round him that the stars swung. All the tortures torn out of forgotten hells could not make him admit that he was heretical. But a few modern phrases have made him boast of it. He says, with a conscious laugh, 'I suppose I am very heretical,' and looks round for applause. The word 'heresy' not only means no longer being wrong; it practically means being clear-headed and coura-geous. The word 'orthodoxy' not only no longer means being right; it practically means being wrong. All this can mean one thing, and one thing only. It means that people care less for whether they are philosophically right. For obviously a man ought to confess himself crazy before he confesses himself heretical. The Bohemian, with a red tie, ought to pique himself on his orthodoxy. The dynamiter, laying a bomb, ought to feel that, whatever else he is, at least he is orthodox.

It is foolish, generally speaking, for a philosopher to set fire to another philosopher in Smithfield Market because they do not agree in their theory of the universe. That was done very frequently in the last decadence of the Middle Ages, and it failed altogether in its object. But there is one thing that is infinitely more absurd and unpractical than burning a man for his philosophy. This is the habit of saying that his philosophy does not matter, and this is done universally in the twentieth century, in the decadence of the great revolutionary period. General theories are everywhere contemned; the doctrine of the Rights of Man is dismissed with the doctrine of the Fall of Man. Atheism itself is too theological for us today. Revolution itself is too much of a system; liberty itself is too much of a restraint. We will have no generalizations. Mr Bernard Shaw has put the view in a perfect epigram: 'The golden rule is that there is no golden rule.' We are more and more to discuss details in art, politics, literature. A man's opinion on tramcars matters; his opinion on Botticelli matters; his opinion on all things does not matter. He may turn over and explore a million objects, but he must not find that strange object, the universe; for if he does he will have a religion, and be lost. Everything matters – except everything.

This was certainly not the idea of those who introduced our freedom. When the old Liberals removed the gags from all the heresies, their idea was that religious and philosophical discoveries might thus be made. Their view was that cosmic truth was so important that everyone ought to bear independent testimony. The modern idea is that cosmic truth is so unimportant that it cannot matter what anyone says. The former freed enquiry as men loose a noble hound; the latter frees enquiry as men fling back into the sea a fish unfit for eating. Never has there been so little discussion about the nature of men as now, when, for the first time, anyone can discuss it. The old restriction meant that only the orthodox were allowed to discuss religion. Modern liberty means that nobody is allowed to discuss it. Good taste, the last and vilest of human superstitions, has succeeded in silencing us where all the rest have failed.

Now, in our time, philosophy or religion, our theory, that is, about ultimate things, has been driven out, more or less simultaneously, from two fields which it used to occupy. General ideals used to dominate literature. They have been driven out by the cry of 'art for art's sake'. General ideals used to dominate politics. They have been driven out by the cry of 'efficiency', which may roughly be translated as 'politics for politics' sake'. Persistently for the last twenty years the ideals of order or liberty have dwindled in our books; the ambitions of wit and eloquence have dwindled in our parliaments. Literature has purposely become less political; politics have purposely become less literary. General theories of the relation of things have thus been extruded from both; and we are in a position to ask, 'What have we gained or lost by this extrusion? Is literature better, is politics better, for having discarded the moralist and the philosopher?'

When everything about a people is for the time growing weak and ineffective, it begins to talk about efficiency. So it is that when a man's body is a wreck he begins, for the first time, to talk about health. Vigorous organisms talk not about their processes, but about their aims. There cannot be any better proof of the physical efficiency of a man than that he talks cheerfully of a journey to the end of the world.

The theory of the unmorality of art has established itself firmly in the strictly artistic classes. They are free to produce anything they like. They are free to write a *Paradise Lost* in which Satan shall conquer God. They are free to write a *Divine Comedy* in which heaven shall be under the floor of hell. And what have they done? Have they produced in their universality anything grander or more beautiful than the things uttered by the fierce Ghibelline Catholic,[1] by the rigid Puritan schoolmaster?[2] We know that they have produced only a few roundels. Milton does not merely beat them at his piety, he beats them at their own irreverence. In all their little books of verse you will not find a finer defiance of God than Satan's. Nor will you find the grandeur of paganism felt as that fiery Christian felt it who described Faranata lifting his head as in disdain of hell. And the reason is very obvious. Blasphemy is an artistic effect, because blasphemy depends upon a philosophical conviction. Blasphemy depends upon belief, and is fading with it. If anyone doubts this, let him sit down seriously and try to think blasphemous thoughts about Thor. I think his family will find him at the end of the day in a state of some exhaustion.

Nothing in this universe is so unwise as that kind of worship of worldly wisdom. A man who is perpetually thinking of whether this race or that race is strong, of whether this cause or that cause is promising, is the man who will never believe in anything long enough to make it succeed. The opportunist politician is like a man who should abandon billiards because he was beaten at billiards, and abandon golf because he was beaten at golf. There is nothing which is so weak for working purposes as this enormous importance attached to immediate victory. There is nothing that fails like success.

And having discovered that opportunism does fail, I have been induced to look at it more largely, and in consequence to see that it must fail. I perceive that it is far more practical to begin at the beginning and discuss theories. For the Christian dogmatists were trying to establish a reign of holiness, and trying to get defined, first of all, what was really holy. But our

1. Alighieri Dante (1265–1321): author of *The Divine Comedy*.
2. John Milton (1608–74): author of *Paradise Lost*.

modern educationists are trying to bring about a religious liberty without attempting to settle what is religion or what is liberty. If the old priests forced a statement on mankind, at least they previously took some trouble to make it lucid. It has been left for the modern mobs of Anglicans and Non-conformists to persecute for a doctrine without even stating it.

For these reasons, and for many more, I for one have come to believe in going back to fundamentals. I revert to the doctrinal methods of the thirteenth century, inspired by the general hope of getting something done.

Suppose that a great commotion arises in the street about something, let us say a lamp post, which many influential persons desire to pull down. A grey-clad monk, who is the spirit of the Middle Ages, is approached upon the matter, and begins to say, in the arid manner of the Schoolmen, 'Let us first of all consider, my brethren, the value of Light. If Light be in itself good ...' At this point he is somewhat excusably knocked down. All the people make a rush for the lamp post, the lamp post is down in ten minutes, and they go about congratulating each other on their unmedieval practicality. But as things go on they do not work out so easily. Some people have pulled the lamp post down because they wanted the electric light; some because they wanted old iron; some because they wanted darkness, because their deeds were evil. Some thought it not enough of a lamp post, some too much; some acted because they wanted to smash municipal machinery; some because they wanted to smash something. And there is war in the night, no man knowing whom he strikes. So, gradually and inevitably, today, tomorrow, or the next day, there comes back the conviction that the monk was right after all, and that all depends on what is the philosophy of Light. Only what we might have discussed under the gas lamp, we now must discuss in the dark.

Heretics, 1905

On Certain Modern Writers and the
Institution of the Family

———

The family may fairly be considered, one would think, an ultimate human institution. Every one would admit that it has been the main cell and central unit of almost all societies hitherto, except, indeed, such societies as that of Lacedæmon,[1] which went in for 'efficiency', and has therefore, perished, and left not a trace behind. Christianity, even enormous as was its revolution, did not alter this ancient and savage sanctity; it merely reversed it. It did not deny the trinity of father, mother and child. It merely read it backwards, making it run child, mother, father. This it called, not the family, but the Holy Family, for many things are made holy by being turned upside down. But some sages of our own decadence have made a serious attack on the family. They have impugned it, as I think wrongly; and its defenders have defended it, and defended it wrongly. The common defence of the family is that, amid the stress and fickleness of life, it is peaceful, pleasant, and at one. But there is another defence of the family which is possible, and to me evident; this defence is that the family is not peaceful and not pleasant and not at one.

It is not fashionable to say much nowadays of the advantages of the small community. We are told that we must go in for

———

1. Ancient Sparta, which exposed weakling children on the mountainside to die.

large empires and large ideas. There is one advantage, however, in the small state, the city or the village, which only the wilfully blind can overlook. The man who lives in a small community lives in a much larger world. He knows much more of the fierce varieties and uncompromising divergences of men. The reason is obvious. In a large community we can choose our companions. In a small community our companions are chosen for us. Thus in all extensive and highly civilized societies groups come into existence founded upon what is called sympathy, and shut out the real world more sharply than the gates of a monastery. There is nothing really narrow about the clan; the thing which is really narrow is the clique. The men of the clan live together because they all wear the same tartan or are all descended from the same sacred cow; but in their souls, by the divine luck of things, there will always be more colours than in any tartan. But the men of the clique live together because they have the same kind of soul, and their narrowness is a narrowness of spiritual coherence and contentment, like that which exists in hell. A big society exists in order to form cliques. A big society is a society for the promotion of narrowness. It is a machinery for the purpose of guarding the solitary and sensitive individual from all experience of the bitter and bracing human compromises. It is, in the most literal sense of the words, a society for the prevention of Christian knowledge.

We can see this change, for instance, in the modern transformation of the thing called a club. When London was smaller, and the parts of London more self-contained and parochial, the club was what it still is in villages, the opposite of what it is now in great cities. Then the club was valued as a place where a man could be sociable. Now the club is valued as a place where a man can be unsociable. The more the enlargement and elaboration of our civilization goes on the more the club ceases to be a place where a man can have a noisy argument, and becomes more and more a place where a man can have what is somewhat fantastically called a quiet chop.

If we were tomorrow morning snowed up in the street in which we live, we should step suddenly into a much larger and much wilder world than we have ever known. And it is the whole effort of the typically modern person to escape from the street in which he lives. First he invents modern hygiene and goes to Margate. Then he invents modern culture and goes to Florence. Then he invents modern imperialism and goes to Timbuktu. He goes to the fantastic borders of the earth. He pretends to shoot tigers. He almost rides on a camel. And in all this he is still essentially fleeing from the street in which he was born; and of this flight he is always ready with his own explanation. He says he is fleeing from his street because it is dull; he is lying. He is really fleeing from his street because it is a great deal too exciting. It is exciting because it is exacting; it is exacting because it is alive. He can visit Venice because to him the Venetians are only Venetians; the people in his own street are men. He can stare at the Chinese because for him the Chinese are a passive thing to be stared at; if he stares at the old lady in the next garden, she becomes active. He is forced to flee, in short, from the too stimulating society of his equals – of free men, perverse, personal, deliberately different from himself. If our neighbours did not mind their own business they would be asked abruptly for their rent, and would rapidly cease to be our neighbours. What we really mean when we say that they cannot mind their own business is something much deeper. We do not dislike them because they have so little force and fire that they cannot be interested in themselves. We dislike them because they have so much force and fire that they can be interested in us as well. What we dread about our neighbours, in short, is not the narrowness of their horizon, but their superb tendency to broaden it. And all aversions to ordinary humanity have this general character. They are not aversions to its feebleness (as is pretended), but to its energy. The misanthropes pretend that they despise humanity for its weakness. As a matter of fact, they hate it for its strength.

Nietzsche's[2] aristocracy has about it all the sacredness that belongs to the weak. When he makes us feel that he cannot endure the innumerable faces, the incessant voices, the over-powering omnipresence which belongs to the mob, he will have the sympathy of anybody who has ever been sick on a steamer or tired in a crowded omnibus. Every man has hated mankind when he was less than a man. Every man has had humanity in his eyes like a blinding fog, humanity in his nostrils like a suffocating smell. But when Nietzsche has the incredible lack of humour and lack of imagination to ask us to believe that this aristocracy is an aristocracy of strong muscles or an aristoc-racy of strong wills, it is necessary to point out the truth. It is an aristocracy of weak nerves.

We make our friends; we make our enemies; but God makes our next-door neighbour. Hence he comes to us clad in all the careless terrors of nature; he is as strange as the stars, as reckless and indifferent as the rain. He is Man, the most terrible of the beasts. That is why the old religions and the old scriptural language showed so sharp a wisdom when they spoke, not of one's duty towards humanity, but one's duty towards one's neighbour. The duty towards humanity may often take the form of some choice which is personal or even pleasurable. That duty may be a hobby; it may even be dissipa-tion. We may work in the East End because we are peculiarly fitted to work in the East End, or because we think we are; we may fight for the cause of international peace because we are very fond of fighting. The most monstrous martyrdom, the most repulsive experience, may be the result of choice or a kind of taste. We may be so made as to be particularly fond of lunatics or specially interested in leprosy. We may love negroes because they are black or German Socialists because they are pedantic. But we have to love our neighbour because he is

2. Friedrich Nietzsche (1844–1900): German philosopher and advocate of the 'superman, beyond good or evil'.

there – a much more alarming reason for a much more serious operation. He is the sample of humanity which is actually given us. Precisely because he may be anybody he is everybody. He is a symbol because he is an accident.

Now, exactly as this principle applies to the empire, to the nation within the empire, to the city within the nation, to the street within the city, so it applies to the home within the street. The institution of the family is to be commended for precisely the same reasons that the institution of the nation, or the institution of the city, are in this matter to be commended. It is a good thing for a man to live in a family for the same reason that it is a good thing for a man to be besieged in a city. It is a good thing for a man to live in a family in the same sense that it is a beautiful and delightful thing for a man to be snowed up in a street. They all force him to realize that life is not a thing from outside, but a thing from inside. Above all, they all insist upon the fact that life, if it be a truly stimulating and fascinating life, is a thing which, of its nature, exists in spite of ourselves. The modern writers who have suggested, in a more or less open manner, that the family is a bad institution, have generally confined themselves to suggesting, with much sharpness, bitterness or pathos, that perhaps the family is not always very congenial. Of course the family is a good institution because it is uncongenial. It is wholesome precisely because it contains so many divergencies and varieties. It is, as the sentimentalists say, like a little kingdom, and, like most other little kingdoms, is generally in a state of something resembling anarchy. It is exactly because our brother George is not interested in our religious difficulties, but is interested in the Trocadero Restaurant, that the family has some of the bracing qualities of the commonwealth. It is precisely because our uncle Henry does not approve of the theatrical ambitions of our sister Sarah that the family is like humanity. The men and women who, for good reasons and bad, revolt against the family, are, for good reasons and bad, simply revolting against mankind. Aunt Elizabeth is unreasonable, like mankind. Papa is excitable, like mankind. Our youngest brother is mischievous, like mankind. Grandpapa is stupid, like the world; he is old, like the world.

Those who wish, rightly or wrongly, to step out of all this, do definitely wish to step into a narrower world. They are dismayed and terrified by the largeness and variety of the family.

The best way that a man could test his readiness to encounter the common variety of mankind would be to climb down a chimney into any house at random, and get on as well as possible with the people inside. And that is essentially what each one of us did on the day that he was born.

This is, indeed, the sublime and special romance of the family. It is romantic because it is a toss-up. It is romantic because it is everything that its enemies call it. It is romantic because it is arbitrary. It is romantic because it is there. So long as you have groups of men chosen rationally, you have some special or sectarian atmosphere. It is when you have groups of men chosen irrationally that you have men. The element of adventure begins to exist; for an adventure is, by its nature, a thing that comes to us. It is a thing that chooses us, not a thing that we choose. Falling in love has been often regarded as the supreme adventure, the supreme romantic accident. Insomuch as there is in it something outside ourselves, something of a sort of merry fatalism, this is very true. Love does take us and transfigure and torture us. It does break our hearts with an unbearable beauty, like the unbearable beauty of music. But in so far as we have certainly something to do with the matter; in so far as we are in some sense prepared to fall in love and in some sense jump into it; in so far as we do to some extent choose and to some extent even judge – in all this falling in love is not truly romantic, is not truly adventurous at all. In this degree the supreme adventure is not falling in love. The supreme adventure is being born. There we do walk suddenly into a splendid and startling trap. There we do see something of which we have dreamed before. Our father and mother do lie in wait for us and leap out on us, like brigands from a bush.

When we step into the family, by the act of being born, we do step into a world which is incalculable, into a world which has its own strange laws, into a world which could do without us, into a world that we have not made.

Heretics, 1905

Concluding Remarks on the Importance of Orthodoxy

Whether the human mind can advance or not, is a question too little discussed, for nothing can be more dangerous than to found our social philosophy on any theory which is debatable but has not been debated. But if we assume, for the sake of argument, that there has been in the past, or will be in the future, such a thing as a growth or improvement of the human mind itself, there still remains a very sharp objection to be raised against the modern version of that improvement. The vice of the modern notion of mental progress is that it is always something concerned with the breaking of bonds, the effacing of boundaries, the casting away of dogmas. But if there be such a thing as mental growth, it must mean the growth into more and more definite convictions, into more and more dogmas. The human brain is a machine for coming to conclusions; if it cannot come to conclusions it is rusty. When we hear of a man too clever to believe, we are hearing of something having almost the character of a contradiction in terms. It is like hearing of a nail that was too good to hold down a carpet; or a bolt that was too strong to keep a door shut. Man can hardly be defined, after the fashion of Carlyle, as an animal who makes tools; ants and beavers and many other animals make tools, in the sense that they make an apparatus. Man can be defined as an animal that makes dogmas. As he piles doctrine on doctrine and conclusion on conclusion in the formation of some tremendous scheme of philosophy and religion, he is, in the only legitimate sense of which the expression is capable, becoming more and more human. When he drops one doctrine after another in a refined scepticism, when he declines to tie himself to a system, when he says that he has outgrown definitions, when he says that he disbelieves in finality, when, in his own imagination, he sits as God, holding no form of creed but contemplating all, then he is by that very process sinking slowly backwards into the vagueness of the vagrant animals and the unconsciousness of the grass. Trees have no dogmas. Turnips are singularly broad-minded.

Heretics, 1905

The Ethics of Elfland

When the businessman rebukes the idealism of his office boy, it is commonly in some such speech as this: 'Ah, yes, when one is young, one has these ideals in the abstract and these castles in the air; but in middle age they all break up like clouds, and one comes down to a belief in practical politics, to using the machinery one has and getting on with the world as it is.' Thus, at least, venerable and philanthropic old men now in their honoured graves used to talk to me when I was a boy. But since then I have grown up and have discovered that these philanthropic old men were telling lies. What has really happened is exactly the opposite of what they said would happen. They said that I should lose my ideals and begin to believe in the methods of practical politicians. Now, I have not lost my ideals in the least; my faith in fundamentals is exactly what it always was. What I have lost is my old childlike faith in practical politics. I am still as much concerned as ever about the Battle of Armageddon; but I am not so much concerned about the General Election. As a babe I leapt up on my mother's knee at the mere mention of it. No; the vision is always solid and reliable. The vision is always a fact. It is the reality that is often a fraud. As much as I ever did, more than I ever did, I believe in Liberalism. But there was a rosy time of innocence when I believed in Liberals.

I take this instance of one of the enduring faiths because, having now to trace the roots of my personal speculation, this may be counted, I think, as the only positive bias. I was brought up a Liberal, and have always believed in democracy, in the elementary liberal doctrine of a self-governing humanity. If anyone finds the phrase vague or threadbare, I can only pause for a moment to explain that the principle of democracy, as I mean it, can be stated in two propositions. The first is this: that the things common to all men are more important than the things peculiar to any men. Ordinary things are more valuable than extraordinary things; nay, they are more extraordinary. Man is something more awful than men; something more strange. The sense of the miracle of humanity itself should be always more vivid to us than any marvels of power, intellect, art or civilization. The mere man on two legs, as such, should be felt as something more heart-breaking than any music, and more startling than any caricature. Death is more tragic even than death by starvation. Having a nose is more comic even than having a Norman nose.

This is the first principle of democracy; that the essential things in men are the things they hold in common, not the things they hold separately. And the second principle is merely this: that the political instinct or desire is one of these things which they hold in common. Falling in love is more poetical than dropping into poetry. The democratic contention is that government (helping to rule the tribe) is a thing like falling in love, and not a thing like dropping into poetry. It is not something analogous to playing the church organ, painting on vellum, discovering the North Pole (that insidious habit), looping the loop, being Astronomer Royal and so on. For these things we do not wish a man to do at all unless he does them well. It is, on the contrary, a thing analogous to writing one's own love letters or blowing one's own nose. These things we want a man to do for himself, even if he does them badly. I am not here arguing the truth of any of these conceptions; I know that some moderns are asking to have their wives chosen by scientists, and they may soon be asking, for all I know, to have their noses blown by nurses. I merely say that mankind does recognize these universal human functions, and that democracy classes government among them. In short, the democratic faith is this: that the most terribly important things must be left to ordinary men themselves – the mating of the sexes, the rearing of the young, the laws of the state. This is democracy; and in this I have always believed.

But there is one thing that I have never from my youth up been able to understand. I have never been able to understand where people got the idea that democracy was in some way opposed to tradition. It is obvious that tradition is only democracy extended through time. It is trusting to a consensus of common human voices rather than to some isolated or arbitrary record. The man who quotes some German historian against the tradition of the Catholic Church, for instance, is strictly appealing to aristocracy. He is appealing to the superiority of one expert against the awful authority of a mob. It is quite easy to see why a legend is treated, and ought to be treated, more respectfully than a book of history. The legend is generally made by the majority of people in the village, who are sane. The book is generally written by the one man in the village who is mad. Those who urge against tradition that men in the past were ignorant may go and urge it at the Carlton Club, along with the statement that voters in the slums are ignorant. It will not do for us. If we attach great importance to the opinion of ordinary men in great unanimity when we are dealing with daily matters, there is no reason why we should disregard it when we are dealing with history or fable.

Tradition may be defined as an extension of the franchise. Tradition means giving votes to the most obscure of all classes, our ancestors. It is the democracy of the dead.

Tradition refuses to submit to the small and arrogant oligarchy of those who merely happen to be walking about. All democrats object to men being disqualified by the accident of birth; tradition objects to their being disqualified by the accident of death. Democracy tells us not to neglect a good man's opinion, even if he is our groom; tradition asks us not to neglect a good man's opinion, even if he is our father. I, at any rate, cannot separate the two ideas of democracy and tradition; it seems evident to me that they are the same idea. We will have the dead at our councils. The ancient Greeks voted by stones; these shall vote by tombstones. It is all quite regular and official, for most tombstones, like most ballot papers, are marked with a cross.

I have first to say, therefore, that if I have had a bias, it was always a bias in favour of democracy, and therefore of tradition. Before we come to any theoretic or logical beginnings I am content to allow for that personal equation; I have always been more inclined to believe the ruck of hard-working people than to believe that special and troublesome literary class to which I belong. I prefer even the fancies and prejudices of the people who see life from the inside to the clearest demonstrations of the people who see life from the outside. I would always trust the old wives' fables against the old maids' facts. As long as wit is mother wit it can be as wild as it pleases.

Now, I have to put together a general position, and I pretend to no training in such things. I propose to do it, therefore, by writing down one after another the three or four fundamental ideas which I have found for myself, pretty much in the way that I found them. Then I shall roughly synthesize them, summing up my personal philosophy or natural religion; then I shall describe my startling discovery that the whole thing had been discovered before. It had been discovered by Christianity. But of these profound persuasions which I have to recount in order, the earliest was concerned with this element of popular tradition. And without the foregoing explanation touching tradition and democracy I could hardly make my mental experience clear. As it is, I do not know whether I can make it clear, but I now propose to try.

My first and last philosophy, that which I believe in with unbroken certainty, I learned in the nursery. I generally learned it from a nurse; that is, from the solemn and star-appointed priestess at once of democracy and tradition. The things I believed most then, the things I believe most now, are the things called fairy tales. They seem to me to be the entirely reasonable things. They are not fantasies: compared with them other things are fantastic. Compared with them religion and rationalism are both abnormal, though religion is abnormally right and rationalism abnormally wrong.

For this reason (we may call it the fairy godmother philosophy) I never could join the young men of my time in feeling what they called the general sentiment of *revolt*. I should have resisted, let us hope, any rules that were evil, and with these and their definition I shall deal in another chapter. But I did not feel disposed to resist any rule merely because it was mysterious. Estates are sometimes held by foolish forms, the breaking of a stick or the payment of a peppercorn; I was willing to hold the huge estate of earth and heaven by any such feudal fantasy. It could not well be wilder than the fact that I was allowed to hold it at all. At this stage I give only one ethical instance to show my meaning. I could never mix in the common murmur of that rising generation against monogamy, because no restriction on sex seemed so odd and unexpected as sex itself. To be allowed, like Endymion, to make love to the moon and then to complain that Jupiter kept his own moons in a harem seemed to me (bred on fairy tales like Endymion's) a vulgar anticlimax. Keeping to one woman is a small price for so much as seeing one woman. To complain that I could only be married once was like complaining that I had only been born once. It was incommensurate with the terrible excitement of which one was talking. It showed, not an exaggerated sensibility to sex, but a curious insensibility to it. A man is a fool who complains that he cannot enter Eden by five gates at once. Polygamy is a lack of the realization of sex; it is like a man plucking five pears in mere absence of mind. The aesthetes touched the last insane limits of language in their eulogy on lovely things. The thistledown made them weep; a burnished beetle brought them to their knees. Yet their emotion never impressed me for an instant, for this reason, that it never occurred to them to pay for their pleasure in any sort of symbolic sacrifice. Men (I felt) might fast forty days for the sake of hearing a blackbird sing. Men might go through fire to find a cowslip. Yet these lovers of beauty could not even keep sober for the blackbird. They would not go through common Christian marriage by way of recompense to the cowslip. Surely one might pay for extraordinary joy in ordinary morals. Oscar Wilde said that sunsets were not valued because we could not pay for sunsets. But Oscar Wilde was wrong; we can pay for sunsets. We can pay for them by not being Oscar Wilde.

Well, I left the fairy tales lying on the floor of the nursery, and I have not found any books so sensible since. I left the nurse guardian of tradition and democracy, and I have not found any modern type so sanely radical or so sanely conservative. But the matter for important comment was here; that when I first went out into the mental atmosphere of the modern world, I found that the modern world was positively opposed on two points to my nurse and to the nursery tales. It has taken me a long time to find out that the modern world is wrong and my nurse was right. The really curious thing was this: that modern thought contradicted this basic creed of my boyhood on its two most essential doctrines. I have explained that the fairy tales founded in me two convictions; first, that this world is a wild and startling place, which might have been quite different, but which is quite delightful; second, that before this wildness and delight one may well be modest and submit to the queerest limitations of so queer a kindness. But I found the whole modern world running like a high tide against both my tendernesses; and the shock of that collision created two sudden and spontaneous sentiments, which I have had ever since and which, crude as they were, have since hardened into convictions.

First, I found the whole modern world talking scientific fatalism; saying that everything is as it must always have been, being unfolded without fault from the beginning. The leaf on the tree is green because it could never have been anything else. Now, the fairy-tale philosopher is glad that the leaf is green precisely because it might have been scarlet. He feels as if it had turned green an instant before he looked at it. He is pleased that snow is white on the strictly reasonable ground that it might have been black. Every colour has in it a bold quality as of choice; the red of garden roses is not only decisive but dramatic, like suddenly spilt blood. He feels that something has been *done*. But the great determinists of the nine-teenth century were strongly against this native feeling that something had happened an instant before. In fact, according to them, nothing ever really had happened since the beginning of the world. Nothing ever had happened since existence had happened; and even about the date of that they were not very sure.

The modern world as I found it was solid for modern Calvinism, for the necessity of things being as they are. But when I came to ask them I found they had really no proof of this unavoidable repetition in things except the fact that the things were repeated. Now, the mere repetition made the things to me rather more weird than more rational. It was as if, having seen a curiously shaped nose in the street and dismissed it as an accident, I had then seen six other noses of the same astonishing shape. I should have fancied for a moment that it must be some local secret society. So one elephant having a trunk was odd; but all elephants having trunks looked like a plot. I speak here only of an emotion, and of an emotion at once stubborn and subtle. But the repetition in Nature seemed sometimes to be an excited repetition, like that of an angry schoolmaster saying the same thing over and over again. The grass seemed signalling to me with all its fingers at once; the crowded stars seemed bent upon being understood. The sun would make me see him if he rose a thousand times. The recurrences of the universe rose to the maddening rhythm of an incantation, and I began to see an idea.

All the towering materialism which dominates the modern mind rests ultimately upon one assumption; a false assumption. It is supposed that if a thing goes on repeating itself it is probably dead; a piece of clockwork. People feel that if the universe was personal it would vary; if the sun were alive it would dance. This is a fallacy even in relation to known fact. For the variation in human affairs is generally brought into them, not by life, but by death; by the dying down or breaking off of their strength or desire. A man varies his movements because of some slight element of failure or fatigue. He gets into an omnibus because he is tired of walking; or he walks because he is tired of sitting still. But if his life and joy were so gigantic that he never tired of going to Islington, he might go to Islington as regularly as the Thames goes to Sheerness. The very speed and ecstasy of his life would have the stillness of death. The sun rises every morning. I do not rise every morning; but the variation is due not to my activity, but to my inaction. Now, to put the matter in a popular phrase, it might be true that the sun rises regularly because he never gets tired of rising. His routine might be due, not to a lifelessness, but to a rush of life. The thing I mean can be seen, for instance, in children, when they find some game or joke that they specially enjoy. A child kicks his legs rhythmically through excess, not absence, of life. Because children have abounding vitality, because they are in spirit fierce and free, therefore they want things repeated and unchanged. They always say, 'Do it again'; and the grown-up person does it again until he is nearly dead. For grown-up people are not strong enough to exult in monotony. But perhaps God is strong enough to exult in monotony. It is possible that God says every morning, 'Do it again' to the sun; and every evening, 'Do it again' to the moon. It may not be automatic necessity that makes all daisies alike; it may be that God makes every daisy separately, but has never got tired of making them. It may be that He has the eternal appetite of infancy; for we have sinned and grown old, and our Father is younger than we. The repetition in Nature may not be a mere recurrence; it may be a theatrical *encore*. Heaven may *encore* the bird who laid an egg. If the human being conceives and brings forth a human child instead of bringing forth a fish, or a bat, or a griffin, the reason may not be that we are fixed in an animal fate without life or purpose. It may be that our little tragedy has touched the gods, that they admire it from their starry galleries, and that at the end of every human drama man is called again and again before the curtain. Repetition may go on for millions of years, by mere choice, and at any instant it may stop. Man may stand on the earth generation after generation, and yet each birth be his positively last appearance.

This was my first conviction; made by the shock of my childish emotions meeting the modern creed in mid-career. I had always vaguely felt facts to be miracles in the sense that they are wonderful: now I began to think them miracles in the stricter sense that they were *wilful*. I mean that that were, or might be, repeated exercises of some will. In short, I had always believed that the world involved magic: now I thought that perhaps it involved a magician. And this pointed a profound emotion always present and subconscious; that this world of ours has some purpose; and if there is a purpose, there is a person. I had always felt life first as a story: and if there is a story there is a story-teller.

But modern thought also hit my second human tradition. It went against the fairy feeling about strict limits and conditions. The one thing it loved to talk about was expansion and largeness. Herbert Spencer[1] would have been greatly annoyed if any one had called him an imperialist, and therefore it is highly regrettable that nobody did. But he was an imperialist of the lowest type. He popularized this contemptible notion that the size of the solar system ought to overawe the spiritual dogma of man. Why should a man surrender his dignity to the solar system any more than to a whale? If mere size proves that man is not the image of God, then a whale may be the image of God; a somewhat formless image; what one might call an impressionist portrait. It is quite futile to argue that man is small compared to the cosmos; for man was always small compared to the nearest tree. But Herbert Spencer, in his headlong imperialism, would insist that we had in some way been conquered and annexed by the astronomical universe. He spoke about men and their ideals exactly as the most insolent Unionist talks about the Irish and their ideals. He turned mankind into a small nationality. And his evil influence can be seen even in the most spirited and honourable of later scientific authors; notably in the early romances of Mr H. G. Wells. Many moralists have in an exaggerated way represented the earth as wicked. But Mr Wells and his school made the heavens wicked. We should lift up our eyes to the stars from whence would come our ruin.

But the expansion of which I speak was much more evil than all this. I have remarked that the materialist, like the mad-man, is in prison; in the prison of one thought. These people seemed to think it singularly inspiring to keep on saying that the prison was very large. The size of this scientific universe gave one no novelty, no relief. The cosmos went on

1. Herbert Spencer (1820–1903): journalist and writer who combined a defence of laissez-faire capitalism with Darwin's 'survival of the fittest'.

for ever, but not in its wildest constellation could there be anything really interesting; anything, for instance, such as forgiveness or free will. The grandeur or infinity of the secret of its cosmos added nothing to it. It was like telling a prisoner in Reading gaol that he would be glad to hear that the gaol now covered half the county. The warder would have nothing to show the man except more and more long corridors of stone lit by ghastly lights and empty of all that is human. So these expanders of the universe had nothing to show us except more and more infinite corridors of space lit by ghastly suns and empty of all that is divine.

In fairyland there had been a real law; a law that could be broken, for the definition of a law is something that can be broken. But the machinery of this cosmic prison was something that could not be broken; for we ourselves were only a part of its machinery. We were either unable to do things or we were destined to do them. The idea of the mystical condition quite disappeared; one can neither have the firmness of keeping laws nor the fun of breaking them. The largeness of this universe had nothing of that freshness and airy outbreak which we have praised in the universe of the poet. This modern universe is literally an empire; that is, it is vast, but it is not free. One went into larger and larger windowless rooms, rooms big with Babylonian perspective; but one never found the smallest window or a whisper of outer air.

Their infernal parallels seemed to expand with distance; but for me all good things comes to a point, swords for instance. So finding the boast of the big cosmos so unsatisfactory to my emotions I began to argue about it a little; and I soon found that the whole attitude was even shallower than could have been expected. According to these people the cosmos was one thing since it had one unbroken rule. Only (they would say) while it is one thing it is also the only thing there is. Why, then, should one worry particularly to call it large? There is nothing to compare it with. It would be just as sensible to call it small. A man may say, 'I like this vast cosmos, with its throng of stars and its crowd of varied creatures.' But if it comes to that why should not a man say, 'I like this cosy little cosmos, with its decent number of stars and as neat a provision of livestock as I wish to see?' One is as good as the other; they are both mere sentiments. It is mere sentiment to rejoice that the sun is larger than the earth; it is quite as sane a sentiment to rejoice that the sun is no larger than it is. A man chooses to have an emotion about the largeness of the world; why should he not choose to have an emotion about its smallness?

It happened that I had that emotion. When one is fond of anything one addresses it by diminutives, even if it is an elephant or a lifeguardsman. The reason is, that anything, however huge, that can be conceived of as complete, can be conceived of as small. If military moustaches did not suggest a sword or tusks a tail, then the object would be vast because it would be immeasurable. But the moment you can imagine a guardsman you can imagine a small guardsman. The moment you really see an elephant you can call it 'Tiny'. If you can make a statue of a thing you can make a statuette of it. These people professed that the universe was one coherent thing; but they were not fond of the universe. But I was frightfully fond of the universe and wanted to address it by a diminutive. I often did so; and it never seemed to mind. Actually and in truth I did feel that these dim dogmas of vitality were better expressed by calling the world small than by calling it large. For about infinity there was a sort of carelessness which was the reverse of the fierce and pious care which I felt touching the pricelessness and the peril of life. They showed only a dreary waste; but I felt a sort of sacred thrift. For economy is far more romantic than extravagance. To them stars were an unending income of halfpence; but I felt about the golden sun and the silver moon as a schoolboy feels if he has one sovereign and one shilling.

These subconscious convictions are best hit off by the colour and tone of certain tales. Thus I have said that stories of magic alone can express my sense that life is not only a pleasure but a kind of eccentric privilege. I may express this other feeling of cosmic cosiness by allusion to another book always read in my boyhood, *Robinson Crusoe*, which I read about this time, and which owes its eternal vivacity to the fact that it celebrates the poetry of limits, nay, even the wild romance of prudence. Crusoe is a man on a small rock with a few comforts just snatched from the sea; the best thing in the book is simply the list of things saved from the wreck. The greatest of poems is an inventory. Every kitchen tool becomes ideal because Crusoe might have dropped it in the sea. It is a good exercise, in empty or ugly hours of the day, to look at anything, the coal scuttle or the bookcase, and think how happy one could be to have brought it out of the sinking ship on to the solitary island. But it is a better exercise still to remember how all things have had this hairbreadth escape: everything has been saved from a wreck. Every man has had one horrible adventure: as a hidden untimely birth he had not been, as infants that never see the light. Men spoke much in my boyhood of restricted or ruined men of genius: and it was common to say that many a man was a Great Might-Have-Been. To me it is a more solid and startling fact that any man in the street is a Great-Might-Not-Have-Been.

But I really felt (the fancy may seem foolish) as if all the order and number of things were the romantic remnant of Crusoe's ship. That there are two sexes and one sun, was like the fact that there were two guns and one axe. It was poignantly urgent that none should be lost; but somehow, it was rather fun that none could be added. The trees and the planets seemed like things saved from the wreck: and when I saw the Matterhorn I was glad that it had not been overlooked in the confusion. I felt economical about the stars as if they were sapphires (they are called so in Milton's Eden): I hoarded the hills. For the universe is a single jewel, and while it is a natural cant to talk of a jewel as peerless and priceless, of this jewel it is literally true. This cosmos is indeed without peer and without price: for there cannot be another one.

Thus ends, in unavoidable inadequacy, the attempt to utter the unutterable things. These are my ultimate attitudes towards life; the soils for the seeds of doctrine. These in some dark way I thought before I could write, and felt before I could think: that we may proceed more easily afterwards, I will roughly recapitulate them now. I felt in my bones, first, that this world does not explain itself. It may be a miracle with a supernatural explanation; it may be a conjuring trick, with a natural explanation. But the explanation of the conjuring trick, if it is to satisfy me, will have to be better than the natural explanations I have heard. The thing is magic, true or false. Second, I came to feel as if magic must have a meaning, and meaning must have someone to mean it. There was something personal in the world, as in a work of art; whatever it meant it meant violently. Third, I thought this purpose beautiful in its old design, in spite of its defects, such as dragons. Fourth, that the proper form of thanks to it is some form of humility and restraint: we should thank God for beer and Burgundy by not drinking too much of them. We owed, also, an obedience to whatever made us. And last, and strangest, there had come into my mind a vague and vast impression that in some way all good was a remnant to be stored and held sacred out of some primordial ruin. Man had saved his good as Crusoe saved his goods: he had saved them from a wreck. All this I felt and the age gave me no encouragement to feel it. And all this time I had not even thought of Christian theology.

Orthodoxy, 1908

The Flag of the World

About the same time I read a solemn flippancy by some free thinker: he said that a suicide was only the same as a martyr. The open fallacy of this helped to clear the question. Obviously a suicide is the opposite of a martyr. A martyr is a man who cares so much for something outside him, that he forgets his own personal life. A suicide is a man who cares so little for anything outside him, that he wants to see the last of everything. One wants something to begin: the other wants everything to end. In other words, the martyr is noble, exactly because (however he renounces the world or execrates all humanity) he confesses this ultimate link with life; he sets his heart outside himself: he dies that something may live. The suicide is ignoble because he has not this link with being: he is a mere destroyer; spiritually, he destroys the universe. And then I remembered the stake and the crossroads, and the queer fact that Christianity had shown this weird harshness to the suicide. For Christianity had shown a wild encouragement of the martyr. Historic Christianity was accused, not entirely without reason, of carrying martyrdom and asceticism to a point, desolate and pessimistic. The early Christian martyrs talked of death with a horrible happiness. They blasphemed the beautiful duties of the body: they smelt the grave afar off like a field of flowers. All this has seemed to many the very poetry of pessimism. Yet there is the stake at the crossroads to show what Christianity thought of the pessimist.

Here it was that I first found that my wandering feet were in some beaten track. Christianity had also felt this opposition of the martyr to the suicide: had it perhaps felt it for the same reason? Had Christianity felt what I felt, but could not (and cannot) express — this need for a first loyalty to things, and then for a ruinous reform of things? Then I remembered that it was actually the charge against Christianity that it combined these two things which I was wildly trying to combine. Christianity was accused, at one and the same time, of being too optimistic about the universe and of being too pessimistic about the world. The coincidence made me suddenly stand still.

All the same, it will be as well if Jones does not worship the sun and moon. If he does, there is a tendency for him to imitate them; to say, that because the sun burns insects alive, he may burn insects alive. He thinks that because the sun gives people sunstroke, he may give his neighbour measles. He thinks that because the moon is said to drive men mad, he may drive his wife mad. This ugly side of mere external optimism had also shown itself in the ancient world. About the time when the Stoic idealism had begun to show the weaknesses of pessimism, the old nature worship of the ancients had begun to show the enormous weaknesses of optimism. Nature worship is natural enough while the society is young, or, in other words, Pantheism is all right as long as it is the worship of Pan. But Nature has another side which experience and sin are not slow in finding out, and it is no flippancy to say of the god Pan that he soon showed the cloven hoof. The only objection to Natural Religion is that somehow it always becomes unnatural. A man loves Nature in the morning for her innocence and amiability, and at night-fall, if he is loving her still, it is for her darkness and her cruelty. He washes at dawn in clear water as did the Wise Man of the Stoics, yet, somehow at the dark end of the day, he is bathing in hot bull's blood, as did Julian the Apostate. The mere pursuit of health always leads to something unhealthy. Physical nature must not be made the direct object of obedience: it must be enjoyed, not worshipped. Stars and mountains must not be taken seriously. If they are, we end where the pagan nature worship ended. Because the earth is kind, we can imitate all her cruelties. Because sexuality is sane, we can all go mad about sexuality. Mere optimism had reached its insane and appropriate termination. The theory that everything was good had become an orgy of everything that was bad.

On the other side our idealist pessimists were represented by the old remnants of the Stoics. Marcus Aurelius[1] and his friends had really given up the idea of any god in the universe and looked only to the god within. They had no hope of any virtue in nature, and hardly any hope of any virtue in society. They had not enough interest in the outer world really to wreck or revolutionize it. They did not love the city enough to set fire to it. Thus the ancient world was exactly in our own desolate dilemma. The only people who really enjoyed this world were busy breaking it up; and the virtuous people did not care enough about them to knock them down. In this dilemma (the same as ours) Christianity suddenly stepped in and offered a singular answer, which the world eventually accepted as *the* answer. It was the answer then, and I think it is the answer now.

This answer was like the slash of a sword: it sundered; it did not in any sense sentimentally unite. Briefly, it divided God from the cosmos. That transcendence and distinctness of the deity which some Christians now want to remove from Christianity, was really the only reason why anyone wanted to

---

1. Marcus Aurelius, Roman Emperor AD 161–180; he also wrote a book of Stoic philosophy called *Meditations*.

be a Christian. It was the whole point of the Christian answer to the unhappy pessimist and the still more unhappy optimist. As I am here only concerned with their particular problem I shall indicate only briefly this great metaphysical suggestion. All descriptions of the creating and sustaining principle in things must be metaphorical, because they must be verbal. Thus the pantheist is forced to speak of God *in* all things as if he were in a box. Thus the evolutionist has, in his very name, the idea of being unrolled like a carpet. All terms, religious and irreligious, are open to this charge. The only question is whether all terms are useless, or whether one can, with such a phrase, cover a distinct *idea* about the origin of things. I think one can, and so evidently does the evolutionist, or he would not talk about evolution. And the root phrase for all Christian theism was this, that God was a creator, as an artist is a creator. A poet is so separate from his poem that he himself speaks of it as a little thing he has 'thrown off'. Even in giving it forth he has flung it away. This principle that all creation and pro-creation is a breaking off is at least consistent through the cosmos as the evolutionary principle that all growth is branching out. A woman loses a child even in having a child. All creation is separation. Birth is as solemn a parting as death.

It was the prime philosophic principle of Christianity that this divorce in the divine act of making (such as severs the poet from the poem or the mother from the new-born child) was the true description of the act whereby the absolute energy made the world. According to most philosophers, God in making the world enslaved it. According to Christianity, in making it, He set it free. God had written, not so much a poem, but rather a play; a play He had planned as perfect, but which had necessarily been left to human actors and stage managers, who had since made a great mess of it. I will discuss the truth of this theorem later. Here I have only to point out with what a startling smoothness it passed the dilemma we have discussed in this chapter. In this way at least one could be both happy and indignant without degrading one's self to be either a pessimist or an optimist. On this system one could fight all the forces of existence without deserting the flag of existence. One could be at peace with the universe and yet be at war with the world. St George could still fight the dragon, however big the monster bulked in the cosmos, though he were bigger than the mighty cities or bigger than the everlasting hills. If he were as big as the world he could yet be killed in the name of the world. St George had not to consider any obvious odds or proportions in the scale of things, but only the original secret of their design. He can shake his sword at the dragon, even if it is everything; even if the empty heavens over his head are only the huge arch of its open jaws.

And then followed an experience impossible to describe. It was as if I had been blundering about since my birth with two huge and unmanageable machines, of different shapes and without apparent connection – the world and the Christian tradition. I had found this hole in the world: the fact that one must somehow find a way of loving the world without trusting it; somehow one must love the world without being worldly. I found this projecting feature of Christian theology, like a sort of hard spike, the dogmatic insistence that God was personal, and had made a world separate from Himself. The spike of dogma fitted exactly into the hole in the world – it had evidently been meant to go there – and then the strange thing began to happen. When once these two parts of the two machines had come together, one after another, all the other parts fitted and fell in with an eerie exactitude. I could hear bolt after bolt over all the machinery falling into its place with a kind of click of relief. Having got one part right, all the other parts were repeating that rectitude, as clock after clock strikes noon. Instinct after instinct was answered by doctrine after doctrine. Or, to vary the metaphor, I was like one who had advanced into a hostile country to take one high fortress.

And when that fort had fallen the whole country surrendered and turned solid behind me. The whole land was lit up, as it were, back to the first fields of my childhood. All those blind fancies of boyhood which in the [previous] chapter I have tried in vain to trace on the darkness, became suddenly transparent and sane. I was right when I felt that roses were red by some sort of choice: it was the divine choice. I was right when I felt that I would almost rather say that grass was the wrong colour than say that it must by necessity have been that colour: it might verily have been any other. My sense that happiness hung on the crazy thread of a condition did mean something when all was said: it meant the whole doctrine of the Fall. Even those dim and shapeless monsters of notions which I have not been able to describe, much less defend, stepped quietly into their places like colossal caryatides of the creed. The fancy that the cosmos was not vast and void, but small and cosy, had a fulfilled significance now, for anything that is a work of art must be small in the sight of the artist; to God the stars might be only small and dear, like diamonds. And my haunting instinct that somehow good was not merely a tool to be used, but a relic to be guarded, like the goods from Crusoe's ship – even that had been the wild whisper of something originally wise, for, according to Christianity, we were indeed the survivors of a wreck, the crew of a golden ship that had gone down before the beginning of the world.

Orthodoxy, 1908

The Paradoxes of Christianity

The real trouble with this world of ours is not that it is an unreasonable world, nor even that it is a reasonable one. The commonest kind of trouble is that it is nearly reasonable, but not quite. Life is not an illogicality; yet it is a trap for logicians. It looks just a little more mathematical and regular than it is; its exactitude is obvious, but its inexactitude is hidden; its wildness lies in wait. I give one coarse instance of what I mean. Suppose some mathematical creature from the moon were to reckon up the human body; he would at once see that the essential thing about it was that it was duplicate. A man is two men, he on the right exactly resembling him on the left. Having noted that there was an arm on the right and one on the left, a leg on the right and one on the left, he might go further and still find on each side the same number of fingers, the same number of toes, twin eyes, twin ears, twin nostrils and even twin lobes of the brain. At last he would take it as a law; and then, where he found a heart on one side, would deduce that there was another heart on the other. And just then, where he most felt he was right, he would be wrong.

It is this silent swerving from accuracy by an inch that is the uncanny element in everything. It seems a sort of secret treason in the universe. An apple or an orange is round enough to get itself called round, and yet is not round after all. The earth itself is shaped like an orange in order to lure some simple astronomer into calling it a globe. A blade of grass is called after the blade of a sword, because it comes to a point; but it doesn't. Everywhere in things there is this element of the quiet and incalculable. It escapes the rationalists, but it never escapes till the last moment. From the grand curve of our earth it could easily be inferred that every inch of it was thus curved. It would seem rational that as a man has a brain on both sides, he should have a heart on both sides. Yet scientific men are still organizing expeditions to find the North Pole, because they are so fond of flat country. Scientific men are also still organizing expeditions to find a man's heart; and when they try to find it, they generally get on the wrong side of him.

Now, actual insight or inspiration is best tested by whether it guesses these hidden malformations or surprises. If our mathematician from the moon saw the two arms and the two ears, he might deduce the two shoulder blades and the two halves of the brain. But if he guessed that the man's heart was in the right place, then I should call him something more than a mathematician. Now, this is exactly the claim which I have since come to propound for Christianity. Not merely that it deduces logical truths, but that when it suddenly becomes illogical, it has found, so to speak, an illogical truth. It not only goes right about things, but it goes wrong (if one may say so) exactly where the things go wrong. Its plan suits the secret irregularities, and expects the unexpected. It is simple about the simple truth; but it is stubborn about the subtle truth. It will admit that a man has two hands, it will not admit (though all the Modernists wail to it) the obvious deduction that he has two hearts. It is my only purpose in this chapter to point this out; to show that whenever we feel there is something odd in Christian theology, we shall generally find that there is something odd in the truth.

I have alluded to an unmeaning phrase to the effect that such and such a creed cannot be believed in our age. Of course, anything can be believed in any age. But, oddly enough, there really is a sense in which a creed, if it is believed at all, can be believed more fixedly in a complex society than in a simple one. If a man finds Christianity true in Birmingham, he has actually clearer reasons for faith than if he had found it true in Mercia. For the more complicated seems the coincidence, the less it can be a coincidence. If snowflakes fell in the shape, say, of the heart of Midlothian, it might be an accident. But if snowflakes fell in the exact shape of the maze at Hampton Court, I think one might call it a miracle. It is exactly as of such a miracle that I have since come to feel of the philosophy of Christianity. The complication of our modern world proves the truth of the creed more perfectly than any of the plain problems of the ages of faith. It was in Notting Hill and Battersea that I began to see that Christianity was true. This is why the faith has that elaboration of doctrines and details which so much distresses those who admire Christianity without believing in it. When once one believes in a creed, one is proud of its complexity, as scientists are proud of the complexity of science. It shows how rich it is in discoveries. If it is right at all, it is a compliment to say that it's elaborately right. A stick might fit a hole or a stone a hollow by accident. But a key and a lock are both complex. And if a key fits a lock, you know it is the right key.

But this involved accuracy of the thing makes it very difficult to do what I now have to do, to describe this accumulation of truth. It is very hard for a man to defend anything of which he is entirely convinced. It is comparatively easy when he is only partially convinced. He is partially convinced because he has found this or that proof of the thing, and he can expound it. But a man is not really convinced of a philosophic theory when he finds that something proves it. He is only really convinced when he finds that everything proves it. And the more converging reasons he finds pointing to this conviction, the more bewildered he is if asked suddenly to sum them up. Thus, if one asked an ordinary intelligent man, on the spur of the moment, 'Why do you prefer civilization to savagery?' he would look wildly round at object after object, and would only be able to answer vaguely, 'Why, there is that bookcase ... and the coals in the coal scuttle ... and pianos ... and policemen.' The whole case for civilization is that the case for it is complex. It has done so many things. But that very multiplicity of proof which ought to make reply overwhelming makes reply impossible.

There is, therefore, about all complete conviction a kind of huge helplessness. The belief is so big that it takes a long time to get it into action. And this hesitation chiefly arises, oddly enough, from an indifference about where one should begin. All roads lead to Rome; which is one reason why many people never get there. In the case of this defence of the Christian conviction I confess that I would as soon begin the argument with one thing as another; I would begin it with a turnip or a taximeter cab. But if I am to be at all careful about making my meaning clear, it will, I think, be wiser to continue the current arguments of the last chapter, which was concerned to urge the first of these mystical coincidences, or rather ratifications. All I had hitherto heard of Christian theology had alienated me from it. I was a pagan at the age of twelve, and a complete agnostic by the age of sixteen; and I cannot understand anyone passing the age of seventeen without having asked himself so simple a question. I did, indeed, retain a cloudy reverence for a cosmic deity and a great historical interest in the Founder of Christianity. But I certainly regarded Him as a man; though perhaps I thought that, even in that point, He had an advantage over some of His modern critics. I read the scientific and sceptical literature of my time – all of it, at least, that I could find written in English and lying about; and I read nothing else; I mean I read nothing else on any other note of philosophy. The penny dreadfuls which I also read were indeed in a healthy and heroic tradition of Christianity; but I did not know this at the time. I never read a line of Christian apologetics. I read as little as I can of them now. It was Huxley[1] and Herbert Spencer and Bradlaugh[2] who brought me back to orthodox theology. They sowed in my mind my first wild doubts of doubt. Our grandmothers were quite right when they said that Tom Paine and the free thinkers unsettled the mind. They do. They unsettled mine horribly. The rationalist made me question whether reason was of any use whatever; and when I had finished Herbert Spencer I had got as far as doubting (for the first time) whether evolution had occurred at all. As I laid down the last of Colonel Ingersoll's atheistic lectures the dreadful thought broke across my mind, 'Almost thou persuadest me to be a Christian.' I was in a desperate way.

This odd effect of the great agnostics in arousing doubts deeper than their own might be illustrated in many ways. I take only one. As I read and re-read all the non-Christian or anti-Christian accounts of the faith, from Huxley to Bradlaugh, a slow and awful impression grew gradually but graphically upon my mind – the impression that Christianity must be a most extraordinary thing. For not only (as I understood) had Christianity the most flaming vices, but it had apparently a mystical talent for combining vices which seemed inconsistent with each other. It was attacked on all sides and for all contradictory reasons. No sooner had one rationalist demonstrated that it was too far to the east than another demonstrated with equal clearness that it was much too far to the west. No sooner had my indignation died down at its angular and aggressive squareness than I was called up again to notice and condemn its enervating and sensual roundness. In case any reader has not

1. Thomas Huxley (1825–95): supporter of Darwin and inventor of the word 'agnostic'.
2. Charles Bradlaugh (1833–91): notorious atheist, elected as an MP in 1880, but refused a seat when he refused to swear an oath.

come across the thing I mean, I will give such instances as I remember at random of this self-contradiction in the sceptical attack. I give four or five of them; there are fifty more.

Thus, for instance, I was much moved by the eloquent attack on Christianity as a thing of inhuman gloom; for I thought (and still think) sincere pessimism the unpardonable sin. Insincere pessimism is a social accomplishment, rather agreeable than otherwise; and fortunately nearly all pessimism is insincere. But if Christianity was, as these people said, a thing purely pessimistic and opposed to life, then I was quite prepared to blow up St Paul's Cathedral. But the extraordinary thing is this. They did prove to me in chapter 1 (to my complete satisfaction) that Christianity was too pessimistic; and then, in chapter 2, they began to prove to me that it was a great deal too optimistic. One accusation against Christianity was that it prevented men, by morbid tears and terrors, from seeking joy and liberty in the bosom of Nature. But another accusation was that it comforted men with a fictitious providence, and put them in a pink-and-white nursery. One great agnostic asked why Nature was not beautiful enough, and why it was hard to be free. Another great agnostic objected that Christian optimism, 'the garment of make-believe woven by pious hands', hid from us the fact that Nature was ugly, and that it was impossible to be free. One rationalist had hardly done calling Christianity a nightmare before another began to call it a fool's paradise. This puzzled me; the charges seemed inconsistent. Christianity could not at once be the black mask on a white world, and also the white mask on a black world. The state of the Christian could not be at once so comfortable that he was a coward to cling to it, and so uncomfortable that he was a fool to stand it. If it falsified human vision it must falsify it one way or another; it could not wear both green and rose-coloured spectacles. I rolled on my tongue with a terrible joy, as did all young men of that time, the taunts which Swinburne hurled at the dreariness of the creed:

> Thou hast conquered, O pale Galilean,
> the world has grown gray with Thy breath.[3]

But when I read the same poet's accounts of paganism (as in 'Atalanta'), I gathered that the world was, if possible, more grey before the Galilean breathed on it than afterwards. The poet maintained, indeed, in the abstract, that life itself was pitch dark. And yet, somehow, Christianity had darkened it. The very man who denounced Christianity for pessimism was himself a pessimist. I thought there must be something wrong. And it did for one wild moment cross my mind that, perhaps, those might not be the very best judges of the relation of religion to happiness who, by their own account, had neither one nor the other.

It must be understood that I did not conclude hastily that the accusations were false or the accusers fools. I simply deduced that Christianity must be something even weirder and wickeder than they made out. A thing might have these two opposite vices; but it must be a rather queer thing if it did. A man might be too fat in one place and too thin in another; but he would be an odd shape. At this point my thoughts were only of the odd shape of the Christian religion; I did not allege any odd shape in the rationalistic mind.

Here is another case of the same kind. I felt that a strong case against Christianity lay in the charge that there is something timid, monkish and unmanly about all that is called 'Christian', especially in its attitude towards resistance and fighting. The great sceptics of the nineteenth century were largely virile. Bradlaugh in an expansive way, Huxley in a reticent way, were decidedly men. In comparison, it did seem tenable that there was something weak and over-patient about Christian counsels. The gospel paradox about the other

3. Swinburne, 'Hymn to Proserpine'.

cheek, the fact that priests never fought, a hundred things made plausible the accusation that Christianity was an attempt to make a man too like a sheep. I read it and believed it, and if I had read nothing different, I should have gone on believing it. But I read something very different. I turned the next page in my agnostic manual, and my brain turned upside down. Now I found that I was to hate Christianity not for fighting too little, but for fighting too much. Christianity, it seemed, was the mother of wars. Christianity had deluged the world with blood. I had got thoroughly angry with the Christian, because he never was angry. And now I was told to be angry with him because his anger had been the most huge and horrible thing in human history; because his anger had soaked the earth and smoked to the sun. The very people who reproached Christianity with the meekness and non-resistance of the monasteries were the very people who reproached it also with the violence and valour of the Crusades. It was the fault of poor old Christianity (somehow or other) both that Edward the Confessor did not fight and that Richard Coeur de Lion did. The Quakers (we were told) were the only characteristic Christians; and yet the massacres of Cromwell and Alva were characteristic Christian crimes. What could it all mean? What was this Christianity which always forbade war and always produced wars? What could be the nature of the thing which one could abuse first because it would not fight, and second because it was always fighting? In what world of riddles was born this monstrous murder and this monstrous meekness? The shape of Christianity grew a queerer shape every instant.

I take a third case; the strangest of all, because it involves the one real objection to the faith. The one real objection to the Christian religion is simply that it is one religion. The world is a big place, full of very different kinds of people. Christianity (it may reasonably be said) is one thing confined to one kind of people; it began in Palestine, it has practically stopped with Europe. I was duly impressed with this argument in my youth, and I was much drawn towards the doctrine often preached in Ethical Societies – I mean the doctrine that there is one great unconscious church of all humanity founded on the omnipresence of the human conscience. Creeds, it was said, divided men; but at least morals united them. The soul might seek the strangest and most remote lands and ages and still find essential ethical common sense. It might find Confucius under Eastern trees, and he would be writing 'Thou shalt not steal.' It might decipher the darkest hieroglyphic on the most primeval desert, and the meaning when deciphered would be 'Little boys should tell the truth.' I believed this doctrine of the brotherhood of all men in the possession of a moral sense, and I believe it still – with other things. And I was thoroughly annoyed with Christianity for suggesting (as I supposed) that whole ages and empires of men had utterly escaped this light of justice and reason. But then I found an astonishing thing. I found that the very people who said that mankind was one church from Plato to Emerson were the very people who said that morality had changed altogether, and that what was right in one age was wrong in another. If I asked, say, for an altar, I was told that we needed none, for men our brothers gave us clear oracles and one creed in their universal customs and ideals. But if I mildly pointed out that one of men's universal customs was to have an altar, then my agnostic teachers turned clean round and told me that men had always been in darkness and the superstitions of savages. I found it was their daily taunt against Christianity that it was the light of one people and had left all others to die in the dark. But I also found that it was their special boast for themselves that science and progress were the discovery of one people, and that all other peoples had died in the dark. Their chief insult to Christianity was actually their chief compliment to themselves, and there seemed to be a strange unfairness about all their relative insistence on the two things. When considering some pagan or agnostic, we were to remember that all men had one religion; when considering some mystic or spiritualist, we were only to consider what absurd religions some men had. We could trust the ethics of Epictetus,[4] because ethics had never changed. We must not trust the ethics of Bossuet,[5] because ethics had changed. They changed in two hundred years, but not in two thousand.

This began to be alarming. It looked not so much as if Christianity was bad enough to include any vices, but rather as if any stick was good enough to beat Christianity with. What again could this astonishing thing be like which people were so anxious to contradict, that in doing so they did not mind contradicting themselves? I saw the same thing on every side. I can give no further space to this discussion of it in detail; but lest anyone supposes that I have unfairly selected three accidental cases I will run briefly through a few others. Thus, certain sceptics wrote that the great crime of Christianity had been its attack on the family; it had dragged women to the loneliness and contemplation of the cloister, away from their homes and their children. But, then, other sceptics (slightly more advanced) said that the great crime of Christianity was forcing the family and marriage upon us; that it doomed women to the drudgery of their homes and children, and forbade them loneliness and contemplation. The charge was actually reversed. Or, again certain phrases in the Epistles or the Marriage Service, were said by the anti-Christians to show contempt for woman's intellect. But I found that the anti-Christians themselves had a contempt for woman's intellect; for it was their great sneer at the Church on the continent that 'only women' went to it. Or again,

4. Epictetus: Greek Stoic philosopher, AD 55–135.
5. Jacques Bossuet (1627–1704): Catholic bishop and theologian at the Court of Louis XIV.

Christianity was reproached with its naked and hungry habits; with its sackcloth and dried peas. But the next minute Christianity was being reproached with its pomp and its ritualism; its shrines of porphyry and its robes of gold. It was abused for being too plain and for being too coloured. Again Christianity had always been accused of restraining sexuality too much, when Bradlaugh the Malthusian discovered that it restrained it too little. It is often accused in the same breath of prim respectability and of religious extravagance. Between the covers of the same atheistic pamphlet I have found the faith rebuked for its disunion, 'One thinks one thing, and one another,' and rebuked also for its union, 'It is difference of opinion that prevents the world from going to the dogs.' In the same conversation a free thinker, a friend of mine, blamed Christianity for despising Jews, and then despised it himself for being Jewish.

I wished to be quite fair then, and I wish to be quite fair now; and I did not conclude that the attack on Christianity was all wrong. I only concluded that if Christianity was wrong, it was very wrong indeed. Such hostile horrors might be combined in one thing, but that thing must be very strange and solitary. There are men who are misers, and also spend-thrifts; but they are rare. There are men sensual and also ascetic; but they are rare. But if this mass of mad contradictions really existed, quakerish and bloodthirsty, too gorgeous and too threadbare, austere, yet pandering preposterously to the lust of the eye, the enemy of women and their foolish refuge, a solemn pessimist and a silly optimist, if this evil existed, then there was in this evil something quite supreme and unique. For I found in my rationalist teachers no explanation of such exceptional corruption. Christianity (theoretically speaking) was in their eyes only one of the ordinary myths and errors of mortals. *They* gave me no key to this twisted and unnatural badness. Such a paradox of evil rose to the stature of the supernatural. It was, indeed, almost as supernatural as the infallibility of the Pope. An historic institution, which never went right, is really quite as much of a miracle as an institution that cannot go wrong. The only explanation which immediately occurred to my mind was that Christianity did not come from heaven, but from hell. Really, if Jesus of Nazareth was not Christ, He must have been Antichrist.

And then in a quiet hour a strange thought struck me like a still thunderbolt. There had suddenly come into my mind another explanation. Suppose we heard an unknown man spoken of by many men. Suppose we were puzzled to hear that some men said he was too tall and some too short; some objected to his fatness, some lamented his leanness; some thought him too dark, and some too fair. One explanation (as has been already admitted) would be that he might be an odd shape. But there is another explanation. He might be the right shape. Outrageously tall men might feel him to be short. Very short men might feel him to be tall. Old bucks who are growing stout might consider him insufficiently filled out; old beaux who were growing thin might feel that he expanded beyond the narrow lines of elegance. Perhaps Swedes (who have pale hair like tow) called him a dark man, while negroes considered him distinctly blond. Perhaps (in short) this extraordinary thing is really the ordinary thing; at least the normal thing, the centre. Perhaps, after all, it is Christianity that is sane and all its critics that are mad — in various ways. I tested this idea by asking myself whether there was about any of the accusers anything morbid that might explain the accusation. I was startled to find that this key fitted a lock. For instance, it was certainly odd that the modern world charged Christianity at once with bodily austerity and with artistic pomp. But then it was also odd, very odd, that the modern world itself combined extreme bodily luxury with an extreme absence of artistic pomp. The modern man thought Becket's[6] robes too rich and his meals too poor. But then the modern man was really exceptional in history;

no man before ever ate such elaborate dinners in such ugly clothes. The modern man found the Church too simple exactly where modern life is too complex; he found the Church too gorgeous exactly where modern life is too dingy. The man who disliked the plain fasts and feasts was made on entrées. The man who disliked vestments wore a pair of preposterous trousers. And surely if there was any insanity involved in the matter at all it was in the trousers, not in the simple falling robe. If there was any insanity at all, it was in the extravagant entrées, not in the bread and wine.

I went over all the cases, and I found the key fitted so far. The fact that Swinburne was irritated at the unhappiness of Christians and yet more irritated at their happiness was easily explained. It was no longer a complication of diseases in Christianity, but a complication of diseases in Swinburne. The restraints of Christians saddened him simply because he was more hedonist than a healthy man should be. The faith of Christians angered him because he was more pessimist than a healthy man should be. In the same way the Malthusians[7] by instinct attacked Christianity; not because there is anything especially anti-Malthusian about Christianity, but because there is something a little anti-human about Malthusianism.

Nevertheless it could not, I felt, be quite true that Christianity was merely sensible and stood in the middle. There was really an element in it of emphasis and even frenzy which had justified the secularists in their superficial criticism. It might be wise, I began more and more to think that it was wise, but it was not merely worldly wise; it was not merely temperate and respectable. Its fierce crusaders and

6. St Thomas à Becket (1118–70): Archbishop of Canterbury, murdered by Henry I for upholding the independence of the Church.
7. Disciples of Thomas Malthus (1766–1834), an economist who forecast that 'overbreeding' by the poor would lead to general destitution and starvation.

meek saints might balance each other; still, the crusaders were very fierce and the saints were very meek, meek beyond all decency. Now, it was just at this point of the speculation that I remembered my thoughts about the martyr and the suicide. In that matter there had been this combination between two almost insane positions which yet somehow amounted to sanity. This was just such another contradiction; and this I had already found to be true. This was exactly one of the paradoxes in which sceptics found the creed wrong; and in this I had found it right. Madly as Christians might love the martyr or hate the suicide, they never felt these passions more madly than I had felt them long before I dreamed of Christianity. Then the most difficult and interesting part of the mental process opened, and I began to trace this idea darkly through all the enormous thoughts of our theology. The idea was that which I had outlined touching the optimist and the pessimist; that we want not an amalgam or compromise, but both things at the top of their energy; love and wrath both burning. Here I shall only trace it in relation to ethics. But I need not remind the reader that the idea of this combination is indeed central in orthodox theology. For orthodox theology has specially insisted that Christ was not a being apart from God and man, like an elf, nor yet a being half human and half not, like a centaur, but both things at once and both things thoroughly, very man and very God. Now let me trace this notion as I found it.

All sane men can see that sanity is some kind of equilibrium; that one may be mad and eat too much, or mad and eat too little. Some moderns have indeed appeared with vague versions of progress and evolution which seeks to destroy the *meson* or balance of Aristotle. They seem to suggest that we are meant to starve progressively, or to go on eating larger and larger breakfasts every morning for ever. But the great truism of the *meson* remains for all thinking men, and these people have not upset any balance except their own. But granted that we have all to keep a balance, the real interest comes in with the question of how that balance can be kept. That was the problem which Paganism tried to solve: that was the problem which I think Christianity solved and solved in a very strange way.

Paganism declared that virtue was in a balance; Christianity declared it was in a conflict: the collision of two passions apparently opposite. Of course they were not really inconsistent; but they were such that it was hard to hold simultaneously. Let us follow for a moment the clue of the martyr and the suicide; and take the case of courage. No quality has ever so much addled the brains and tangled the definitions of merely rational sages. Courage is almost a contradiction in terms. It means a strong desire to live taking the form of a readiness to die. 'He that will lose his life, the same shall save it,' is not a piece of mysticism for saints and heroes. It is a piece of every-day advice for sailors or mountaineers. It might be printed in an Alpine guide or a drill book. This paradox is the whole principle of courage; even of quite earthly or quite brutal courage. A man cut off by the sea may save his life if he will risk it on the precipice. He can only get away from death by continually stepping within an inch of it. A soldier surrounded by enemies, if he is to cut his way out, needs to combine a strong desire for living with a strange carelessness about dying. He must not merely cling to life, for then he will be a coward, and will not escape. He must not merely wait for death, for then he will be a suicide, and will not escape. He must seek his life in a spirit of furious indifference to it; he must desire life like water and yet drink death like wine. No philosopher, I fancy, has ever expressed this romantic riddle with adequate lucidity, and I certainly have not done so. But Christianity has done more: it has marked the limits of it in the awful graves of the suicide and the hero, showing the distance between him who dies for the sake of living and him who dies for the sake of dying. And it has held up ever since above the European lances the banner of the mystery of chivalry: the Christian courage, which is a disdain of death; not the Chinese courage, which is a disdain of life.

And now I began to find that this duplex passion was the Christian key to ethics everywhere. Everywhere the creed made a moderation out of the still crash of two impetuous emotions. Take, for instance, the matter of modesty, of the balance between mere pride and mere prostration. The average pagan, like the average agnostic, would merely say that he was content with himself, but not insolently self-satisfied, that there were many better and many worse, that his deserts were limited, but he would see that he got them. In short, he would walk with his head in the air; but not necessarily with his nose in the air. This is a manly and rational position, but it is open to the objection we noted against the compromise between optimism and pessimism – the 'resignation' of Matthew Arnold. Being a mixture of two things, it is a dilution of two things; neither is present in its full strength or contributes its full colour. This proper pride does not lift the heart like the tongue of trumpets; you cannot go clad in crimson and gold for this. On the other hand, this mild rationalist modesty does not cleanse the soul with fire and make it clear like crystal; it does not (like a strict and searching humility) make a man as a little child, who can sit at the feet of the grass. It does not make him look up and see marvels; for Alice must grow small if she is to be Alice in Wonderland. Thus it loses both the poetry of being proud and the poetry of being humble. Christianity sought by this same strange expedient to save both of them.

It separated the two ideas and then exaggerated them both. In one way Man was to be haughtier than he had ever been before; in another way he was to be humbler than he had ever been before. In so far as I am Man I am the chief of creatures. In so far as I am *a* man I am the chief of sinners. All humility that had meant pessimism, that had meant man taking a vague or mean view of his whole destiny – all that was to go. We were to hear no more the wail of Ecclesiastes that humanity had no pre-eminence over the brute, or the awful cry of Homer that man was only the saddest of all the beasts of the field. Man was a statue of God walking about the garden. Man had pre-eminence over all the brutes; man was only sad because he was not a beast, but a broken god. The Greek had spoken of men creeping on the earth, as if clinging to it. Now Man was to tread on the earth as if to subdue it. Christianity thus held a thought of the dignity of man that could only be expressed in crowns rayed like the sun and fans of peacock plumage. Yet at the same time it could hold a thought about the abject smallness of man that could only be expressed in fasting and fantastic submission, in the grey ashes of St Dominic and the white snows of St Bernard. When one came to think of *one's self*, there was vista and void enough for any amount of bleak abnegation and bitter truth. There the real- istic gentleman could let himself go – as long as he let himself go at himself. There was an open playground for the happy pessimist. Let him say anything against himself short of blas- pheming the original aim of his being; let him call himself a fool and even a damned fool (though that is Calvinistic); but he must not say that fools are not worth saving. He must not say that a man, *qua* man, can be valueless. Here again, in short, Christianity got over the difficulty of combining furious opposites, by keeping them both, and keeping them both furious. The Church was positive on both points. One can hardly think too little of one's self. One can hardly think too much of one's soul.

Take another case: the complicated question of charity, which some highly uncharitable idealists seem to think quite easy. Charity is a paradox, like modesty and courage. Stated baldly, charity certainly means one of two things – pardoning unpardonable acts, or loving unlovable people. But if we ask ourselves (as we did in the case of pride) what a sensible pagan would feel about such a subject, we shall probably be beginning at the bottom of it. A sensible pagan would say that there were some people one could forgive, and some one couldn't: a slave who stole wine could be laughed at; a slave who betrayed his benefactor could be killed, and cursed even after he was killed. In so far as the act was pardonable, the man was pardonable. That again is rational, and even refreshing; but it is a dilution. It leaves no place for a pure horror of injustice, such as that which is a great beauty in the innocent. And it leaves no place for a mere tenderness for men as men, such as is the whole fascination of the charitable. Christianity came in here as before. It came in startlingly with a sword, and clove one thing from another. It divided the crime from the criminal. The criminal we must forgive unto seventy times seven. The crime we must not forgive at all. It was not enough that slaves who stole wine inspired partly anger and partly kindness. We must be much more angry with theft than before, and yet much kinder to thieves than before. There was room for wrath and love to run wild. And the more I considered Christianity, the more I found that while it had established a rule and order, the chief aim of that order was to give room for good things to run wild.

Mental and emotional liberty are not so simple as they look. Really they require almost as careful a balance of laws and conditions as do social and political liberty. The ordinary aesthetic anarchist who sets out to feel everything freely gets knotted at last in a paradox that prevents him feeling at all. He breaks away from home limits to follow poetry. But in ceasing to feel home limits he has ceased to feel the *Odyssey*. He is free from national prejudices and outside patriotism. But being outside patriotism he is outside *Henry V*. Such a literary man is simply outside all literature: he is more of a prisoner than any bigot. For if there is a wall between you and the world, it makes little difference whether you describe yourself as locked in or as locked out. What we want is not the universality that is outside all normal sentiments; we want the universality that is inside all normal sentiments. It is all the difference between being free from them, as a man is free from a prison, and being free of them as a man is free of a city. I am free from Windsor Castle (that is, I am not forcibly detained there), but I am by no means free of that building. How can man be approximately free of fine emotions, able to swing them in a clear space without breakage or wrong? *This* was the achievement of this Christian paradox of the parallel passions. Granted the primary dogma of the war between divine and diabolic, the revolt and ruin of the world, their optimism and pessimism, as pure poetry, could be loosened like cataracts.

St Francis, in praising all good, could be a more shouting optimist than Walt Whitman. St Jerome, in denouncing all evil, could paint the world blacker than Schopenhauer.[8] Both passions were free because both were kept in their place. The optimist could pour out all the praise he liked on the gay music of the march, the golden trumpets, and the purple banners going into battle. But he must not call the fight needless. The pessimist might draw as darkly as he chose the sickening marches or the sanguine wounds. But he must not call the fight hopeless. So it was with all the other moral problems, with pride, with protest and with compassion. By defining its main doctrine, the Church not only kept seemingly inconsistent things side by side, but, what was more, allowed them to break out in a sort of artistic violence otherwise possible only to anarchists. Meekness grew more dramatic than madness. Historic Christianity rose into a high and strange *coup de théâtre* of morality – things that are to virtue what the crimes of Nero are to vice. The spirits of indignation and of charity took terrible and attractive forms,

8. Arthur Schopenhauer (1788–1860): German philosopher of pessimism.

ranging from that monkish fierceness that scourged like a dog the first and greatest of the Plantagenets, to the sublime pity of St Catherine, who, in the official shambles, kissed the bloody head of the criminal. Poetry could be acted as well as composed. This heroic and monumental manner in ethics has entirely vanished with supernatural religion. They, being humble, could parade themselves; but we are too proud to be prominent. Our ethical teachers write reasonably for prison reform; but we are not likely to see Mr Cadbury, or any eminent philanthropist, go into Reading Gaol and embrace the strangled corpse before it is cast into the quicklime. Our ethical teachers write mildly against the power of millionaires; but we are not likely to see Mr Rockefeller, or any modern tyrant, publicly whipped in Westminster Abbey.

Thus, the double charges of the secularists, though throwing nothing but darkness and confusion on themselves, throw a real light on the faith. It *is* true that the historic Church has at once emphasized celibacy and emphasized the family; has at once (if one may put it so) been fiercely for having children and fiercely for not having children. It has kept them side by side like two strong colours, red and white, like the red and white upon the shield of St George. It has always had a healthy hatred of pink. It hates that combination of two colours which is the feeble expedient of the philosophers. It hates that evolution of black into white which is tantamount to a dirty grey. In fact, the whole theory of the Church on virginity might be symbolized in the statement that white is a colour: not merely the absence of a colour. All that I am urging here can be expressed by saying that Christianity sought in most of these cases to keep two colours co-existent but pure. It is not a mixture like russet or purple; it is rather like a shot silk, for a shot silk is always at right angles, and is in the pattern of the cross.

So it is also, of course, with the contradictory charges of the anti-Christians about submission and slaughter. It *is* true that the Church told some men to fight and others not to fight; and it *is* true that those who fought were like thunderbolts and those who did not fight were like statues. All this simply means that the Church preferred to use its Supermen and to use its Tolstoyans. There must be *some* good in the life of battle, for so many good men have enjoyed being soldiers. There must be *some* good in the idea of non-resistance, for so many good men seem to enjoy being Quakers. All that the Church did (so far as that goes) was to prevent either of these good things from ousting the other. They existed side by side. The Tolstoyans, having all the scruples of monks, simply became monks. The Quakers became a club instead of becoming a sect. Monks said all that Tolstoy says; they poured out lucid lamentations about the cruelty of battles and the vanity of revenge. But the Tolstoyans are not quite right enough to run the whole world; and in the ages of faith they were not allowed to run it. The world did not lose the last charge of Sir James Douglas or the banner of Joan the Maid. And sometimes this pure gentleness and this pure fierceness met and justified their juncture; the paradox of all the prophets was fulfilled, and, in the soul of St Louis, the lion lay down with the lamb. But remember that this text is too lightly interpreted. It is constantly assured, especially in our Tolstoyan tendencies, that when the lion lies down with the lamb the lion becomes lamb-like. But that is brutal annexation and imperialism on the part of the lamb. That is simply the lamb absorbing the lion instead of the lion eating the lamb. The real problem is: can the lion lie down with the lamb and still retain his royal ferocity? *That* is the problem the Church attempted; *that* is the miracle she achieved.

This is what I have called guessing the hidden eccentricities of life. This is knowing that a man's heart is to the left and not in the middle. This is knowing not only that the earth is round, but knowing exactly where it is flat. Christian doctrine detected the oddities of life. It not only discovered the law, but it foresaw the exceptions. Those underrate Christianity who say that it discovered mercy; anyone might discover mercy. In fact everyone did. But to discover a plan for being merciful and also severe — *that* was to anticipate a strange need of human nature. For no one wants to be forgiven for a big sin as if it were a little one. Anyone might say that we should be neither quite miserable nor quite happy. But to find out how far one *may* be quite miserable without making it impossible to be quite happy — that was a discovery in psychology. Anyone might say, 'Neither swagger nor grovel'; and it would have been a limit. But to say, 'Here you can swagger and there you can grovel' — that was an emancipation.

This was the big fact about Christian ethics; the discovery of the new balance. Paganism had been like a pillar of marble, upright because proportioned with symmetry. Christianity was like a huge and ragged and romantic rock, which, though it sways on its pedestal at a touch, yet, because its exaggerated excrescences exactly balance each other, is enthroned there for a thousand years. In a Gothic cathedral the columns were all different, but they were all necessary. Every support seemed an accidental and fantastic support; every buttress was a flying buttress. So in Christendom apparent accidents balanced. Becket wore a hair shirt under his gold and crimson, and there is much to be said for the combination; for Becket got the benefit of the hair shirt while the people in the street got the benefit of the crimson and gold. It is at least better than the manner of the modern millionaire, who has the black and the drab outwardly for others, and the gold next his heart. But the balance was not always in one man's body as in Becket's; the balance was often distributed over the whole body of Christendom. Because a man prayed and fasted on the Northern snows, flowers could be flung at his festival in the Southern cities; and because fanatics drank water on the sands of Syria, men could still drink cider in the orchards of England. This is what makes Christendom at once so much more perplexing and so much more interesting than the Pagan empire; just as Amiens Cathedral is not better but more interesting than the Parthenon. If anyone wants a modern proof of all this, let him consider the curious fact that, under Christianity, Europe (while remaining a unity) has broken up into individual nations. Patriotism is a perfect example of this deliberate balancing of one emphasis against another emphasis. The instinct of the Pagan empire would have said, 'You shall all be Roman citizens, and grow alike; let the German grow less slow and reverent; the Frenchmen less experimental and swift.' But the instinct of Christian Europe says, 'Let the German remain slow and reverent, that the Frenchman may the more safely be swift and experimental. We will make an equipoise out of these excesses. The absurdity called Germany shall correct the insanity called France.'

Last and most important, it is exactly this which explains what is so inexplicable to all the modern critics of the history of Christianity. I mean the monstrous wars about small points of theology, the earthquakes of emotion about a gesture or a word. It was only a matter of an inch; but an inch is everything when you are balancing. The Church could not afford to swerve a hair's breadth on some things if she was to continue her great and daring experiment of the irregular equilibrium. Once let one idea become less powerful and some other idea would become too powerful. It was no flock of sheep the Christian shepherd was leading, but a herd of bulls and tigers, of terrible ideals and devouring doctrines, each one of them strong enough to turn to a false religion and lay waste the world. Remember that the Church went in specifically for dangerous ideas; she was a lion tamer. The idea of birth through a Holy Spirit, of the death of a divine being, of the forgiveness of sins, or the fulfilment of prophecies, are ideas which, anyone can see, need but a touch to turn them into something blasphemous or ferocious. The smallest link was let drop by the artificers of the

Mediterranean, and the lion of ancestral pessimism burst his chain in the forgotten forests of the north. Of these theological equalizations I have to speak afterwards. Here it is enough to notice that if some small mistake were made in doctrine, huge blunders might be made in human happiness. A sentence phrased wrong about the nature of symbolism would have broken all the best statues in Europe. A slip in the definitions might stop all the dances; might wither all the Christmas trees or break all the Easter eggs. Doctrines had to be defined within strict limits, even in order that man might enjoy general human liberties. The Church had to be careful, if only that the world might be careless.

This is the thrilling romance of Orthodoxy. People have fallen into a foolish habit of speaking of orthodoxy as something heavy, humdrum and safe. There never was anything so perilous or so exciting as orthodoxy. It was sanity: and to be sane is more dramatic than to be mad. It was the equilibrium of a man behind madly rushing horses, seeming to stoop this way and to sway that, yet in every attitude having the grace of statuary and the accuracy of arithmetic. The Church in her early days went fierce and fast with any warhorse; yet it is utterly unhistoric to say that she merely went mad along one idea, like a vulgar fanaticism. She swerved to left and right, so as exactly to avoid enormous obstacles. She left on one hand the huge bulk of Arianism, buttressed by all the worldly powers to make Christianity too worldly. The next instant she was swerving to avoid an orientalism, which would have made it too unworldly. The orthodox Church never took the tame course or accepted the conventions; the orthodox Church was never respectable. It would have been easier to have accepted the earthly power of the Arians. It would have been easy, in the Calvinistic seventeenth century, to fall into the bottomless pit of predestination. It is easy to be a madman; it is easy to be a heretic. It is always easy to let the age have its head; the difficult thing is to keep one's own. It is always easy to be a modernist; as it is easy to be a snob. To have fallen into any of those open traps of error and exaggeration which fashion after fashion and sect after sect set along the historic path of Christendom – that would indeed have been simple. It is always simple to fall; there are an infinity of angles at which one falls, only one at which one stands. To have fallen into any one of the fads from Gnosticism to Christian Science would indeed have been obvious and tame. But to have avoided them all has been one whirling adventure; and in my vision the heavenly chariot flies thundering through the ages, the dull heresies sprawling and prostrate, the wild truth reeling but erect.

Orthodoxy, 1908

The End of the World

The shepherds were dying because their gods were dying.
Paganism lived upon poetry; that poetry already considered
under the name of mythology. But everywhere, and especially
in Italy, it had been a mythology and a poetry rooted in the
countryside; and that rustic religion had been largely responsible for the rustic happiness. Only as the whole society grew
in age and experience, there began to appear that weakness in
all mythology already noted in the chapter under that name.
This religion was not quite a religion. In other words, this
religion was not quite a reality. It was the young world's riot
with images and ideas like a young man's riot with wine or
love-making; it was not so much immoral as irresponsible;
it had no foresight of the final test of time. Because it was
creative to any extent it was credulous to any extent. It belonged to the artistic side of man, yet even considered artistically it had long become overloaded and entangled. The
family trees sprung from the seed of Jupiter were a jungle
rather than a forest; the claims of the gods and demigods
seemed like things to be settled rather by a lawyer or a professional herald than by a poet. But it is needless to say that it was
not only in the artistic sense that these things had grown
more anarchic. There had appeared in more and more flagrant
fashion that flower of evil that is really implicit in the very
seed of nature worship, however natural it may seem. I have

said that I do not believe that natural worship necessarily begins with this particular passion; I am not of the de Rougemont school of scientific folklore. I do not believe that mythology must begin in eroticism. But I do believe that mythology must end in it. I am quite certain that mythology did end in it. Moreover, not only did the poetry grow more immoral, but the immorality grew more indefensible. Greek vices, oriental vices, hints of the old horrors of the Semitic demons, began to fill the fancies of decaying Rome, swarming like flies on a dung heap. The psychology of it is really human enough, to anyone who will try that experiment of seeing history from the inside. There comes an hour in the afternoon when the child is tired of 'pretending'; when he is weary of being a robber or a Red Indian. It is then that he torments the cat. There comes a time in the routine of an ordered civilization when the man is tired of playing at mythology and pretending that a tree is a maiden or that the moon made love to a man. The effect of this staleness is the same everywhere; it is seen in all drug-taking and dram-drinking and every form of the tendency to increase the dose. Men seek stranger sins or more startling obscenities as stimulants to their jaded sense. They seek after mad oriental religions for the same reason. They try to stab their nerves to life, if it were with the knives of the priests of Baal. They are walking in their sleep and try to wake themselves up with nightmares.

At that stage even of paganism therefore the peasant songs and dances sound fainter and fainter in the forest. For one thing, the peasant civilization was fading, or had already faded, from the whole countryside. The Empire at the end was organized more and more on that servile system which generally goes with the boast of organization; indeed it was almost as servile as the modern schemes for the organization of industry. It is proverbial that what would once have been a peasantry became a mere populace of the town dependent for bread and circuses; which may again suggest to some a mob dependent upon doles and cinemas. In this as in many other respects, the modern return to heathenism has been a return not even to the heathen youth but rather to the heathen old age. But the causes of it were spiritual in both cases; and especially the spirit of paganism had departed with its familiar spirits.

The heart had gone out of it with its household gods, who went along with the gods of the garden and the field and the forest. The Old Man of the Forest was too old; he was already dying. It is said truly in a sense that Pan died because Christ was born. It is almost as true in another sense that men knew that Christ was born because Pan was already dead. A void was made by the vanishing of the whole mythology of mankind, which would have asphyxiated like a vacuum if it had not been filled with theology. But the point for the moment is that the mythology could not have lasted like a theology in any case. Theology is thought, whether we agree with it or not. Mythology was never thought, and nobody could really agree with it or disagree with it. It was a mere mood of glamour, and when the mood went it could not be recovered. Men not only ceased to believe in the gods, but they realized that they had never believed in them. They had sung their praises; they had danced round their altars. They had played the flute; they had played the fool.

So came the twilight upon Arcady, and the last notes of the pipe sound sadly from the beechen grove. In the great Virgilian poems there is already something of the sadness; but the loves and the household gods linger in lovely lines like that which Mr Belloc took for a test of understanding: *incipe, parve puer, risu cognoscere matrem.*[1] But with them as with us, the human family itself began to break down under servile

1. The quotation is not quite accurate. The original means 'Begin with a smile to your mother, O little boy. For else you are not worthy of a god's table or of a goddess's bed.'

organization and the herding of the towns. The urban mob became enlightened; that is, it lost the mental energy that could create myths. All round the circle of the Mediterranean cities the people mourned for the loss of gods and were consoled with gladiators. And meanwhile something similar was happening to that intellectual aristocracy of antiquity that had been walking about and talking at large ever since Socrates and Pythagoras. They began to betray to the world the fact that they were walking in a circle and saying the same thing over and over again. Philosophy began to be a joke; it also began to be a bore. That unnatural simplification of everything into one system or another, which we have noted as the fault of the philosopher, revealed at once its finality and its futility. Everything was virtue or everything was happiness or everything was fate or everything was good or everything was bad; anyhow, everything was everything and there was no more to be said; so they said it. Everywhere the sages had degenerated into sophists: that is, into hired rhetoricians or askers of riddles.

It is essential to recognize that the Roman Empire was recognized as the highest achievement of the human race; and also as the broadest. A dreadful secret seemed to be written as in obscure hieroglyphics across those mighty works of marble and stone, those colossal amphitheatres and aqueducts. Man could do no more.

For it was not the message blazed on the Babylonian wall, that one king was found wanting or his one kingdom given to a stranger. It was no such good news as the news of invasion and conquest. There was nothing left that could conquer Rome; but there was also nothing left that could improve it. It was the strongest thing that was growing weak. It was the best thing that was going to the bad. It is necessary to insist again and again that many civilizations had met in one civilization of the Mediterranean sea; that it was already universal with a stale and sterile universality. The peoples had pooled their resources and still there was not enough. The empires had gone into partnership and they were still bankrupt. No philosopher who was really philosophical could think anything except that, in that central sea, the wave of the world had risen to its highest, seeming to touch the stars. But the wave was already stooping; for it was only the wave of the world.

That mythology and that philosophy into which paganism has already been analysed had thus both of them been drained most literally to the dregs. If with the multiplication of magic the third department, which we have called the demons, was even increasingly active, it was never anything but destructive. There remains only the fourth element, or rather the first; that which had been in a sense forgotten because it was the first. I mean the primary and overpowering yet impalpable impression that the universe after all has one origin and one aim; and because it has an aim must have an author. What became of this great truth in the background of men's minds, at this time, it is perhaps more difficult to determine. Some of the Stoics undoubtedly saw it more and more clearly as the clouds of mythology cleared and thinned away; and great men among them did much even to the last to lay the foundations of a concept of the moral unity of the world. The Jews still held their secret certainty of it jealously behind high fences of exclusiveness; yet it is intensely characteristic of the society and the situation that some fashionable figures, especially fashionable ladies, actually embraced Judaism. But in the case of many others I fancy there entered at this point a new negation. Atheism became really possible in that abnormal time; for atheism is abnormality. It is not merely the denial of a dogma. It is the reversal of a subconscious assumption in the soul; the sense that there is a meaning and a direction in the world it sees.

The Everlasting Man, 1925

The God in the Cave

Men like Bossuet and Pascal could be as stern and logical as any Calvinist or Utilitarian. How would St Joan of Arc, a woman waving on men to war with the sword, have fared among the Quakers or the Dukhobors or the Tolstoyan sect of pacifists? Yet any number of Catholic saints have spent their lives in preaching peace and preventing wars. It is the same with all the modern attempts at Syncretism. They are never able to make something larger than the Creed without leaving something out. I do not mean leaving out something divine but something human; the flag or the inn or the boy's tale of battle or the hedge at the end of the field. The Theosophists build a pantheon; but it is only a pantheon for pantheists. They call a Parliament of Religions as a reunion of all the peoples; but it is only a reunion of all the prigs. Yet exactly such a pantheon had been set up two thousand years before by the shores of the Mediterranean; and Christians were invited to set up the image of Jesus side by side with the image of Jupiter, of Mithras, of Osiris, of Atys, or of Ammon. It was the refusal of the Christians that was the turning point of history. If the Christians had accepted, they and the whole world would have certainly, in a grotesque but exact metaphor, gone to pot. They would all have been boiled down to one lukewarm liquid in that great pot of cosmopolitan corruption in which all the other myths and mysteries were already melting. It was an awful and an appalling escape. Nobody understands the nature of the Church, or the ringing note of the creed descending from antiquity, who does not realize that the whole world once very nearly died of broad-mindedness and the brotherhood of all religions.

Here it is the important point that the Magi, who stand for mysticism and philosophy, are truly conceived as seeking something new and even as finding something unexpected. That tense sense of crisis which still tingles in the Christmas story, and even in every Christmas celebration, accentuates the idea of a search and a discovery. The discovery is, in this case, truly a scientific discovery. For the other mystical figures in the miracle play, for the angel and the mother, the shepherds and the soldiers of Herod, there may be aspects both simpler and more supernatural, more elemental or more emotional. But the Wise Men must be seeking wisdom; and for them there must be a light also in the intellect. And this is the light: that the Catholic creed is catholic and that nothing else is catholic. The philosophy of the Church is universal. The philosophy of the philosophers was not universal. Had Plato and Pythagoras and Aristotle stood for an instant in the light that came out of that little cave, they would have known that their own light was not universal. It is far from certain, indeed, that they did not know it already. Philosophy also, like mythology, had very much the air of a search. It is the realization of this truth that gives its traditional majesty and mystery to the figures of the Three Kings; the discovery that religion is broader than philosophy and that this is the broadest of religions, contained within this narrow space. The Magicians were gazing at the strange pentacle with the human triangle reversed; and they have never come to the end of their calculations about it. For it is the paradox of that group in the cave, that while our emotions about it are of childish simplicity, our thoughts about it can branch with a never-ending complexity. And we can never reach the end even of our own ideas about the child who was a father and the mother who was a child.

We might well be content to say that mythology had come with the shepherds and philosophy with the philosophers; and that it only remained for them to combine in the recognization of religion. But there was a third element that must not be ignored and one which that religion for ever refuses to ignore, in any revel or reconciliation. There was present in the primary scenes of the drama that Enemy that had rotted the legends with lust and frozen the theories into atheism, but which answered the direct challenge with something of that more direct method which we have seen in the conscious cult of the demons. In the description of that demon worship, of the devouring detestation of innocence shown in the works of its witchcraft and the most inhuman of its human sacrifice, I have said less of its indirect and secret penetration of the saner paganism; the soaking of mythological imagination with sex; the rise of imperial pride into insanity. But both the indirect and the direct influence make themselves felt in the drama of Bethlehem. A ruler under the Roman suzerainty, probably equipped and surrounded with the Roman ornament and order though himself of eastern blood, seems in that hour to have felt stirring within him the spirit of strange things. We all know the story of how Herod, alarmed at some rumour of a mysterious rival, remembered the wild gesture of the capricious despots of Asia and ordered a massacre of suspects of the new generation of the populace. Everyone knows the story; but not everyone has perhaps noted its place in the story of the strange religions of men. Not everybody has seen the significance even of its very contrast with the Corinthian columns and Roman pavement of that conquered and superficially civilized world. Only, as the purpose in his dark spirit began to show and shine in the eyes of the Idumean, a seer might perhaps have seen something like a great grey ghost that looked over his shoulder; have seen behind him, filling the dome of night and hovering for the last time over history, that vast and fearful face that was Moloch of the Carthaginians; awaiting his last tribute from a ruler of the races of Shem. The demons also, in that first festival of Christmas, feasted after their own fashion.

Unless we understand the presence of that Enemy, we shall not only miss the point of Christianity, but even miss the point of Christmas. Christmas for us in Christendom has become one thing, and in one sense even a simple thing. But, like all the truths of that tradition, it is in another sense a very complex thing. Its unique note is the simultaneous striking of many notes; of humility, of gaiety, of gratitude, of mystical fear, but also of vigilance and of drama. It is not only an occasion for the peacemakers any more than for the merrymakers; it is not only a Hindu peace conference any more than it is only a Scandinavian winter feast. There is something defiant in it also; something that makes the abrupt bells at midnight sound like the great guns of a battle that has just been won. All this indescribable thing that we call the Christmas atmosphere only hangs in the air as something like a lingering fragrance or fading vapour from the exultant explosion of that one hour in the Judean hills nearly two thousand years ago. But the saviour is still unmistakable, and it is something too subtle or too solitary to be covered by our use of the word peace. By the very nature of the story the rejoicings in the cavern were rejoicings in a fortress or an outlaw's den; properly understood it is not unduly flippant to say they were rejoicings in a dug-out. It is not only true that such a subterranean chamber was a hiding place from enemies; and that the enemies were already scouring the stony plain that lay above it like a sky. It is not only that the very horse-hoofs of Herod might in that sense have passed like thunder over the sunken head of Christ. It is also that there is in that image a true idea of an outpost, of a piercing through the rock and an entrance into an enemy territory. There is in this buried divinity an idea of *undermining* the world; of shaking the towers and palaces from below; even as Herod the great king felt that earthquake under him and swayed with his swaying palace.

That is perhaps the mightiest of the mysteries of the cave. It is already apparent that though men are said to have looked for hell under the earth, in this case it is rather heaven that is under the earth. And there follows in this strange story the idea of an upheaval of heaven. That is the paradox of the whole position; that henceforth the highest thing can only work from below. Royalty can only return to its own by a sort of rebellion. Indeed the Church from her beginnings, and perhaps especially in her beginnings, was not so much a principality as a revolution against the prince of the world. This sense that the world had been conquered by the great usurper, and was in his possession, has been much deplored or derided by those optimists who identify enlightenment with ease. But it was responsible for all that thrill of defiance and a beautiful danger that made the good news seem to be really both good and new. It was in truth against a huge unconscious usurpation that it raised a revolt, and originally so obscure a revolt. Olympus still occupied the sky like a motionless cloud moulded into many mighty forms; philosophy still sat in the high places and even on the thrones of the kings, when Christ was born in the cave and Christianity in the catacombs.

In both cases we may remark the same paradox of revolution; the sense of something despised and of something feared. The cave in one aspect is only a hole or corner into which the outcasts are swept like rubbish; yet in the other aspect it is a hiding place of something valuable which the tyrants are seeking like treasure. In one sense they are there because the innkeeper would not even remember them, and in another because the king can never forget them. We have already noted that this paradox appeared also in the treatment of the early Church. It was important while it was still insignificant, and certainly while it was still impotent. It was important solely because it was intolerable; and in that sense it is true to say that it was intolerable because it was intolerant. It was resented, because, in its own still and almost secret way, it had declared war. It had risen out of the ground to wreck the heaven and earth of heathenism. It did not try to destroy all that creation of gold and marble; but it contemplated a world without it. It dared to look right through it as though the gold and marble had been glass. Those who charged the Christians with burning down Rome with firebrands were slanderers; but they were at least far nearer to the nature of Christianity than those among the moderns who tell us that the Christians were a sort of ethical society, being martyred in a languid fashion for telling men they had a duty to their neighbours, and only mildly disliked because they were meek and mild.

Herod had his place, therefore, in the miracle play of Bethlehem because he is the menace to the Church Militant and shows it from the first as under persecution and fighting for its life. For those who think this a discord, it is a discord that sounds simultaneously with the Christmas bells. For those who think the idea of the Crusade is one that spoils the idea of the Cross, we can only say that for them the idea of the Cross is spoiled; the idea of the Cross is spoiled quite literally in the Cradle. It is not here to the purpose to argue with them on the abstract ethics of fighting; the purpose in this place is merely to sum up the combination of ideas that make up the Christian and Catholic idea, and to note that all of them are already crystallized in the first Christmas story. They are three distinct and commonly contrasted things which are neverthe-less one thing; but this is the only thing which can make them one. The first is the human instinct for a heaven that shall be as literal and almost as local as a home. It is the idea pursued by all poets and pagans making myths; that a particular place must be the shrine of the god or the abode of the blest; that fairyland is a land; or that the return of the ghost must be the resurrection of the body. I do not here reason about the refusal of rationalism to satisfy this need. I only say that if the rationalists refuse to satisfy it, the pagans will not be satisfied. This is present in the story of Bethlehem and Jerusalem as it is present in the story of Delos and Delphi; and as it is *not* present in the whole universe of Lucretius or the whole universe of Herbert Spencer. The second element is a philosophy *larger* than other philosophies; larger than that of Lucretius and infinitely larger than that of Herbert Spencer. It looks at the world through a hundred windows where the ancient Stoic or the modern agnostic only looks through one. It sees life with thousands of eyes belonging to thousands of different sorts of people, where the other is only the individual standpoint of a Stoic or an agnostic. It has something for all moods of man, it finds work for all kinds of men, it understands secrets of psychology, it is aware of depths of evil, it is able to distinguish between real and unreal marvels and miraculous exceptions, it trains itself in tact about hard cases, all with a multiplicity and subtlety and imagination about the varieties of life which is far beyond the bald or breezy platitudes of most ancient or modern moral philosophy. In a word, there is more in it; it finds more in existence to think about; it gets more out of life. Masses of this material about our many-sided life have been added since the time of St Thomas Aquinas. But St Thomas Aquinas alone would have found himself limited in the world of Confucius or of Comte. And the third point is this: that while it is local enough for poetry and larger than any other philosophy, it is also a challenge and a fight. While it is deliberately broadened to embrace every aspect of truth, it is still stiffly embattled against every mode of error. It gets every kind of man to fight for it, it gets every kind of weapon to fight with, it widens its knowledge of the things that are fought for and against with every art of curiosity or sympathy; but it never forgets that it is fighting. It proclaims peace on earth and never forgets why there was war in heaven.

This is the trinity of truths symbolized here by the three types in the old Christmas story: the shepherds and the kings and that other king who warred upon the children. It is simply not true to say that other religions and philosophies are in this respect its rivals. It is not true to say that any one of them combines these characters; it is not true to say that any one of them pretends to combine them. Buddhism may profess to be equally mystical; it does not even profess to be equally military. Islam may profess to be equally military; it does not even profess to be equally metaphysical and subtle. Confucianism may profess to satisfy the need of the philosophers for order and reason; it does not even profess to satisfy the need of the mystics for miracle and sacrament and the consecration of concrete things. There are many evidences of this presence of a spirit at once universal and unique. One will serve here which is the symbol of the subject of this chapter; that no other story, no pagan legend or philosophical anecdote or historical event, does in fact affect any of us with that peculiar and even poignant impression produced on us by the word Bethlehem. No other birth of a god or childhood of a sage seems to us to be Christmas or anything like Christmas. It is either too cold or too frivolous, or too formal and classical, or too simple and savage, or too occult and complicated. Not one of us, whatever his opinions, would ever go to such a scene with the sense that he was going home. He might admire it because it was poetical, or because it was philosophical, or any number of other things in separation; but not because it was itself. The truth is that there is a quite peculiar and individual character about the hold of this story on human nature; it is not in its psychological substance at all like a mere legend or the life of a great man. It does not exactly in the ordinary sense turn our minds to greatness; to those extensions and exaggerations of humanity which are turned into gods and heroes, even by the healthiest sort of hero worship. It does not exactly work outwards, adventurously, to the wonders to be found at the ends of the earth. It is rather something that surprises us from behind, from the hidden and personal part of our being; like that which can sometimes take us off our guard in the pathos of small objects or the blind pieties of the poor. It is rather as if a man had found an inner room in the very heart of his own house which he had never suspected; and seen a light from within. It is as if he found something at the back of his own heart that betrayed him into good. It is not made of what the world would call strong materials; or rather it is made of materials whose strength is in that winged levity with which they brush us and pass. It is all that is in us but a brief tenderness that is there made eternal; all that means no more than a momentary softening that is in some strange fashion become a strengthening and a repose; it is the broken speech and the lost word that are made positive and suspended unbroken; as the strange kings fade into a far country and the mountains resound no more with the feet of the shepherds; and only the night and the cavern lie in fold upon fold over something more human than humanity.

The Everlasting Man, 1925

The Riddles of the Gospel

To understand the nature of this chapter, it is necessary to recur to the nature of this book. The argument which is meant to be the backbone of the book is of the kind called the *reductio ad absurdum*. It suggests that the results of assuming the rationalist thesis are more irrational than ours; but to prove it we must assume that thesis. Thus in the first section I often treated man as merely an animal, to show that the effect was more impossible than if he were treated as an angel. In the sense in which it was necessary to treat man merely as an animal, it is necessary to treat Christ merely as a man. I have to suspend my own beliefs, which are much more positive; and assume this limitation even in order to remove it. I must try to imagine what would happen to a man who did really read the story of Christ as the story of a man; and even of a man of whom he had never heard before. And I wish to point out that a really impartial reading of that kind would lead, if not immediately to belief, at least to a bewilderment of which there is really no solution except in belief. In this chapter, for this reason, I shall bring in nothing of the spirit of my own creed; I shall exclude the very style of diction, and even of lettering, which I should think fitting in speaking in my own person. I am speaking as an imaginary heathen human being, honestly staring at the gospel story for the first time.

Now it is not at all easy to regard the New Testament as a

New Testament. It is not at all easy to realize the good news as new. Both for good and evil familiarity fills us with assumptions and associations; and no man of our civilization, whatever he thinks of our religion, can really read the thing as if he had never heard of it before. Of course it is in any case utterly unhistorical to talk as if the New Testament were a neatly bound book that had fallen from heaven. It is simply the selection made by the authority of the Church from a mass of early Christian literature. But apart from any such question, there is a psychological difficulty in feeling the New Testament as new. There is a psychological difficulty in seeing those well-known words simply as they stand and without going beyond what they intrinsically stand for. And this difficulty must indeed be very great; for the result of it is very curious. The result of it is that most modern critics and most current criticism, even popular criticism, makes a comment that is the exact reverse of the truth. It is so completely the reverse of the truth that one could almost suspect that they had never read the New Testament at all.

We have all heard people say a hundred times over, for they seem never to tire of saying it, that the Jesus of the New Testament is indeed a most merciful and humane lover of humanity, but that the Church has hidden this human character in repellent dogmas and stiffened it with ecclesiastical terrors till it has taken on an inhuman character. This is, I venture to repeat, very nearly the reverse of the truth. The truth is that it is the image of Christ in the churches that is almost entirely mild and merciful. It is the image of Christ in the Gospels that is a good many other things as well. The figure in the Gospels does indeed utter in words of almost heart-breaking beauty His pity for our broken hearts. But they are very far from being the only sort of words that He utters. Nevertheless they are almost the only kind of words that the Church in her popular imagery ever represents Him as uttering. That popular imagery is inspired by a perfectly sound popular instinct. The mass of the poor are broken, and the mass of the people are poor, and for the mass of mankind the main thing is to carry the conviction of the incredible compassion of God. But nobody with his eyes open can doubt that it is chiefly this idea of compassion that the popular machinery of the Church does seek to carry. The popular imagery carries a great deal to excess the sentiment of 'Gentle Jesus, meek and mild'. It is the first thing that the outsider feels and criticizes in a *pietà* or a shrine of the Sacred Heart. As I say, while the art may be insufficient, I am not sure that the instinct is unsound. In any case there is something appalling, something that makes the blood run cold, in the idea of having a statue of Christ in wrath. There is something insupportable even to the imagination in the idea of turning the corner of a street or coming out into the spaces of a market-place to meet the petrifying petrifaction of *that* figure as it turned upon a generation of vipers, or that face as it looked at the face of a hypocrite. The Church can reasonably be justified therefore if she turns the most merciful face or aspect towards men; but it is certainly the most merciful aspect that she does turn. And the point is here that it is very much more specially and exclusively merciful than any impression that could be formed by a man merely reading the New Testament for the first time. A man simply taking the words of the story as they stand would form quite another impression; an impression full of mystery and possibly of inconsistency; but certainly not merely an impression of mildness. It would be intensely interesting; but part of the interest would consist in its leaving a good deal to be guessed at or explained. It is full of sudden gestures evidently significant except that we hardly know what they signify; of enigmatic silences; of ironical replies. The outbreaks of wrath, like storms above our atmosphere, do not seem to break out exactly where we should expect them, but to follow some higher weather chart of their own. The Peter whom popular

Church teaching presents is very rightly the Peter to whom Christ said in forgiveness, 'Feed my lambs.' He is not the Peter upon whom Christ turned as if he were the devil, crying in that obscure wrath, 'Get thee behind Me, Satan.' Christ lamented with nothing but love and pity over Jerusalem which was to murder Him. We do not know what strange spiritual atmosphere or spiritual insight led Him to sink Bethsaida lower in the pit than Sodom. I am putting aside for the moment all questions of doctrinal inferences or expositions, orthodox or otherwise; I am simply imagining the effect on a man's mind if he did really do what these critics are always talking about doing; if he did really read the New Testament without reference to orthodoxy and even without reference to doctrine. He would find a number of things which fit in far less with the current unorthodoxy than they do with the current orthodoxy. He would find, for instance, that if there are any descriptions that deserved to be called realistic, they are precisely the descriptions of the supernatural. If there is one aspect of the New Testament Jesus in which He may be said to present Himself eminently as a practical person, it is in the aspect of an exorcist. There is nothing meek and mild, there is nothing even in the ordinary sense mystical, about the tone of the voice that says, 'Hold thy peace and come out of him.' It is much more like the tone of a very business-like lion tamer or a strong-minded doctor dealing with a homicidal maniac. But this is only a side issue for the sake of illustration; I am not now raising these controversies, but considering the case of the imaginary man from the moon to whom the New Testament is new.

Now the first thing to note is that if we take it merely as a human story, it is in some ways a very strange story. I do not refer here to its tremendous and tragic culmination or to any implications involving triumph in that tragedy. I do not refer to what is commonly called the miraculous element; for on that point philosophies vary and modern philosophies very decidedly waver. Indeed the educated Englishman of today may be said to have passed from an old fashion, in which he would not believe in any miracles unless they were ancient, and adopted a new fashion in which he will not believe in any miracles unless they are modern. He used to hold that miraculous cures stopped with the first Christians and is now inclined to suspect that they began with the first Christian Scientists. But I refer here rather specially to unmiraculous and even to unnoticed and inconspicuous parts of the story. There are a great many things about it which nobody would have invented, for they are things that nobody has ever made any particular use of; things which if they were remarked at all have remained rather as puzzles. For instance, there is that long stretch of silence in the life of Christ up to the age of thirty. It is of all silences the most immense and imaginatively impressive. But it is not the sort of thing that anybody is particularly likely to invent in order to prove something; and nobody so far as I know has ever tried to prove anything in particular from it. It is impressive, but it is only impressive as a fact; there is nothing particularly popular or obvious about it as a fable. The ordinary trend of hero worship and myth making is much more likely to say the precise opposite. It is much more likely to say (as I believe some of the gospels rejected by the Church do say) that Jesus displayed a divine precocity and began His mission at a miraculously early age. And there is indeed something strange in the thought that He who of all humanity needed least preparation seems to have had most. Whether it was some mode of the divine humility, or some truth of which we see the shadow in the longer domestic tutelage of the higher creatures of the earth, I do not propose to speculate; I mention it simply as an example of the sort of thing that does in any case give rise to speculations, quite apart from recognized religious speculations. Now the whole story is full of these things. It is not by any means, as baldly presented in print, a story that it is easy to get to the bottom of. It is anything but what these people talk of as a simple Gospel. Relatively speaking, it is the Gospel that has the mysticism and the Church that has the rationalism. As I should put it, of course, it is the Gospel that is the riddle and the Church that is the answer. But whatever be the answer, the Gospel as it stands is almost a book of riddles.

First, a man reading the gospel sayings would not find platitudes. If he had read even in the most respectful spirit the majority of ancient philosophers and of modern moralists, he would appreciate the unique importance of saying that he did not find platitudes. It is more than can be said even of Plato. It is much more than can be said of Epictetus or Seneca or Marcus Aurelius or Apollonius of Tyana. And it is immeasurably more than can be said of most of the agnostic moralists and the preachers of the ethical societies; with their songs of service and their religion of brotherhood. The morality of most moralists, ancient and modern, has been one solid and polished cataract of platitudes flowing for ever and ever. That would certainly not be the impression of the imaginary independent outsider studying the New Testament. He would be conscious of nothing so commonplace and in a sense of nothing so continuous as that stream. He would find a number of strange claims that might sound like the claim to be the brother of the sun and moon; a number of very startling pieces of advice; a number of stunning rebukes; a number of strangely beautiful stories. He would see some very gigantesque figures of speech about the impossibility of threading a needle with a camel or the possibility of throwing a mountain into the sea. He would see a number of very daring simplifications of the difficulties of life; like the advice to shine upon everybody indifferently as does the sunshine or not to worry about the future any more than the birds. He would find on the other hand some passages of almost impenetrable darkness, so far as he is concerned, such as the moral of the parable of the Unjust Steward. Some of these things might strike him as fables and some as truths; but none as truisms. For instance, he would not find the ordinary platitudes in favour of peace. He would find several paradoxes in favour of peace. He would find several ideals of non-resistance, which taken as they stand would be rather too pacific for any pacifist. He would be told in one passage to treat a robber *not* with passive resistance, but rather with positive and enthusiastic encouragement, if the terms be taken literally; heaping up gifts upon the man who had stolen goods. But he would not find a word of all that obvious rhetoric against war which has filled countless books and odes and orations; not a word about the wickedness of war, the wastefulness of war, the appalling scale of the slaughter in war and all the rest of the familiar frenzy; indeed not a word about war at all. There is nothing that throws any particular light on Christ's attitude towards organized warfare, except that He seems to have been rather fond of Roman soldiers. Indeed it is another perplexity, speaking from the same external and human standpoint, that He seems to have got on much better with Romans than He did with Jews. But the question here is a certain tone to be appreciated by merely reading a certain text; and we might give any number of instances of it.

The statement that the meek shall inherit the earth is very far from being a meek statement. I mean it is not meek in the ordinary sense of mild and moderate and inoffensive. To justify it, it would be necessary to go very deep into history and anticipate things undreamed of then and by many unrealized even now; such as the way in which the mystical monks reclaimed the lands which the practical kings had lost. If it was a truth at all, it was because it was a prophecy. But certainly it was not a truth in the sense of a truism. The blessing upon the meek would seem to be a very violent statement; in the sense of doing violence to reason and probability. And with this we come to another important stage in the speculation. As a prophecy it really was fulfilled; but it was only fulfilled long afterwards. The monasteries were the most practical and prosperous estates and experiments in reconstruction after the barbaric deluge; the meek did really inherit the earth. But nobody could have known anything of the sort at the time – unless indeed there was One who knew. Something of the same thing may be said about the incident of Martha and Mary; which has been interpreted in retrospect and from the inside by the mystics of the Christian contemplative life. But it was not at all an obvious view of it; and most moralists, ancient and modern, could be trusted to make a rush for the obvious. What torrents of effortless eloquence would have flowed from them to swell any slight superiority on the part of Martha; what splendid sermons about the Joy of Service and the Gospel of Work and the World Left Better Than We Found It, and generally all the ten thousand platitudes that can be uttered in favour of taking trouble – by people who need take no trouble to utter them. If in Mary the mystic and child of love Christ was guarding the seed of something more subtle, who was likely to understand it at the time? Nobody else could have seen Clare and Catherine and Teresa shining above the little roof at Bethany. It is so in another way with that magnificent menace about bringing into the world a sword to sunder and divide. Nobody could have guessed then either how it could be fulfilled or how it could be justified. Indeed some free thinkers are still so simple as to fall into the trap and be shocked at a phrase so deliberately defiant. They actually complain of the paradox for not being a platitude.

But the point here is that if we *could* read the gospel reports as things as new as newspaper reports, they would puzzle us and perhaps terrify us much *more* than the same things as developed by historical Christianity. For instance: Christ after a clear allusion to the eunuchs of eastern courts, said these would be eunuchs of the kingdom of heaven. If this does not mean the voluntary enthusiasm of virginity, it could only be made to mean something much more unnatural or uncouth. It is the historical religion that humanizes it for us by experience of Franciscans or of Sisters of Mercy. The mere statement standing by itself might very well suggest a rather dehumanized atmosphere; the sinister and inhuman silence of the Asiatic harem and divan. This is but one instance out of scores; but the moral is that the Christ of the Gospel might actually seem more strange and terrible than the Christ of the Church.

I am dwelling on the dark and dazzling or defiant or mysterious side of the gospel words, not because they had not obviously a more obvious and popular side, but because this is the answer to a common criticism on a vital point. The free thinker frequently says that Jesus of Nazareth was a man of His time, even if He was in advance of His time; and that we cannot accept His ethics as final for humanity. The free thinker then goes on to criticize His ethics, saying plausibly enough that men cannot turn the other cheek, or that they must take thought for the morrow, or that the self-denial is too ascetic or the monogamy too severe. But the Zealots and the Legionaries did not turn the other cheek any more than we do, if so much. The Jewish traders and Roman tax gatherers took thought for the morrow as much as we, if not more. We cannot pretend to be abandoning the morality of the past for one more suited to the present. It is certainly not the morality of another age, but it might be of another world.

In short, we can say that these ideals are impossible in themselves. Exactly what we cannot say is that they are impossible for us. They are rather notably marked by a mysticism which, if it be a sort of madness, would always have struck the same sort of people as mad. Take, for instance, the case of marriage and the relations of the sexes. It might very well have been true that a Galilean teacher taught things natural to a Galilean environment; but it is not. It might rationally be expected that a man in the time of Tiberius would have advanced a view conditioned by the time of Tiberius;

but he did not. What He advanced was something quite different; something very difficult; but something no more difficult now than it was then. When, for instance, Mahomet made his polygamous compromise we may reasonably say that it was conditioned by a polygamous society. When he allowed a man four wives he was really doing something suited to the circumstances, which might have been less suited to other circumstances. Nobody will pretend that the four wives were like the four winds, something seemingly a part of the order of nature; nobody will say that the figure four was written for ever in stars upon the sky. But neither will anyone say that the figure four is an inconceivable ideal; that it is beyond the power of the mind of man to count up to four; or to count the number of his wives and see whether it amounts to four. It is a practical compromise carrying with it the character of a particular society. If Muhammad had been born in Acton in the nineteenth century, we may well doubt whether he would instantly have filled that suburb with harems of four wives apiece. As he was born in Arabia in the sixth century, he did in his conjugal arrangements suggest the conditions of Arabia in the sixth century. But Christ in His view of marriage does not in the least suggest the conditions of Palestine in the first century. He does not suggest anything at all, except the sacramental view of marriage as developed long afterwards by the Catholic Church. It was quite as difficult for people then as for people now. It was much more puzzling to people then than to people now. Jews and Romans and Greeks did not believe, and did not even understand enough to disbelieve, the mystical idea that the man and the woman had become one sacramental substance. We may think it an incredible or impossible ideal; but we cannot think it any more incredible or impossible than they would have thought it. In other words, whatever else is true, it is not true that the controversy has been altered by time. Whatever else is true, it is emphatically not true that the ideas of Jesus of

Nazareth were suitable to His time, but are no longer suitable to our time. Exactly how suitable they were to His time is perhaps suggested in the end of His story.

The same truth might be stated in another way by saying that if the story be regarded as merely human and historical, it is extraordinary how very little there is in the recorded words of Christ that ties Him at all to His own time. I do not mean the details of a period, which even a man of the period knows to be passing. I mean the fundamentals which even the wisest man often vaguely assumes to be eternal. For instance, Aristotle was perhaps the wisest and most wide-minded man who ever lived. He founded himself entirely upon fundamentals, which have been generally found to remain rational and solid through all social and historical changes. Still, he lived in a world in which it was thought as natural to have slaves as to have children. And therefore he did permit himself a serious recognition of a difference between slaves and free men. Christ as much as Aristotle lived in a world that took slavery for granted. He did not particularly denounce slavery. He started a movement that could exist in a world with slavery. But He started a movement that could exist in a world without slavery. He never used a phrase that made His philosophy depend even upon the very existence of the social order in which He lived. He spoke as one conscious that everything was ephemeral, including the things that Aristotle thought eternal. By that time the Roman Empire had come to be merely the *orbis terrarum*, another name for the world. But He never made His morality dependent on the existence of the Roman Empire or even on the existence of the world. 'Heaven and earth shall pass away; but my words shall not pass away.'

The truth is that when critics have spoken of the local limitations of the Galilean, it has always been a case of the local limitations of the critics. He did undoubtedly believe in certain things that one particular modern sect of materialists do not believe. But they were not things particularly peculiar to His time. It would be nearer the truth to say that the denial of them is quite peculiar to our time. Doubtless it would be nearer still to the truth to say merely that a certain solemn social importance, in the minority disbelieving them, is peculiar to our time. He believed, for instance, in evil spirits or in the psychic healing of bodily ills; but not because He was a Galilean born under Augustus. It is absurd to say that a man believed things because he was a Galilean under Augustus when he might have believed the same things if he had been an Egyptian under Tutankhamun or an Indian under Genghis Khan. But with this general question of the philosophy of diabolism or of divine miracles I deal elsewhere. It is enough to say that the materialists have to prove the impossibility of miracles against the testimony of all mankind, not against the prejudices of provincials in North Palestine under the first Roman Emperors. What they have to prove, for the present argument, is the presence in the gospels of those particular prejudices of those particular provincials. And, humanly speaking, it is astonishing how little they can produce even to make a beginning of proving it.

So it is in this case of the sacrament of marriage. We may not believe in sacraments, as we may not believe in spirits, but it is quite clear that Christ believed in this sacrament in His own way and not in any current or contemporary way. He certainly did not get His argument against divorce from the Mosaic law or the Roman law or the habits of the Palestinian people. It would appear to His critics then exactly what it appears to His critics now: an arbitrary and transcendental dogma coming from nowhere save in the sense that it came from Him. I am not at all concerned here to defend that dogma; the point here is that it is just as easy to defend it now as it was to defend it then. It is an ideal altogether outside time; difficult at any period; impossible at no period. In other words, if anyone says it is what might be expected of a man walking about in that place at that period, we can quite fairly answer that it is much *more* like what might be the mysterious utterance of a being beyond man, if he walked alive among men.

I maintain therefore that a man reading the New Testament frankly and freshly would *not* get the impression of what is now often meant by a human Christ. The merely human Christ is a made-up figure, a piece of artificial selection, like the merely evolutionary man. Moreover there have been too many of these human Christs found in the same story, just as there have been too many keys to mythology found in the same stories. Three or four separate schools of rationalism have worked over the ground and produced three or four equally rational explanations of His life. The first rational explanation of His life was that He never lived. And this in turn gave an opportunity for three or four different explanations; as that He was a sun-myth or a corn-myth, or any other kind of myth that is also a monomania. Then the idea that He was a divine being who did not exist gave place to the idea that He was a human being who did exist. In my youth it was the fashion to say that He was merely an ethical teacher in the manner of the Essenes, who had apparently nothing very much to say that Hillel or a hundred other Jews might not have said; as that it is a kindly thing to be kind and an assistance to purification to be pure. Then somebody said He was a madman with a Messianic delusion. Then others said He was indeed an original teacher because He cared about nothing but Socialism; or (as others said) about nothing but Pacifism. Then a more grimly scientific character appeared who said that Jesus would never have been heard of at all except for His prophecies of the end of the world. He was important merely as a Millennarian like Dr Cumming; and created a provincial scare by announcing the exact date of the crack of doom. Among other variants on the same theme was the theory that He was a spiritual healer and nothing else; a view implied by Christian Science, which has really to expound a Christianity without the Crucifixion in order to explain the curing of Peter's wife's mother or the daughter of a centurion. There is another theory that concentrates entirely on the business of diabolism and what it would call the contemporary superstition about demoniacs; as if Christ, like a young deacon taking his first orders, had got as far as exorcism and never got any further. Now each of these explanations in itself seems to me singularly inadequate; but taken together they do suggest something of the very mystery which they miss. There must surely have been something not only mysterious but many-sided about Christ if so many smaller Christs can be carved out of Him. If the Christian Scientist is satisfied with Him as a spiritual healer, and the Christian Socialist is satisfied with Him as a social reformer, so satisfied that they do not even expect Him to be anything else, it looks as if He really covered rather more ground than they could be expected to expect. And it does seem to suggest that there might be more than they fancy in these other mysterious attributes of casting out devils or prophesying doom.

Above all, would not such a new reader of the New Testament stumble over something that would startle him much more than it startles us? I have here more than once attempted the rather impossible task of reversing time and the historic method; and in fancy looking forward to the facts, instead of backward through the memories. So I have imagined the monster that man might have seemed at first to the mere nature around Him. We should have a worse shock if we really imagined the nature of Christ named for the first time. What should we feel at the first whisper of a certain suggestion about a certain man? Certainly it is not for us to blame anybody who should find that first wild whisper merely impious and insane. On the contrary, stumbling on that rock of scandal is the first step. Stark staring incredulity is a far more loyal tribute to that truth than a modernist metaphysic that would make it out merely a matter of degree. It were better to rend our robes with a great cry against blasphemy, like Caiaphas in the judgement, or to lay hold of the man as a maniac possessed of devils like the kinsmen and the crowd, rather than to stand stupidly debating fine shades of pantheism in the presence of so catastrophic a claim. There is more of the wisdom that is one with surprise in any simple person, full of the sensitiveness of simplicity, who should expect the grass to wither and the birds to drop dead out of the air, when a strolling carpenter's apprentice said calmly and almost carelessly, like one looking over His shoulder: 'Before Abraham was, I am.'

The Everlasting Man, 1925

The Strangest Story in the World

Even in the matter of mere literary style, if we suppose ourselves thus sufficiently detached to look at it in that light, there is a curious quality to which no critic seems to have done justice. It had among other things a singular air of piling tower upon tower by the use of the *a fortiori*; making a pagoda of degrees like the seven heavens. I have already noted that almost inverted imaginative vision which pictured the impossible penance of the Cities of the Plain. There is perhaps nothing so perfect in all language or literature as the use of these three degrees in the parable of the lilies of the field; in which He seems first to take one small flower in His hand and note its simplicity and even its impotence; then suddenly expands it in flamboyant colours into all the palaces and pavilions full of a great name in national legend and national glory; and then, by yet a third overturn, shrivels it to nothing once more with a gesture as if flinging it away '... and if God so clothes the grass that today is and tomorrow is cast into the oven – how much more ...' It is like the building of a good Babel tower by white magic in a moment and in the movement of a hand; a tower heaved suddenly up to heaven on the top of which can be seen afar off, higher than we had fancied possible, the figure of man; lifted by three infinities above all other things, on a starry ladder of light logic and swift imagination. Merely in a literary sense it would be more of a masterpiece than most of the masterpieces in the libraries; yet it seems to have been uttered almost at random while a man might pull a flower. But merely in a literary sense also, this use of the comparative in several degrees has about it a quality which seems to me to hint of much higher things than the modern suggestion of the simple teaching of pastoral or communal ethics. There is nothing that really indicates a subtle and in the true sense a superior mind so much as this power of comparing a lower thing with a higher and yet that higher with a higher still; of thinking on three planes at once. There is nothing that wants the rarest sort of wisdom so much as to see, let us say, that the citizen is higher than the slave and yet that the soul is infinitely higher than the citizen or the city. It is not by any means a faculty that commonly belongs to these simplifiers of the Gospel; those who insist on what they call a simple morality and others call a sentimental morality. It is not at all covered by those who are content to tell everybody to remain at peace. On the contrary, there is a very striking example of it in the apparent inconsistency between Christ's sayings about peace and about a sword. It is precisely this power which perceives that while a good peace is better than a good war, even a good war is better than a bad peace. These far-flung comparisons are nowhere so common as in the Gospels; and to me they suggest something very vast. So a thing solitary and solid, with the added dimension of depth or height, might tower over the flat creatures living only on a plane.

This quality of something that can only be called subtle and superior, something that is capable of long views and even of double meanings, is not noted here merely as a counterblast to the commonplace exaggerations of amiability and mild idealism. It is also to be noted in connection with the more tremendous truth touched upon at the end of the last chapter. For this is the very last character that commonly goes with mere megalomania; especially such steep and staggering megalomania as might be involved in that claim. This quality that can only be called intellectual distinction is not, of course, an evidence of divinity. But it is an evidence of a probable distaste for vulgar and vainglorious claims to divinity. A man of that sort, if he were only a man, would be the last man in the world to suffer from that intoxication by one notion from nowhere in particular, which is the mark of the self-deluding sensationalist in religion. Nor is it even avoided by denying that Christ did make this claim. Of no such man as that, of no other prophet or philosopher of the same intellectual order, would it be even possible to pretend that he had made it. Even if the Church had mistaken His meaning, it would still be true that no other historical tradition except the Church had ever even made the same mistake. Muhammadans did not misunderstand Muhammad and suppose he was Allah. Jews did not misinterpret Moses and identify him with Jehovah. Why was this claim alone exaggerated unless this alone was made? Even if Christianity was one vast universal blunder, it is still a blunder as solitary as the Incarnation.

The purpose of these pages is to fix the falsity of certain vague and vulgar assumptions; and we have here one of the most false. There is a sort of notion in the air everywhere that all the religions are equal because all the religious founders were rivals; that they are all fighting for the same starry crown. It is quite false. The claim to that crown, or anything like that crown, is really so rare as to be unique. Muhammad did not make it any more than Micah or Malachi. Confucius did not make it any more than Plato or Marcus Aurelius. Buddha never said he was Bramah. Zoroaster no more claimed to be Ormuz than to be Ahriman. The truth is that, in the common run of cases, it is just as we should expect it to be, in common sense and certainly in Christian philosophy. It is exactly the other way. Normally speaking, the greater a man is, the less likely he is to make the very greatest claim. Outside the unique case we are considering, the only kind of man who ever does make that kind of claim is a very small man; a secretive or self-centred monomaniac. Nobody can imagine Aristotle claiming to be the father of gods and men, come down from the sky; though we might imagine some insane Roman Emperor like Caligula claiming it for him, or more probably for himself. Nobody can imagine Shakespeare talking as if he were literally divine; though we might imagine some crazy American crank finding it as a cryptogram in Shakespeare's works, or preferably in his own works. It is possible to find here and there human beings who make this supremely superhuman claim. It is possible to find them in lunatic asylums; in padded cells; possibly in strait waistcoats. But what is much more important than their mere materialistic fate in our very materialistic society, under very crude and clumsy laws about lunacy, the type we know as tinged with this, or tending towards it, is a diseased and disproportionate type; narrow yet swollen and morbid to monstrosity. It is by rather an unlucky metaphor that we talk of a madman as cracked; for in a sense he is not cracked enough. He is cramped rather than cracked; there are not enough holes in his head to ventilate it. This impossibility of letting in daylight on a delusion does sometimes cover and conceal a delusion of divinity. It can be found, not among prophets and sages and founders of religions, but only among a low set of lunatics. But this is exactly where the argument becomes intensely interesting; because the argument proves too much. For nobody supposes that Jesus of Nazareth was *that* sort of person. No modern critic in his five wits thinks that the preacher of the Sermon on the Mount was a horrible half-witted imbecile that might be scrawling stars on the walls of a cell. No atheist or blasphemer believes that the author of the Parable of the Prodigal Son was a monster with one mad idea, like a cyclops with one eye. Upon any possible historical criticism he must be put higher in the scale of human beings than that. Yet by all analogy we have really to put him there or else in the highest place of all.

In fact, those who can really take it (as I here hypothetically take it) in a quite dry and detached spirit, have here a most curious and interesting human problem. It is so intensely interesting, considered as a human problem, that it is in a spirit quite disinterested, so to speak, that I wish some of them had turned that intricate human problem into something like an intelligible human portrait. If Christ was simply a human character, He really was a highly complex and contradictory human character. For He combined exactly the two things that lie at the two extremes of human variation. He was exactly what the man with a delusion never is: He was wise; He was a good judge. What He said was always unexpected; but it was always unexpectedly magnanimous and often unexpectedly moderate. Take a thing like the point of the parable of the tares and the wheat. It has the quality that unites sanity and subtlety. It has not the simplicity of a madman. It has not even the simplicity of a fanatic. It might be uttered by a philosopher a hundred years old, at the end of a century of Utopias. Nothing could be less like this quality of seeing beyond and all round obvious things, than the condition of the egomaniac with the one sensitive spot on his brain. I really do not see how these two characters could be convincingly combined, except in the astonishing way in which the creed combines them. For until we reach the full acceptance of the fact as a fact, however marvellous, all mere approximations to it are actually further and further away from it. Divinity is great enough to be divine; it is great enough to call itself divine. But as humanity grows greater, it grows less and less likely to do so. God is God, as the Muslims say; but a great man knows he is not God, and the greater he is the better he knows it. That is the paradox; everything that is merely approaching to that point is merely receding from it. Socrates, the wisest man, knows that he knows nothing. A lunatic may think he is omniscience, and a fool may talk as if he were omniscient. But Christ is in another sense omniscient if he not only knows, but knows that he knows.

Even on the purely human and sympathetic side, therefore, the Jesus of the New Testament seems to me to have in a great many ways the note of something superhuman; that is, of something human and more than human. But there is another quality running through all His teachings which seems to me neglected in most modern talk about them as teachings; and that is the persistent suggestion that He has not really come to teach. If there is one incident in the record which affects me personally as grandly and gloriously human, it is the incident of giving wine for the wedding feast. That is really human in the sense in which a whole crowd of prigs, having the appearance of human beings, can hardly be described as human. It rises superior to all superior persons. It is as human as Herrick and as democratic as Dickens. But even in that story there is something else that has that note of things not fully explained; and in a way here very relevant. I mean the first hesitation, not on any ground touching the nature of the miracle, but on that of the propriety of working any miracles at all, at least at that stage: 'My time is not yet come.' What did that mean? At least it certainly meant a general plan or purpose in the mind, with which certain things did or did not fit in. And if we leave out that solitary strategic plan, we not only leave out the point of the story, but the story.

We often hear of Jesus of Nazareth as a wandering teacher; and there is a vital truth in that view in so far as it emphasizes an attitude towards luxury and convention which most respectable people would still regard as that of a vagabond. It is expressed in His own great saying about the holes of the foxes and the nests of the birds, and, like many of His great sayings, it is felt as less powerful than it is, through lack of appreciation of that great paradox by which He spoke of His own humanity as in some way collectively and representatively human; calling Himself simply the Son of Man; that is, in effect, calling Himself simply Man. It is fitting that the New

Man or the Second Adam should repeat in so ringing a voice and with so arresting a gesture the great fact which came first in the original story: that man differs from the brutes by everything, even by deficiency; that he is in a sense less normal and even less native; a stranger upon the earth. It is well to speak of His wanderings in this sense and in the sense that He shared the drifting life of the most homeless and hopeless of the poor. It is assuredly well to remember that He would quite certainly have been moved on by the police, and almost certainly arrested by the police, for having no visible means of subsistence. For our law has in it a turn of humour or touch of fancy which Nero and Herod never happened to think of; that of actually punishing homeless people for not sleeping at home.

But in another sense the word 'wandering' as applied to His life is a little misleading. As a matter of fact, a great many of the pagan sages and not a few of the pagan sophists might truly be described as wandering teachers. In some of them their rambling journeys were not altogether without a parallel in their rambling remarks. Apollonius of Tyana, who figured in some fashionable cults as a sort of ideal philosopher, is represented as rambling as far as the Ganges and Ethiopia, more or less talking all the time. There was actually a school of philosophers called the Peripatetics; and most even of the great philosophers give us a vague impression of having very little to do except to walk and talk. The great conversations which give us our glimpses of the great minds of Socrates or Buddha or even Confucius often seem to be parts of a never-ending picnic; and especially, which is the important point, to have neither beginning nor end. Socrates did indeed find the conversation interrupted by the incident of his execution. But it is the whole point and the whole particular merit, of the position of Socrates that death was only an interruption and an incident. We miss the real moral importance of the great philosopher if we miss that point; that he stares at the executioner with an innocent surprise, and almost an innocent annoyance, at finding anyone so unreasonable as to cut short a little conversation for the elucidation of truth. He is looking for truth and not looking for death. Death is but a stone in the road which can trip him up. His work in life is to wander on the roads of the world and talk about truth for ever. Buddha, on the other hand, did arrest attention by one gesture; it was the gesture of renunciation, and therefore in a sense of denial. But by one dramatic negation he passed into a world of negation that was not dramatic; which he would have been the first to insist was not dramatic. Here again we miss the particular moral importance of the great mystic if we do not see the distinction; that it was his whole point that he had done with drama, which consists of desire and struggle and generally of defeat and disappointment. He passes into peace and lives to instruct others how to pass into it. Henceforth his life is that of the ideal philosopher; certainly a far more really ideal philosopher than Apollonius of Tyana; but still a philosopher in the sense that it is not his business to do anything but rather to explain everything; in his case, we might almost say, mildly and softly to explode everything. For the messages are basically different. Christ said, 'Seek first the kingdom, and all these things shall be added unto you.' Buddha said, 'Seek first the kingdom, and then you will need none of these things.'

Now, compared to these wanderers the life of Jesus went as swift and straight as a thunderbolt. It was above all things dramatic; it did above all things consist in doing something that had to be done. It emphatically would not have been done if Jesus had walked about the world for ever doing nothing except tell the truth. And even the external movement of it must not be described as a wandering in the sense of forgetting that it was a journey. This is where it was a fulfilment of the myths rather than of the philosophies; it is a journey with a goal and an object, like Jason going to find the

Golden Fleece, or Hercules the golden apples of the Hesperides. The gold that He was seeking was death. The primary thing that He was going to do was to die. He was going to do other things equally definite and objective; we might almost say equally external and material. But from first to last the most definite fact is that He is going to die. No two things could possibly be more different than the death of Socrates and the death of Christ. We are meant to feel that the death of Socrates was, from the point of view of his friends at least, a stupid muddle and miscarriage of justice interfering with the flow of a humane and lucid, I had almost said a light, philosophy. We are meant to feel that Death was the bride of Christ as Poverty was the bride of St Francis. We are meant to feel that His life was in that sense a sort of love affair with death, a romance of the pursuit of the ultimate sacrifice. From the moment when the star goes up like a birthday rocket to the moment when the sun is extinguished like a funeral torch, the whole story moves on wings with the speed and direction of a drama, ending in an act beyond words.

Therefore the story of Christ is the story of a journey, almost in the manner of a military march; certainly in the manner of the quest of a hero moving to his achievement or his doom. It is a story that begins in the paradise of Galilee, a pastoral and peaceful land having really some hint of Eden, and gradually climbs the rising country into the mountains that are nearer to the storm clouds and the stars, as to a Mountain of Purgatory. He may be met as if straying in strange places, or stopped on the way for discussion or dispute; but His face is set towards the mountain city. That is the meaning of that great culmination when He crested the ridge and stood at the turning of the road and suddenly cried aloud, lamenting over Jerusalem. Some light touch of that lament is in every patriotic poem; or if it is absent, the patriotism stinks with vulgarity. That is the meaning of the stirring and startling incident at the gates of the Temple, when the tables were hurled like lumber down the steps, and the rich merchants driven forth with bodily blows; the incident that must be at least as much of a puzzle to the pacifists as any paradox about non-resistance can be to any of the militarists. I have compared the quest to the journey of Jason, but we must never forget that in a deeper sense it is rather to be compared to the journey of Ulysses. It was not only a romance of travel but a romance of return; and of the end of a usurpation. No healthy boy reading the story regards the rout of the Ithacan suitors as anything but a happy ending. But there are doubtless some who regard the rout of the Jewish merchants and money-changers with that refined repugnance which never fails to move them in the presence of violence, and especially of violence against the well-to-do. The point here, however, is that all these incidents have in them a character of mounting crisis. In other words, these incidents are not incidental. When Apollonius the ideal philosopher is brought before the judgement seat of Domitian and vanishes by magic, the miracle is entirely incidental. It might have occurred at any time in the wandering life of the Tyanean; indeed, I believe it is doubtful in date as well as in substance. The ideal philosopher merely vanished, and resumed his ideal existence somewhere else for an indefinite period. It is characteristic of the contrast perhaps that Apollonius was supposed to have lived to an almost miraculous old age. Jesus of Nazareth was less prudent in His miracles. When Jesus was brought before the judgement seat of Pontius Pilate, He did not vanish. It was the crisis and the goal; it was the hour and the power of darkness. It was the supremely supernatural act, of all His miraculous life, that He did not vanish.

Every attempt to amplify that story has diminished it. The task has been attempted by many men of real genius and eloquence as well as by only too many vulgar sentimentalists and self-conscious rhetoricians. The tale has been retold with

patronizing pathos by elegant sceptics and with fluent enthusiasm by boisterous best-sellers. It will not be retold here. The
grinding power of the plain words of the Gospel story is like
the power of millstones; and those who can read them simply
enough will feel as if rocks had been rolled upon them.
Criticism is only words about words; and of what use are words
about such words as these? What is the use of word-painting
about the dark garden filled suddenly with torchlight and
furious faces? 'Are you come out with swords and staves as
against a robber? All day I sat in your temple teaching, and you
took me not.' Can anything be added to the massive and gathered restraint of that irony; like a great wave lifted to the sky
and refusing to fall? 'Daughters of Jerusalem, weep not for me,
but weep for yourselves and for your children.' As the High
Priest asked what further need he had of witnesses, we might
well ask what further need we have of words. Peter in a panic
repudiated Him: 'and immediately the cock crew; and Jesus
looked upon Peter, and Peter went out and wept bitterly.' Has
anyone any further remarks to offer? Just before the murder
He prayed for all the murderous race of men, saying, 'They
know not what they do'; is there anything to say to that, except
that we know as little what we say? Is there any need to repeat
and spin out the story of how the tragedy trailed up the Via
Dolorosa and how they threw Him in haphazard with two
thieves in one of the ordinary batches of execution; and how in
all that horror and howling wilderness of desertion one voice
spoke in homage, a startling voice from the very last place
where it was looked for, the gibbet of the criminal; and he said
to that nameless ruffian, 'This night shalt thou be with me in
Paradise'? Is there anything to put after that but a full stop? Or
is any one prepared to answer adequately that farewell gesture
to all flesh which created for His Mother a new Son?

It is more within my powers, and here more immediately
to my purpose, to point out that in that scene were symbolically gathered all the human forces that have been vaguely

sketched in this story. As kings and philosophers and the popular element had been symbolically present at His birth, so they were more practically concerned in His death; and with that we come face to face with the essential fact to be realized. All the great groups that stood about the Cross represent in one way or another the great historical truth of the time: that the world could not save itself. Man could do no more. Rome and Jerusalem and Athens and everything else were going down like a sea turned into a slow cataract. Externally indeed the ancient world was still at its strongest; it is always at that moment that the inmost weakness begins. But in order to understand that weakness we must repeat what has been said more than once: that it was not the weakness of a thing originally weak. It was emphatically the strength of the world that was turned to weakness, and the wisdom of the world that was turned to folly.

In this story of Good Friday it is the best things in the world that are at their worst. That is what really shows us the world at its worst. It was, for instance, the priests of a true monotheism and the soldiers of an international civilization. Rome, the legend, founded upon fallen Troy and triumphant over fallen Carthage, had stood for a heroism which was the nearest that any pagan ever came to chivalry. Rome had defended the household gods and the human decencies against the ogres of Africa and the hermaphrodite monstrosities of Greece. But in the lightning flash of this incident, we see great Rome, the imperial republic, going downward under her Lucretian doom. Scepticism has eaten away even the confident sanity of the conquerors of the world.

But there was present in this ancient population an evil more peculiar to the ancient world. We have noted it already as the neglect of the individual, even of the individual voting the condemnation and still more of the individual condemned. It was the soul of the hive; a heathen thing. The cry of this spirit also was heard in that hour, 'It is well that one man die for the people.' Yet this spirit in antiquity of devotion to the city and to the state had also been in itself and in its time a noble spirit. It had its poets and its martyrs; men still to be honoured for ever. It was failing through its weakness in not seeing the separate soul of a man, the shrine of all mysticism; but it was only failing as everything else was failing. The mob went along with the Sadducees and the Pharisees, the philosophers and the moralists. It went along with the imperial magistrates and the sacred priests, the scribes and the soldiers, that the one universal human spirit might suffer a universal condemnation; that there might be one deep, unanimous chorus of approval and harmony when Man was rejected of men.

There were solitudes beyond where none shall follow. There were secrets in the inmost and invisible part of that drama that have no symbol in speech; or in any severance of a man from men. Nor is it easy for any words less stark and single-minded than those of the naked narrative even to hint at the horror of exaltation that lifted itself above the hill. Endless expositions have not come to the end of it, or even to the beginning. And if there be any sound that can produce a silence, we may surely be silent about the end and the extremity; when a cry was driven out of that darkness in words dreadfully distinct and dreadfully unintelligible, which man shall never understand in all the eternity they have purchased for him; and for one annihilating instant an abyss that is not for our thoughts had opened even in the unity of the absolute; and God had been forsaken of God.

They took the body down from the cross and one of the few rich men among the first Christians obtained permission to bury it in a rock tomb in his garden, the Romans setting a military guard lest there should be some riot and attempt to recover the body. There was once more a natural symbolism in these natural proceedings; it was well that the tomb should be sealed with all the secrecy of ancient eastern sepulture and guarded by the authority of the Caesars.

The Everlasting Man, 1925

The Five Deaths of the Faith

It is not the purpose of this book to trace the subsequent history of Christianity, especially the later history of Christianity; which involves controversies of which I hope to write more fully elsewhere. It is devoted only to the suggestion that Christianity, appearing amid heathen humanity, had all the character of a unique thing and even of a supernatural thing. It was not like any of the other things; and the more we study it the less it looks like any of them. But there is a certain rather peculiar character which marked it henceforward even down to the present moment, with a note on which this book may well conclude.

I have said that Asia and the ancient world had an air of being too old to die. Christendom has had the very opposite fate. Christendom has had a series of revolutions and in each one of them Christianity has died. Christianity has died many times and risen again; for it had a God who knew the way out of the grave. But the first extraordinary fact which marks this history is this: that Europe has been turned upside down over and over again; and that at the end of each of these revolutions the same religion has again been found on top. The Faith is always converting the age, not as an old religion but as a new religion. This truth is hidden from many by a convention that is too little noticed. Curiously enough, it is a convention of the sort which those who ignore it claim especially to detect

and denounce. They are always telling us that priests an
ceremonies are not religion and that religious organization
can be a hollow sham; but they hardly realize how true it is.

The faith is not a survival. It is not as if the Druids had
managed somehow to survive somewhere for two thousand
years. That is what might have happened in Asia or ancient
Europe, in that indifference or tolerance in which mytholo-
gies and philosophies could live for ever side by side. It has not
survived; it has returned again and again in this Western world
of rapid change and institutions perpetually perishing.
Europe, in the tradition of Rome, was always trying revolution and reconstruction; rebuilding a universal republic. And
it always began by rejecting this old stone and ended by
making it the head of the corner; by bringing it back from the
rubbish heap to make it the crown of the capitol. Some stones
of Stonehenge are standing and some are fallen; and as the
stone falleth so shall it lie. There has not been a Druidic
renaissance every century or two, with the young Druids
crowned with fresh mistletoe, dancing in the sun on Salisbury
Plain. Stonehenge has not been rebuilt in every style of architecture from the rude round Norman to the last rococo of
the Baroque. The sacred place of the Druids is safe from the
vandalism of restoration.

But the Church in the West was not in a world where
things were too old to die, but in one in which they were
always young enough to get killed. The consequence was that
superficially and externally she often did get killed; nay, she
sometimes wore out even without getting killed. And there
follows a fact I find it somewhat difficult to describe, yet
which I believe to be very real and rather important. As a
ghost is the shadow of a man, and in that sense the shadow of
life, so at intervals there passed across this endless life a sort of
shadow of death. It came at the moment when it would have
perished had it been perishable. It withered away everything
that was perishable. If such animal parallels were worthy of

the occasion, we might say that the snake shuddered and shed a skin and went on, or even that the cat went into convulsions as it lost only one of its nine hundred and ninety-nine lives. It is truer to say, in a more dignified image, that a clock struck and nothing happened; or that a bell tolled for an execution that was everlastingly postponed.

What was the meaning of all that dim but vast unrest of the twelfth century when, as it has been so finely said, Julian stirred in his sleep? Why did there appear so strangely early, in the twilight of dawn after the Dark Ages, so deep a scepticism as that involved in urging nominalism against realism? For realism against nominalism was really realism against rationalism, or something more destructive than what we call rationalism. The answer is that just as some might have thought the Church simply a part of the Roman Empire, so others later might have thought the Church only a part of the Dark Ages. The Dark Ages ended as the Empire had ended; and the Church should have departed with them, if she had been also one of the shades of night. It was another of those spectral deaths or simulations of death. I mean that if nominalism had succeeded, it would have been as if Arianism had succeeded; it would have been the beginning of a confession that Christianity had failed. For nominalism is a far more fundamental scepticism than mere atheism. Such was the question that was openly asked as the Dark Ages broadened into that daylight that we call the modern world. But what was the answer? The answer was Aquinas in the chair of Aristotle, taking all knowledge for his province; and tens of thousands of lads, down to the lowest ranks of peasant and serf, living in rags and on crusts about the great colleges, to listen to the scholastic philosophy.

In considering the war of the Albigensians, we come to the breach in the heart of Europe and the landslide of a new philosophy that nearly ended Christendom for ever. In that case the new philosophy was also a very new philosophy; it was pessimism. It was none the less like modern ideas because it was as old as Asia; most modern ideas are. It was the Gnostics returning; but why did the Gnostics return? Because it was the end of an epoch, like the end of the Empire; and should have been the end of the Church. It was Schopenhauer hovering over the future; but it was also Manichaeus rising from the dead; that men might have death and that they might have it more abundantly.

The faith has not only often died but it has often died of old age. It has not only been often killed but it has often died a natural death; in the sense of coming to a natural and necessary end. It is obvious that it has survived the most savage and the most universal persecutions from the shock of the Diocletian fury to the shock of the French Revolution. But it has a more strange and even a more weird tenacity; it has survived not only war but peace. It has not only died often but degenerated often and decayed often; it has survived its own weakness and even its own surrender. We need not repeat what is so obvious about the beauty of the end of Christ in its wedding of youth and death. But this is almost as if Christ had lived to the last possible span, had been a white-haired sage of a hundred and died of natural decay, and then had risen again rejuvenated, with trumpets and the rending of the sky. It was said truly enough that human Christianity in its recurrent weakness was sometimes too much wedded to the powers of the world: but if it was wedded it has very often been widowed. It is a strangely immortal sort of widow. An enemy may have said at one moment that it was but an aspect of the power of the Caesars; and it sounds as strange today as to call it an aspect of the Pharaohs. An enemy might say that it was the official faith of feudalism; and it sounds as convincing now as to say that it was bound to perish with the ancient Roman villa. All these things did indeed run their course to its normal end; and there seemed no course for the religion but to end with them. It ended and it began again.

'Heaven and earth shall pass away, but my words shall not pass away.' The civilization of antiquity was the whole world: and men no more dreamed of its ending than of the ending of daylight. They could not imagine another order unless it were in another world. The civilization of the world has passed away and those words have not passed away. In the long night of the Dark Ages feudalism was so familiar a thing that no man could imagine himself without a lord: and religion was so woven into that network that no man would have believed they could be torn asunder. Feudalism itself was torn to rags and rotted away in the popular life of the true Middle Ages; and the first and freshest power in that new freedom was the old religion. Feudalism had passed away, and the words did not pass away. The whole medieval order, in many ways so complete and almost cosmic a home for man, wore out gradually in its turn: and here at least it was thought that the words would die. They went forth across the radiant abyss of the Renaissance and in fifty years were using all its light and learning for new religious foundations, new apologetics, new saints. It was supposed to have been withered up at last in the dry light of the Age of Reason; it was supposed to have disappeared ultimately in the earthquake of the Age of Revolution. Science explained it away; and it was still there. History disinterred it in the past; and it appeared suddenly in the future. Today it stands once more in our path; and even as we watch it, it grows.

If our social relations and records retain their continuity, if men really learn to apply reason to the accumulating facts of so crushing a story, it would seem that sooner or later even its enemies will learn from their incessant and interminable disappointments not to look for anything so simple as its death. They may continue to war with it, but it will be as they war with nature; as they war with the landscape, as they war with the skies. 'Heaven and earth shall pass away, but my words shall not pass away.' They will watch for it to stumble; they will watch for it to err; they will no longer watch for it to end. Insensibly, even unconsciously, they will in their own silent anticipations fulfil the relative terms of that astounding prophecy; they will forget to watch for the mere extinction of what has so often been vainly extinguished; and will learn instinctively to look first for the coming of the comet or the freezing of the star.

The Everlasting Man, 1925

The Aristotelian Revolution

Among the students thronging into the lecture rooms there was one student, conspicuous by his tall and bulky figure, and completely failing or refusing to be conspicuous for anything else. He was so dumb in the debates that his fellows began to assume an American significance in the word dumbness; for in that land it is a synonym for dullness. It is clear that, before long, even his imposing stature began to have only the ignominious immensity of the big boy left behind in the lowest form. He was called the Dumb Ox. He was the object, not merely of mockery, but of pity. One good-natured student pitied him so much as to try to help him with his lessons, going over the elements of logic like an alphabet in a hornbook. The dunce thanked him with pathetic politeness; and the philanthropist went on swimmingly, till he came to a passage about which he was himself a little doubtful; about which, in point of fact, he was wrong. Whereupon the dunce, with every appearance of embarrassment and disturbance, pointed out a possible solution which happened to be right. The benevolent student was left staring, as at a monster, at this mysterious lump of ignorance and intelligence; and strange whispers began to run round the schools.

A regular religious biographer of Thomas Aquinas (who, needless to say, was the dunce in question) has said that by the end of this interview 'his love of truth overcame his humility';

which, properly understood, is precisely true. But it does not, in the secondary psychological and social sense, describe all the welter of elements that went on within that massive head. All the relatively few anecdotes about Aquinas have a very peculiar vividness if we visualize the type of man; and this is an excellent example. Amid those elements was something of the difficulty which the generalizing intellect has in adapting itself suddenly to a tiny detail of daily life; there was something of the shyness of really well-bred people about showing off.

Aquinas was still generally known only as one obscure and obstinately unresponsive pupil, among many more brilliant and promising pupils, when the great Albert broke silence with his famous cry and prophecy: 'You call him a Dumb Ox; I tell you this Dumb Ox shall bellow so loud that his bellowings will fill the world.'

We have all heard of the humility of the man of science; of many who were very genuinely humble; and of some who were very proud of their humility. It will be the somewhat too recurrent burden of this brief study that Thomas Aquinas really did have the humility of the man of science; as a special variant of the humility of the saint. It is true that he did not himself contribute anything concrete in the experiment or detail of physical science; in this, it may be said, he even lagged behind the last generation, and was far less of an experimental scientist than his tutor, Albertus Magnus. But for all that, he was historically a great friend to the freedom of science. The principles he laid down, properly understood, are perhaps the best that can be produced for protecting science from mere obscurantist persecution. For instance: in the matter of the inspiration of Scripture, he fixed first on the obvious fact, which was forgotten by four furious centuries of sectarian battle, that the meaning of Scripture is very far from self-evident; and that we must often interpret it in the light of other truths. If a literal interpretation is really and flatly contradicted by an obvious fact, why then we can only say that the literal interpretation must be a false interpretation. But the fact must really be an obvious fact. And unfortunately, nineteenth-century scientists were just as ready to jump to the conclusion that any guess about nature was an obvious fact, as were seventeenth-century sectarians to jump to the conclusion that any guess about Scripture was the obvious explanation. Thus, private theories about what the Bible ought to mean, and premature theories about what the world ought to mean, have met in loud and widely advertised controversy, especially in the Victorian time; and this clumsy collision of two very impatient forms of ignorance was known as the quarrel of Science and Religion.

But St Thomas had the scientific humility in this very vivid and special sense: that he was ready to take the lowest place, for the examination of the lowest things. He did not, like a modern specialist, study the worm as if it were the world; but he was willing to begin to study the reality of the world in the reality of the worm. His Aristotelianism simply meant that the study of the humblest fact will lead to the study of the highest truth. That for him the process was logical and not biological, was concerned with philosophy rather than science, does not alter the essential idea; that he believed in beginning at the bottom of the ladder. But he also gave, by his view of Scripture and Science, and other questions, a sort of charter for pioneers more purely practical than himself. He practically said that if they could really prove their practical discoveries, the traditional interpretation of Scripture must give way before those discoveries. He could hardly, as the common phrase goes, say fairer than that. If the matter had been left to him, and men like him, there never would have been any quarrel between Science and Religion. He did his very best to map out two provinces for them; and to trace a just frontier between them.

It is often cheerfully remarked that Christianity has failed, by which is meant that it has never had that sweeping, imperial and imposed supremacy, which has belonged to each of the great revolutions, every one of which has subsequently failed. There was never a moment when men could say that every man was a Christian, as they might say for several months that every man was a Royalist or a Republican or a Communist. But if sane historians want to understand the sense in which the Christian character has succeeded, they could not find a better case than the massive moral pressure of a man like St Thomas, in support of the buried rationalism of the heathens, which had as yet only been dug up for the amusement of the heretics. It was, quite strictly and exactly, because a new kind of man was conducting rational enquiry in a new kind of way, that men forgot the curse that had fallen on the temples of the dead demons and the palaces of the dead despots; forgot even the new fury out of Arabia against which they were fighting for their lives; because the man who was asking them to return to sense, or to return to their senses, was not a sophist but a saint. Aristotle had described the magnanimous man, who is great and knows that he is great. But Aristotle would never have recovered his own greatness, but for the miracle that created the more magnanimous man – who is great and knows that he is small.

There is a certain historical importance in what some would call the heaviness of the style employed. It carries a curious impression of candour, which really did have, I think, a considerable effect upon contemporaries. The saint has sometimes been called a sceptic. The truth is that he was very largely tolerated as a sceptic because he was obviously a saint. When he seemed to stand up as a stubborn Aristotelian, hardly distinguishable from the Arabian heretics, I do seriously believe that what protected him was very largely the prodigious power of his simplicity and his obvious goodness and love of truth. Those who went out against the haughty confidence of the heretics were stopped, and brought up all standing, against a sort of huge humility which was like a mountain; or perhaps like that immense valley that is the mould of a mountain.

After the hour of triumph came the moment of peril. It is always so with alliances, and especially because Aquinas was fighting on two fronts. His main business was to defend the faith against the abuse of Aristotle; and he boldly did it by supporting the use of Aristotle. He knew perfectly well that armies of atheists and anarchists were roaring applause in the background at his Aristotelian victory over all he held most dear. Nevertheless, it was never the existence of atheists, any more than Arabs or Aristotelian pagans, that disturbed the extraordinary controversial composure of Thomas Aquinas. The real peril that followed on the victory he had won for Aristotle was vividly presented in the curious case of Siger of Brabant, and it is well worth study for anyone who would begin to comprehend the strange history of Christendom.

Siger of Brabant, following on some of the Arabian Aristotelians, advanced a theory which most modern newspaper readers would instantly have declared to be the same as the theory of St Thomas. That was what finally roused St Thomas to his last and most emphatic protest. He had won his battle for a wider scope of philosophy and science; he had cleared the ground for a general understanding about faith and enquiry, an understanding that has generally been observed among Catholics, and certainly never deserted without disaster. It was the idea that the scientist should go on exploring and experimenting freely, so long as he did not claim an infallibility and finality which it was against his own principles to claim. Meanwhile the Church should go on developing and defining about supernatural things, so long as she did not claim a right to alter the deposit of faith, which it was against her own principles to claim. And when he had said this, Siger of Brabant got up and said something so horribly like it, and so horribly unlike, that (like Anti Christ) he might have deceived the very elect.

Siger of Brabant said this: the Church must be right theologically; but she can be wrong scientifically. There are two truths: the truth of the supernatural world, and the truth of the natural world, which contradicts the supernatural world. While we are being naturalists, we can suppose that Christianity is all nonsense; but then, when we remember that we are Christians, we must admit that Christianity is true even if it is nonsense. In other words, Siger of Brabant split the human head in two, like the blow in an old legend of battle, and declared that a man has two minds, with one of which he must entirely believe and with the other may utterly disbelieve. To many this would at least seem like a parody of Thomism. As a fact, it was the assassination of Thomism. It was not two ways of finding the same truth; it was an untruthful way of pretending that there are two truths. And it is extraordinarily interesting to note that this is the one occasion when the Dumb Ox really came out like a wild bull. When he stood up to answer Siger of Brabant, he was altogether transfigured, and the very style of his sentences, which is a thing like the tone of a man's voice, is suddenly altered. He had never been angry with any of the enemies who disagreed with him. But these enemies had attempted the worst treachery: they had made him agree with them.

Those who complain that theologians draw fine distinctions could hardly find a better example of their own folly. In fact, a fine distinction can be a flat contradiction. It was notably so in this case. St Thomas was willing to allow the one truth to be approached by two paths, precisely *because* he was sure there was only one truth. Because the faith was the one truth, nothing discovered in nature could ultimately contradict the faith. Because the faith was the one truth, nothing really deduced from the faith could ultimately contradict the facts. It was in truth a curiously daring confidence in the reality of his religion. And this last group of enemies suddenly sprang up, to tell him they entirely agreed with him in saying that there are two contradictory truths. Truth, in the medieval phrase, carried two faces under one hood; and these double-faced sophists practically dared to suggest that it was the Dominican hood.

So, in his last battle and for the first time, he fought as with a battle-axe. There is a ring in the words altogether beyond the almost impersonal patience he maintained in debate with so many enemies. 'Behold our refutation of the error. It is not based on documents of faith, but on the reasons and statements of the philosophers themselves. If then anyone there be who, boastfully taking pride in his supposed wisdom, wishes to challenge what we have written, let him not do it in some corner nor before children who are powerless to decide on such difficult matters. Let him reply openly if he dare. He shall find me there confronting him, and not only my negligible self, but many another whose study is truth. We shall do battle with his errors or bring a cure to his ignorance.'

The Dumb Ox is bellowing now; like one at bay and yet terrible and towering over all the baying pack.

St Thomas Aquinas, 1933

A Meditation on the Manichees

This book is meant only to be the sketch of a man; but it must at least lightly touch, later on, upon a method and a meaning; or what our journalism has an annoying way of calling a message. A few very inadequate pages must be given to the man in relation to his theology and his philosophy; but the thing of which I mean to speak here is something at once more general and more personal even than his philosophy. I have therefore introduced it here, before we come to anything like technical talk about his philosophy. It was something that might alternatively be called his moral attitude, or his temperamental predisposition, or the purpose of his life so far as social and human effects were concerned; for he knew better than most of us that there is but one purpose in this life, and it is one that is beyond this life. But if we wanted to put in a picturesque and simplified form what he wanted for the world, and what was his work in history, apart from theoretical and theological definitions, we might well say that it really was to strike a blow and settle the Manichees.

The full meaning of this may not be apparent to those who do not study theological history; and perhaps even less apparent to those who do. Indeed, it may seem equally irrelevant to the history and the theology. In history St Dominic and Simon de Montfort between them had already pretty well settled the Manichees. And in theology, of course, an encyclopaedic doctor like Aquinas dealt with a thousand other heresies besides the Manichean heresy. Nevertheless, it does represent his main position and the turn he gave to the whole history of Christendom.

I think it well to interpose this chapter, though its scope may seem more vague than the rest, because there is a sort of big blunder about St Thomas and his creed, which is an obstacle for most modern people in even beginning to understand them. It arises roughly thus. St Thomas, like other monks, and especially other saints, lived a life of renunciation and austerity; his fasts, for instance, being in marked contrast to the luxury in which he might have lived if he chose. This element stands high in his religion, as a manner of asserting the will against the power of nature, of thanking the Redeemer by partially sharing His sufferings, of making a man ready for anything as a missionary or martyr, and similar ideals. These happen to be rare in the modern industrial society of the West, outside his communion; and it is therefore assumed that they are the whole meaning of that communion. Because it is uncommon for an alderman to fast forty days, or a politician to take a Trappist vow of silence, or a man about town to live a life of strict celibacy, the average outsider is convinced, not only that Catholicism is nothing except asceticism, but that asceticism is nothing except pessimism. He is so obliging as to explain to Catholics why they hold this heroic virtue in respect; and is ever ready to point out that the philosophy behind it is an oriental hatred of anything connected with nature, and a purely Schopenhauerian disgust with the Will to Live. I read in a 'high-class' review of Miss Rebecca West's book on St Augustine, the astounding statement that the Catholic Church regards sex as having the nature of sin. How marriage can be a sacrament if sex is a sin, or why it is the Catholics who are in favour of birth and their foes who are in favour of birth control, I will leave the critic to worry out for himself. My concern is not with that part of the argument, but with another.

The ordinary modern critic, seeing this ascetic ideal in an authoritative Church, and not seeing it in most other inhabitants of Brixton or Brighton, is apt to say, 'This is the result of Authority; it would be better to have Religion without Authority.' But in truth, a wider experience outside Brixton or Brighton would reveal the mistake. It is rare to find a fasting alderman or a Trappist politician; but it is still more rare to see nuns suspended in the air on hooks or spikes; it is unusual for a Catholic Truth Society orator in Hyde Park to begin his speech by gashing himself all over with knives; a stranger calling at an ordinary presbytery will seldom find the parish priest lying on the floor with a fire lighted on his chest and scorching him, while he utters spiritual ejaculations. Yet all these things are done all over Asia, for instance, by voluntary enthusiasts acting solely on the great impulse of Religion; of Religion, in their case, not commonly imposed by any immediate Authority; and certainly not imposed by this particular Authority. In short, a real knowledge of mankind will tell anybody that Religion is a very terrible thing; that it is truly a raging fire; and that Authority is often quite as much needed to restrain it as to impose it.

Now, nobody will begin to understand the Thomist philosophy, or indeed the Catholic philosophy, who does not realize that the primary and fundamental part of it is entirely the praise of Life; the praise of Being; the praise of God as the Creator of the World. Everything else follows a long way after that, being conditioned by various complications like the Fall or the vocation of heroes. The trouble occurs because the Catholic mind moves upon two planes; that of the Creation and that of the Fall. The nearest parallel is, for instance, that of England invaded; there might be strict martial law in Kent because the enemy had landed in Kent, and relative liberty in Hereford; but this would not affect the affection of an English patriot for Hereford or Kent, and strategic caution in Kent would not affect the love of Kent. For the love of England would remain, both of the parts to be redeemed by discipline and the parts to be enjoyed in liberty. Any extreme of Catholic asceticism is a wise, or unwise, precaution against the evil of the Fall; it is *never* a doubt about the good of the Creation. And *that* is where it really does differ, not only from the rather excessive eccentricity of the gentleman who hangs himself on hooks, but from the whole cosmic theory which is the hook on which he hangs. In the case of many oriental religions, it really is true that the asceticism is pessimism; that the ascetic tortures himself to death out of an abstract hatred of life; that he does not merely mean to control nature as he should, but to contradict nature as much as he can. And though it takes a milder form than hooks in millions of the religious populations of Asia, it is a fact far too little realized, that the dogma of the denial of life does really rule as a first principle on so vast a scale. One historic form it took was that great enemy of Christianity from its beginnings: the Manichees.

What is called the Manichean philosophy has had many forms; indeed, it has attacked what is immortal and immutable with a very curious kind of immortal mutability. It is like the legend of the magician who turns himself into a snake or a cloud; and the whole has that nameless note of irresponsibility, which belongs to much of the metaphysics and morals of Asia, from which the Manichean mystery came. But it is always in one way or another a notion that nature is evil; or that evil is at least rooted in nature. The essential point is that as evil has roots in nature, so it has rights in nature. Wrong has as much right to exist as right. As already stated, this notion took many forms. Sometimes it was a dualism, which made evil an equal partner with good; so that neither could be called an usurper. More often it was a general idea that demons had made the material world; and if there were any good spirits, they were concerned only with the spiritual world. The idea was that the creator of the earth was primarily the creator of the evil, whether we call him a devil or a god.

Since there are a good many Manicheans among the Moderns, as we may remark in a moment, some may agree with this view; some may be puzzled about it; some may only be puzzled about why we should object to it. To understand the medieval controversy, a word must be said of the Catholic doctrine, which is as modern as it is medieval. That 'God looked on all things and saw that they were good' contains a subtlety which the popular pessimist cannot follow; or is too hasty to notice. It is the thesis that there are no bad things; but only bad uses of things. If you will, there are no bad things but only bad thoughts; and especially bad intentions. But it is possible to have bad intentions about good things; and good things, like the world and the flesh, have been twisted by a bad intention called the devil. But he cannot make *things* bad; they remain as on the first day of creation. The work of heaven alone was material; the making of a material world. The work of hell is entirely spiritual.

This error then had many forms; but especially, like nearly every error, it had two forms: a fiercer one which was outside the Church and attacking the Church, and a subtler one, which was inside the Church and corrupting the Church. There has never been a time when the Church was not torn between that invasion and that treason. It was so, for instance, in the Victorian time. Darwinian 'competition', in commerce or race conflict, was every bit as brazen an atheist assault in the nineteenth century, as the Bolshevist No-God movement in the twentieth century. To brag of brute prosperity, to admire the most muddy millionaires who had cornered wheat by a trick, to talk about the 'unfit' (in imitation of the scientific thinker who would finish them off because he cannot even finish his own sentence – unfit for what?) – all that is as simply and openly Anti-Christian as the Black Mass. Yet some weak and worldly Catholics did use this cant in defence of Capitalism, in their first rather feeble resistance to Socialism. At least they did, until the great Encyclical of the Pope on the

Rights of Labour put a stop to all their nonsense. The evil is always both within and without the Church; but in a wilder form outside and a milder form inside. So it was again in the seventeenth century, when there was Calvinism outside and Jansenism inside. And so it was in the thirteenth century, when the obvious danger outside was in the revolution of the Albigensians; but the potential danger inside was in the very traditionalism of the Augustinians. For the Augustinians derived only from Augustine; and Augustine derived partly from Plato; and Plato was right, but not quite right. It is a mathematical fact that if a line be not perfectly directed towards a point, it will actually go further away from it as it comes nearer to it. After a thousand years of extension, the miscalculation of Platonism had come very near to Manichaeism.

Popular errors are nearly always right. They nearly always refer to some ultimate reality, about which those who correct them are themselves incorrect. It is a very queer thing that 'Platonic Love' has come to mean for the unlettered something rather purer and cleaner than it means for the learned. Yet even those who realize the great Greek evil may well realize that perversity often comes out of the wrong sort of purity. Now it was the inmost lie of the Manichees that they identified purity with sterility. It is singularly contrasted with the language of St Thomas, which always connects purity with fruitfulness; whether it be natural or supernatural. And, queerly enough, as I have said, there does remain a sort of reality in the vulgar colloquialism that the affair between Sam and Susan is 'quite Platonic'. It is true that, quite apart from the local perversion, there was in Plato a sort of idea that people would be better without their bodies; that their heads might fly off and meet in the sky in merely intellectual marriage, like cherubs in a picture. The ultimate phase of this 'Platonic' philosophy was what inflamed poor D.H. Lawrence into talking nonsense, and he was probably unaware that the

Catholic doctrine of marriage would say much of what he said, without talking nonsense. Anyhow, it is historically important to see that Platonic love did somewhat distort both human and divine love, in the theory of the early theologians. Many medieval men, who would indignantly deny the Albigensian doctrine of sterility, were yet in an emotional mood to abandon the body in despair; and some of them to abandon everything in despair.

In truth, this vividly illuminates the provincial stupidity of those who object to what they call 'creeds and dogmas'. It was precisely the creed and dogma that saved the sanity of the world. These people generally propose an alternative religion of intuition and feeling. If, in the really Dark Ages, there had been a religion of feeling, it would have been a religion of black and suicidal feeling. It was the rigid creed that resisted the rush of suicidal feeling. The critics of asceticism are probably right in supposing that many a Western hermit did *feel* rather like an Eastern fakir. But he could not really *think* like an Eastern fakir; because he was an orthodox Catholic. And what kept his thought in touch with healthier and more humanistic thought was simply and solely the Dogma. He could not deny that a good God had created the normal and natural world; he could not say that the devil had made the world; because he was not a Manichee. A thousand enthusiasts for celibacy, in the day of the great rush to the desert or the cloister, might have called marriage a sin, if they had only considered their individual ideals, in the modern manner, and their own immediate feelings about marriage. Fortunately, they had to accept the Authority of the Church, which had definitely said that marriage was not a sin. A modern emotional religion might at any moment have turned Catholicism into Manichaeism. But when Religion would have maddened men, Theology kept them sane.

In this sense St Thomas stands up simply as the great orthodox theologian, who reminded men of the creed of

Creation, when many of them were still in the mood of mere destruction. It is futile for the critics of medievalism to quote a hundred medieval phrases that may be supposed to sound like mere pessimism, if they will not understand the central fact; that medieval men did not care about being medieval and did not accept the authority of a mood, because it was melancholy, but did care very much about orthodoxy, which is not a mood. It was because St Thomas could *prove* that his glorification of the Creator and His creative joy was more orthodox than any atmospheric pessimism, that he dominated the Church and the world, which accepted that truth as a test. But when this immense and impersonal importance is allowed for, we may agree that there was a personal element as well. Like most of the great religious teachers, he was fitted individually for the task that God had given him to do. We can if we like call that talent instinctive; we can even descend to calling it temperamental.

Anybody trying to popularize a medieval philosopher must use language that is very modern and very unphilosophical. Nor is this a sneer at modernity; it arises from the moderns having dealt so much in moods and emotions, especially in the arts, that they have developed a large but loose vocabulary, which deals more with atmosphere than with actual attitude or position. As noted elsewhere, even the modern philosophers are more like the modern poets, in giving an individual tinge even to truth, and often looking at all life through different-coloured spectacles. To say that Schopenhauer had the blues, or that William James had a rather rosier outlook, would often convey more than calling the one a pessimist or the other a pragmatist. This modern moodiness has a value, though the moderns overrate it; just as medieval logic had its value, though it was overrated in the later Middle Ages. But the point is that to explain the medievals to the moderns, we must often use this modern language of mood. Otherwise the character will be missed, through certain prejudices and ignorances about all such medieval characters. Now there is something that lies all over the work of St Thomas Aquinas like a great light; which is something quite primary and perhaps unconscious with him, which he would perhaps have passed over as an irrelevant personal quality, and which can now only be expressed by a rather cheap journalistic term which he would probably have thought quite senseless.

Nevertheless, the only working word for that atmosphere is Optimism. And in a rather larger and more luminous sense than in the case of these men, the term was basically true of Thomas Aquinas. He did, with a most solid and colossal conviction, believe in Life; and in something like what Stevenson called the great theorem of the livableness of life. It breathes somehow in his very first phrases about the reality of Being. If the morbid Renaissance intellectual is supposed to say, 'To be or not to be – that is the question,' then the massive medieval doctor does most certainly reply in a voice of thunder, 'To be – that is the answer.'

In the theology of St Thomas, it is proved by the tremendous truth that supports all that theology; or any other Christian theology. There really was a new reason for regarding the senses, and the sensations of the body, and the experiences of the common man, with a reverence at which great Aristotle would have stared, and no man in the ancient world could have begun to understand. The Body was no longer what it was when Plato and Porphyry and the old mystics had left it for dead. It had hung upon a gibbet. It had risen from a tomb. It was no longer possible for the soul to despise the senses, which had been the organs of something that was more than man. Plato might despise the flesh; but God had not despised it. The senses had truly become sanctified; as they are blessed one by one at a Catholic baptism. 'Seeing is believing' was no longer the platitude of a mere idiot, or common individual, as in Plato's world; it was mixed up with real conditions of real belief. Those revolving mirrors that send messages to the brain of man, that light that breaks upon the brain, these had truly revealed to God Himself the path to Bethany or the light on the high rock of Jerusalem. These ears that resound with common noises had reported also to the secret knowledge of God the noise of the crowd that strewed palms and the crowd that cried for Crucifixion. After the Incarnation had become the idea that is central in our civilization, it was inevitable that there should be a return to materialism; in the sense of the serious value of matter and the making of the body. When once Christ had risen, it was inevitable that Aristotle should rise again.

Those are three real reasons, and very sufficient reasons, for the general support given by the saint to a solid and objective philosophy. And yet there was something else, very vast and vague, to which I have tried to give a faint expression by the interposition of this chapter. It is difficult to express it fully, without the awful peril of being popular, or what the Modernists quite wrongly imagine to be popular; in short, passing from religion to religiosity. But there is a general tone and temper of Aquinas, which it is as difficult to avoid as daylight in a great house of windows. It is that *positive* position of his mind, which is filled and soaked as with sunshine, with the warmth of the wonder of created things. There is a certain private audacity, in his communion, by which men add to their private names the tremendous titles of the Trinity and the Redemption; so that some nun may be called 'of the Holy Ghost'; or a man bear such a burden as the title of St John of the Cross. In this sense, the man we study may specially be called St Thomas of the Creator.

St Thomas Aquinas, 1933

The Permanent Philosophy

St Thomas Aquinas closely resembles the great Professor Huxley, the Agnostic who invented the word Agnosticism. He is like him in his way of starting the argument, and he is unlike everybody else, before and after, until the Huxleyan age. He adopts almost literally the Huxleyan definition of the agnostic method: 'To follow reason as far as it will go'; the only question is – where does it go? He lays down the almost startlingly modern or materialist statement: 'Everything that is in the intellect has been in the senses.' This is where he began, as much as any modern man of science, nay, as much as any modern materialist who can now hardly be called a man of science; at the very opposite end of enquiry from that of the mere mystic. The Platonists, or at least the Neo-Platonists, all tended to the view that the mind was lit entirely from within; St Thomas insisted that it was lit by five windows, that we call the windows of the senses. But he wanted the light from without to shine on what was within. He wanted to study the nature of Man, and not merely of such moss and mushrooms as he might see through the window, and which he valued as the first enlightening experience of man. And starting from this point, he proceeds to climb the House of Man, step by step and story by story, until he has come out on the highest tower and beheld the largest vision.

In other words, he is an anthropologist, with a complete theory of Man, right or wrong. Now the modern anthropologists, who called themselves agnostics, completely failed to be anthropologists at all. Under their limitations, they could not get a complete theory of Man, let alone a complete theory of nature. They began by ruling out something which they called the Unknowable. The incomprehensibility was almost comprehensible, if we could really understand the Unknowable in the sense of the Ultimate. But it rapidly became apparent that all sorts of things were Unknowable, which were exactly the things that a man has got to know. It is necessary to know whether he is responsible or irresponsible, perfect or imperfect, perfectible or unperfectible, mortal or immortal, doomed or free: not in order to understand God, but in order to understand Man. Nothing that leaves these things under a cloud of religious doubt can possibly pretend to be a Science of Man; it shrinks from anthropology as completely as from theology. Has a man free will; or is his sense of choice an illusion? Has he a conscience, or has his conscience any authority; or is it only the prejudice of the tribal past? Is there any real hope of settling these things by human reason; and has *that* any authority? Is he to regard death as final; and is he to regard miraculous help as possible? Now it is all nonsense to say that these are unknowable in any remote sense, like the distinction between the Cherubim and the Seraphim, or the Procession of the Holy Ghost. The Schoolmen may have shot too far beyond our limits in pursuing the cherubim and seraphim. But in asking whether a man can choose or whether a man will die, they were asking ordinary questions in natural history; like whether a cat can scratch or whether a dog can smell. Nothing calling itself a complete Science of Man can shirk them. And the great agnostics did shirk them. They may have said they had no scientific evidence; in that case they failed to produce even a scientific hypothesis. What they generally did produce was a wildly unscientific contradiction. Most Monist moralists simply said that Man has no choice; but he must think and act heroically as if he had. Huxley made morality, and even Victorian morality, in the exact sense, supernatural. He said it had arbitrary rights above nature, a sort of theology without theism.

I do not know for certain why St Thomas was called the Angelic Doctor: whether it was that he had an angelic temper, or the intellectualism of an angel; or whether there was a later legend that he concentrated on angels – especially on the points of needles. If so, I do not quite understand how this idea arose; history has many examples of an irritating habit of labelling somebody in connection with something, as if he never did anything else. Who was it who began the inane habit of referring to Dr Johnson as 'our lexicographer', as if he never did anything but write a dictionary?

St Thomas was interested in the problem of the angel, as he was interested in the problem of the Man, because it was a problem; and especially because it was a problem of an inter-mediate creature. I do not pretend to deal here with this mysterious quality, as he conceives it to exist in that inscrutable intellectual being, who is less than God but more than Man. But it was this quality of a link in the chain, or a rung in the ladder, which mainly concerned the theologian in developing his own particular theory of degrees. Above all, it is this which chiefly moves him when he finds so fasci-nating the central mystery of Man. And for him the point is always that Man is not a balloon going up into the sky, nor a mole burrowing merely in the earth; but rather a thing like a tree, whose roots are fed from the earth, while its highest branches seem to rise almost to the stars.

The importance of Thomism to the twentieth century is that it may give us back a cosmos. We can give here only the rudest sketch of how Aquinas, like the agnostics, beginning in the cosmic cellars, yet climbed to the cosmic towers.

Without pretending to span within such limits the essential Thomist idea, I may be allowed to throw out a sort of rough version of the fundamental question, which I think I have known myself, consciously or unconsciously, since my childhood. When a child looks out of the nursery window and sees anything, say the green lawn of the garden, what does he actually know, or does he know anything? There are all sorts of nursery games of negative philosophy played round this question. A brilliant Victorian scientist delighted in declaring that the child does not see any grass at all, but only a sort of green mist reflected in a tiny mirror of the human eye. This piece of rationalism has always struck me as almost insanely irrational. If he is not sure of the existence of the grass, which he sees through the glass of a window, how on earth can he be sure of the existence of the retina, which he sees through the glass of a microscope? If sight deceives, why can it not go on deceiving? Men of another school answer that grass is a mere green impression on the mind; and that the child can be sure of nothing except the mind. They declare that he can only be conscious of his own consciousness, which happens to be the one thing that we know the child is not conscious of at all. In that sense, it would be far truer to say that there is grass and no child, than to say that there is a conscious child but no grass. St Thomas Aquinas, suddenly intervening in this nursery quarrel, says emphatically that the child is aware of *Ens*. Long before he knows that grass is grass, or self is self, he knows that something is something. Perhaps it would be best to say very emphatically (with a blow on the table), 'There *is* an Is.' That is as much monkish credulity as St Thomas asks of us at the start. Very few unbelievers start by asking us to believe so little. And yet, upon this sharp pinpoint of reality, he rears by long logical processes that have never really been successfully overthrown, the whole cosmic system of Christendom.

Thus, Aquinas insists very profoundly, but very practically, that there *instantly* enters, with this idea of affirmation, the idea of contradiction. It is instantly apparent, even to the child, that there cannot be both affirmation and contradiction. Whatever you call the thing he sees, a lawn or a mirage or a sensation or a state of consciousness, when he sees it, he knows it is not true that he does not see it. Or whatever you call what he is supposed to be doing, seeing or dreaming or being conscious of an impression, he knows that if he is doing it, it is a lie to say he is not doing it. Therefore there has already entered *something* beyond even the first fact of being; there follows it like its shadow the first fundamental creed or commandment: that a thing cannot be and not be. Henceforth, in common or popular language, there is a false and true. I say in popular language, because Aquinas is nowhere more subtle than in pointing out that being is not strictly the same as truth; seeing truth must mean the appreciation of being by some mind capable of appreciating it. But in a general sense there has entered that primeval world of pure actuality, the division and dilemma that brings the ultimate sort of war into the world; the everlasting duel between Yes and No. This is the dilemma that many sceptics have darkened the universe and dissolved the mind, solely in order to escape. They are those who maintain that there is something that is both Yes and No. I do not know whether they pronounce it Yo.

The next step following on this acceptance of actuality or certainty, or whatever we call it in popular language, is much more difficult to explain in that language. But it represents exactly the point at which nearly all other systems go wrong; and in taking the third step abandon the first. Aquinas has affirmed that our first sense of fact is a fact; and he cannot go back on it without falsehood. But when we come to look at the fact or facts, as we know them, we observe that they have a rather queer character, which has made many moderns grow strangely and restlessly sceptical about them. For instance, they are largely in a state of change, from being one thing to being another; or their qualities are relative to other things; or they appear to move incessantly; or they appear to vanish entirely. At this point, as I say, many sages lose hold of the first principle of reality, which they would concede at first; and fall back on saying that there is nothing except change; or nothing except comparison; or nothing except flux; or in effect that there is nothing at all. Aquinas turns the whole argument the other way, keeping in line with his first realization of reality. There is no doubt about the being of being, even if it does sometimes look like becoming; that is because what we see is not the fullness of being; or (to continue a sort of colloquial slang) we never see being being as much as it can. Ice is melted into cold water and cold water is heated into hot water; it cannot be all three at once. But this does not make water unreal or even relative; it only means that its being is limited to being one thing at a time. But the fullness of being is everything that it can be; and without it the lesser or approximate forms of being cannot be explained as anything; unless they are explained away as nothing.

This crude outline can only at the best be historical rather than philosophical. It is impossible to compress into it the metaphysical proofs of such an idea; especially in the medieval metaphysical language. But this distinction in philosophy is tremendous as a turning point in history. Most thinkers, on realizing the apparent mutability of being, have really forgotten their own realization of the being, and believed only in the mutability. They cannot even say that a thing changes into another thing; for them there is no instant in the process at which it is a thing at all. It is only a change. It would be more logical to call it nothing changing into nothing, than to say (on these principles) that there ever was or will be a moment when the thing is itself. St Thomas maintains that the ordinary thing at any moment is something; but it is not everything that it could be. There is a fullness of being, in which it could be everything that it can be. Thus, while most sages come at last to nothing but naked change, he comes to the ultimate thing that is unchangeable, because it is all the other things at once. While they describe a change which is really a change in nothing, he describes a changelessness which includes the changes of everything. Things change because they are not complete; but their reality can only be explained as part of something that is complete. It is God.

Historically, at least, it was round this sharp and crooked corner that all the sophists have followed each other, while the great Schoolman went up the high road of experience and expansion, to the beholding of cities, to the building of cities. They all failed at this early stage because, in the words of the old game, they took away the number they first thought of. The recognition of something, of a thing or things, is the first act of the intellect. But because the examination of a thing shows it is not a fixed or final thing, they inferred that there is nothing fixed or final. Thus, in various ways, they all began to see a thing as something thinner than a thing; a wave; a weakness; an abstract instability. St Thomas, to use the same rude figure, saw a thing that was thicker than a thing; that was even more solid than the solid but secondary facts he had started by admitting as facts. Since we know them to be real, any elusive or bewildering element in their reality cannot really be unreality; and must be merely their relation to the real reality. A hundred human philosophies, ranging over the earth from Nominalism to Nirvana and Maya, from formless Evolutionism to mindless Quietism, all come from this first break in the Thomist chain, the notion that, because what we see does not satisfy us, or explain itself, it is not even what we see. That cosmos is a contradiction in terms and strangles itself; but Thomism cuts itself free. The defect we see, in what is, is simply that it is not all that is. God is more actual even than Man; more actual even than Matter; for God with all His powers at every instant is immortally in action.

St Thomas says, quite straightforwardly, that he himself believes this world has a beginning and end, because such seems to be the teaching of the Church, the validity of which mystical message to mankind he defends elsewhere with dozens of quite different arguments. Anyhow, the Church said the world would end, and apparently the Church was right; always supposing (as we are always supposed to suppose) that the latest men of science are right. But Aquinas says he sees no particular reason, in reason, why this world should not be a world without end; or even without beginning. And he is quite certain that, if it were entirely without end or beginning, there would still be exactly the same logical need of a Creator. Anybody who does not see that, he gently implies, does not really understand what is meant by a Creator.

For what St Thomas means is not a medieval picture of an old king; but this second step in the great argument about *Ens* or Being, the second point which is so desperately difficult to put correctly in popular language. That is why I have introduced it here in the particular form of the argument that there must be a Creator even if there is no Day of Creation. Looking at Being as it is now, as the baby looks at the grass, we see a second thing about it: in quite popular language, it *looks* secondary and dependent. Existence exists; but it is not sufficiently self-existent; and would never become so merely by going on existing. The same primary sense which tells us it is Being, tells us that it is not perfect Being; not merely imperfect in the popular controversial sense of containing sin or sorrow, but imperfect as Being, less actual than the actuality it implies. For instance, its Being is often only Becoming; beginning to Be or ceasing to Be; it implies a more constant or complete thing of which it gives in itself no example. That is the meaning of that basic medieval phrase, 'Everything that is moving is moved by another'; which, in the clear subtlety of St Thomas, means inexpressibly more than the mere Deistic 'somebody wound up the clock' with which it is probably often confounded. Anyone who thinks deeply will see that motion has about it an essential incompleteness, which approximates to something more complete. The actual argument is rather technical, and concerns the fact that potentiality does not explain itself; moreover, in any case unfolding must be of something folded.

In a sketch that aims only at the baldest simplification, this does seem to me the simplest truth about St Thomas the philosopher. He is one, so to speak, who is faithful to his first love; and it is love at first sight. I mean that he immediately recognized a real quality in things; and afterwards resisted all the disintegrating doubts arising from the nature of those things. That is why I emphasize, even in the first few pages, the fact that there is a sort of purely Christian humility and fidelity underlying his philosophic realism. St Thomas could as truly say, of having seen merely a stick or a stone, what St Paul said of having seen the rending of the secret heavens, 'I was not disobedient to the heavenly vision.' For though the stick or the stone is an earthly vision, it is through them that St Thomas finds his way to heaven; and the point is that he is obedient to the vision, he does not go back on it. Nearly all the other sages who have led or misled mankind do, on one excuse or another, go back on it. They dissolve the stick or the stone in chemical solutions of scepticism; either in the medium of mere time and change, or in the difficulties of classification of unique units, or in the difficulty of recognizing variety while admitting unity.

He has seen grass; and will not say he has not seen grass, because it today is and tomorrow is cast into the oven. That is the substance of all scepticism about change, transition, transformism and the rest. He will not say that there is no grass but only growth. If grass grows and withers, it can only mean that it is part of a greater thing, which is even more real; not that the grass is less real than it looks. St Thomas has a really logical right to say, in the words of the modern mystic, A.E.: 'I begin by the grass to be bound again to the Lord.'

He has seen grass and grain; and he will not say that they do not differ, because there is something common to grass and grain. Nor will he say that, because there is something common to grass and grain, they do not really differ. He will not say, with the extreme Nominalists, that because grain can be differentiated into all sorts of fruitage, or grass trodden into mire with any kind of weed, therefore there can be no *classification* to distinguish weeds from slime or to draw a fine distinction between cattle food and cattle. He will not say with the extreme Platonists, on the other hand, that he saw the perfect fruit in his own head by shutting his eyes, *before* he saw any difference between grain and grass. He saw one thing and then another thing, and then a common quality; but he does not really pretend that he saw the quality before the thing.

He has seen grass and gravel; that is to say, he has seen things really different, things not classified together like grass and grain. The first flash of fact shows us a world of really strange things; not merely strange to us, but strange to each other. The separate things need have nothing in common except Being. Everything is Being; but it is not true that everything is Unity. It is here, as I have said, that St Thomas does definitely, one might say defiantly, part company with the Pantheist and the Monist. All things are; but among the things that are is the thing called difference, quite as much as the thing called similarity. And here again we begin to be bound again to the Lord, not only by the universality of grass, but by the incompatibility of grass and gravel. For this world of different and varied beings is especially the world of the Christian Creator, the world of created things, like things made by an artist; as compared with the world that is only one thing, with a sort of shimmering and shifting veil of misleading change, which is the conception of so many of the ancient religions of Asia and the modern sophistries of Germany.

To sum up: the reality of things, the mutability of things, the diversity of things, and all other such things that can be attributed to things, is followed carefully by the medieval philosopher, without losing touch with the original point of the reality. The *deceitfulness* of things which has had so sad an effect on so many sages, has almost a contrary effect on this sage. If things deceive us, it is by being more real than they seem. As ends in themselves they always deceive us; but as things tending to a greater end, they are even more real than we think them. If they seem to have a relative unreality (so to speak) it is because they are potential and not actual; they are unfulfilled, like packets of seeds or boxes of fireworks. They have it in them to be more real than they are. And there is an upper world of what the Schoolman called Fruition, or Fulfilment, in which all this relative relativity becomes actuality; in which the trees burst into flower or the rockets into flame.

Here I leave the reader, on the very lowest rung of those ladders of logic, by which St Thomas besieged and mounted the House of Man. It is enough to say that by arguments as honest and laborious, he climbed up to the turrets and talked with angels on the roofs of gold.

St Thomas Aquinas, 1933

Postscript

Letter to Chesterton by Albino Luciani, Pope John Paul I

Dear Chesterton,

On Italian television during the past few weeks we have been seeing Father Brown, your surprising detective-priest – a character who is typically yours. A pity we haven't also had Professor Lucifer and the monk Michael. I'd very much have liked to see them as you described them in *The Ball and the Cross*, sitting beside each other on the flying ship.

When the flying ship is above St Paul's Cathedral, the Professor gives 'a shriek indescribable' as they pass the cross on the ball set on top of the dome.

' "I once knew a man like you, Lucifer," ' says Michael. ' "...This man also took the view that the symbol of Christianity was a symbol of savagery and all unreason. His history is rather amusing. It is also a perfect allegory of what happens to rationalists like yourself. He began, of course, by refusing to allow a crucifix in his house, or round his wife's neck, or even in a picture. He said, as you say, that it was an arbitrary and fantastic shape, that it was a monstrosity, loved because it was paradoxical. Then he began to grow fiercer and more eccentric; he would batter the crosses by the roadside; for he lived in a Roman Catholic country. Finally in a height of frenzy he climbed the steeple of the Parish Church and tore down the cross, waving it in the air, and uttering wild soliloquies up there under the stars. Then one still summer evening as he was wending his way homewards, along a lane, the devil of his madness came upon him with a violence and transfiguration which changes the world. He was standing smoking, for a moment, in front of an interminable line of palings, when his eyes were opened. Not a light shifted, not a leaf stirred, but he saw as if by a sudden change in the eyesight that this paling was an army of innumerable crosses linked together over hill and dale. And he whirled up his heavy stick and went at it as if at an army. Mile after mile along his homeward path he broke it down and tore it up. For he hated the cross and every paling is a wall of crosses. When he returned to his house he was a literal madman. He sat upon a chair and then started up from it for the crossbars of the carpentry repeated the intolerable image. He flung himself upon a bed only to remember that this, too, like all workmanlike things, was constructed on the accursed plan. He broke his furniture because it was made of crosses. He burnt his house because it was made of crosses. He was found in the river." '

'Lucifer was looking at him with a bitten lip,' you continue.

'"Is that story really true?" he asked.

'"Oh, no," said Michael, airily. "It is a parable. It is a parable of you and all your rationalists. You begin by breaking up the Cross; but you end by breaking up the habitable world."'

The monk's conclusion, which is yours, dear Chesterton, is quite right. Take God away and what is left, what do men become? What sort of a world are we reduced to living in? 'Why, the world of progress!' I hear someone say. 'The world of affluence!' Yes, but this famous progress isn't all it was once cracked up to be. It contains other things in itself; missiles, bacteriological and atomic weapons, the present process of pollution – all things that, unless they are dealt with in time, threaten to plunge the whole human race into catastrophe.

In other words, progress that involves men who love one another, thinking of themselves as brothers and as children of the one Father, God, can be a magnificent thing. Progress that involves men who don't recognize a single Father in God becomes a constant danger: without a parallel moral progress, which is continuous and internal, it develops what is lowest and cruellest in man, making him a machine possessed by machines, a number manipulated by numbers; he becomes what Papini called 'a raving savage, who, to satisfy his predatory, destructive, and licentious instincts, no longer uses a club, but has the immense forces of nature and mechanical invention to draw upon.'

Yes, I know there are plenty of people who think the opposite of this. They consider religion a consoling dream, invented by oppressed people who imagine another world, a non-existent world in which they can later find what is stolen from them today by their oppressors. These oppressors have arranged the whole thing for their own benefit, to keep the oppressed underfoot and to quieten the instinct towards a class struggle, an instinct that, were it not for religion, would urge them to fight.

It is no good reminding these people that the Christian religion itself favours the revival of proletarian awareness, that it exalts the poor and foresees a just future, 'Yes,' they reply, 'Christianity does awaken the awareness of the poor, but then it paralyses it by preaching patience, and by substituting faith in God and trust in the gradual reform of society for the class struggle.'

Many also think that God and religion, by fixing people's hopes and efforts on a future, distant paradise, *alienate* man, and prevent him committing himself to a nearby paradise, to achieving one here on earth.

It is no good reminding them that, according to the recent Council, a Christian, just because he is a Christian, must feel all the more committed to support progress for the good of all, and social advancement for everyone. 'All the same,' they say, 'you think of progress through a transitory world, waiting for a definitive paradise which will never be achieved. We want our paradise here, as a result of all our struggles. We can see the beginning of it already, whereas your God is actually called "dead" by some theologians. We agree with Heine, who wrote: "Do you hear the bells? Down on yours knees! We are taking the last sacraments to a dying God."'

Dear Chesterton, you and I go down on our knees before a God who is more present than ever. Only he can give a satisfactory answer to the questions, which, for everyone, are the most important of all: Who am I? Where did I come from? Where am I going?

As to the heaven that will be enjoyed on earth and only on earth, and in the near future, after the famous 'class struggle', I'd like to quote someone much more gifted than me and, without denying your merits, than you too, dear Chesterton: Dostoevsky.

You remember his Ivan Karamazov. He was an atheist, a friend of the devil. Well, he protested with all an atheist's vehemence against the paradise achieved through effort, suffering and the martyrdom of countless generations. To think of our descendants being happy thanks to the unhappiness of their ancestors! Ancestors who struggle without ever receiving their share of joy, often without even the comfort of a glimpse of paradise when they emerge from the hell they have gone through! Multitudes exterminated, wounded and sacrificed merely to provide the soil in which to grow the future trees of life! Impossible! says Ivan. It would be a pitiless, monstrous justice.

And he was right.

The sense of justice that lies in every man, whatever his faith, demands that the good we do and the evil we suffer should be rewarded, that the hunger for life found in everyone should be satisfied. Where and how, if there is no other life? And from whom, if not from God? And from what God, if not the one of whom St Francis de Sales wrote: 'Do not fear God, who wishes you no harm, but love Him a great deal, who wishes you so much good.'

What many people fight is not the true God but the false idea they have made of God: a God who protects the rich, who only asks and demands, who is jealous of our growing prosperity, who spies continuously on our sins from above, to give Himself the pleasure of punishing us.

Dear Chesterton, you know God isn't like that; you know that He's both good and just; the father of prodigal sons, who wishes them all to be, not sad and wretched, but great and free, and creators of their own destiny. Our God is not man's rival, He wants us to be His friends, he has called us to share in His divine nature and in His external happiness. And He does not ask anything excessive of us: He is content with very little, because He knows quite well that we haven't got very much.

Dear Chesterton, I'm sure, as you are, that this God will make Himself ever more known and loved: by everyone, including those who reject Him, not because they are evil (they may be better than both of us!), but because they look at Him from a mistaken point of view. If they continue not to believe in Him, He replies: 'Well, I believe in you!'

Bibliography of Major Works
by G.K. Chesterton

———

Listed here are Chesterton's works which appeared in book form, excluding general anthologies, reprints and pamphlets.

Year	Title	Publisher
1900	*Greybeards at Play* (Poetry)	Brimley Johnson
	The Wild Knight (Poetry)	Brimley Johnson
1901	*The Defendant* (Collected Essays)	Brimley Johnson
1902	*G.F.Watts* (Biography)	Duckworth
	Twelve Types (Collected Essays)	A.L. Humphreys
1903	*Robert Browning* (Biography)	Macmillan
1904	*The Napoleon of Notting Hill* (Novel)	John Lane
1905	*The Club of Queer Trades* (Stories)	Hodder & Stoughton
	Heretics (Philosophy/Theology)	John Lane
1906	*Charles Dickens* (Biography)	Methuen
1908	*The Man Who Was Thursday* (Novel)	Arrowsmith
	Orthodoxy (Philosophy/Theology)	John Lane
	All Things Collected (Collected Essays)	Methuen
1909	*George Bernard Shaw* (Biography)	John Lane
	Tremendous Trifles (Collected Essays)	Methuen
1910	*The Ball and the Cross* (Novel)	Wells Gardiner
	What's Wrong With the World (Social Criticism)	Cassell
	William Blake (Biography)	Duckworth

	Alarms and Discursions (Collected Essays)	Methuen
	Five Types (Collected Essays)	A.L. Humphreys
1911	*The Innocence of Father Brown* (Stories)	Cassell
	Appreciations and Criticism of the Works of Charles Dickens (Literary Criticism)	Dent
	The Ballad of the White Horse (Poetry)	Methuen
	Manalive (Novel)	Arrowsmith
1912	*A Miscellany of Men* (Collected Essays)	Methuen
	The Victorian Age in Literature (Literary Criticism)	Williams & Norgate/ Home University Library
1913	*Magic* (Drama)	Secker
1914	*The Wisdom of Father Brown* (Stories)	Cassell
	The Flying Inn (Novel)	Methuen
1917	*A Short History of England* (History)	Chatto & Windus
1919	*Irish Impressions* (Travel)	Collins
1920	*The Uses of Diversity* (Collected Essays)	Methuen
	The New Jerusalem (Travel)	Hodder & Stoughton
	The Superstition of Divorce (Social Criticism)	Chatto & Windus
1922	*Eugenics and Other Evils* (Social Criticism)	Cassell
	What I Saw in America (Travel)	Hodder & Stoughton
1923	*Fancies versus Fads* (Collected Essays)	Methuen
	St Francis of Assisi (Theology)	Hodder & Stoughton
1925	*The Everlasting Man* (Theology)	Hodder & Stoughton
	Tales of the Long Bow (Stories)	Cassell
	William Cobbett (Biography)	Hodder & Stoughton

1926	*The Incredulity of Father Brown* (Stories)	Cassell
	The Outline of Sanity (Social Criticism)	Methuen
1927	*Robert Louis Stevenson* (Biography)	Hodder & Stoughton
	Collected Poems	Cecil Palmer
	The Secret of Father Brown (Stories)	Cassell
1928	*Generally Speaking* (Collected Essays)	Methuen
1929	*The Poet and the Lunatics* (Stories)	Cassell
	The Thing (Collected Religious Essays)	Sheed & Ward
	GK as MC (i.e. as Master of Ceremonies: a collection of GKC's introductions to other writer's books)	Methuen
1930	*Come to Think of It* (Collected Essays)	Methuen
	The Resurrection of Rome (Travel)	Hodder & Stoughton
1931	*All is Grist* (Collected Essays)	Methuen
1932	*Chaucer* (Biography)	Faber & Faber
	Sidelights on New London & Newer York (Travel)	Sheed & Ward
1933	*All I Survey* (Collected Essays)	Methuen
	St Thomas Aquinas (Theology)	Hodder & Stoughton
	Collected Poems	Methuen
1934	*Avowals and Denials* (Collected Essays)	Methuen
1935	*The Scandal of Father Brown* (Stories)	Cassell
	The Well and the Shallows (Collected Religious Essays)	Sheed & Ward
1936	*As I Was Saying* (Collected Essays)	Methuen
	Autobiography	Hutchinson
1937	*The Paradoxes of Mr Pond* (Stories)	Cassell

Posthumous Collections

Chesterton completed the *Autobiography* and *The Paradoxes of Mr Pond* himself, although both appeared after his death. His devoted secretary Dorothy Collins compiled a number of new collections of his writings of which the most important are:

Year	Title	Publisher
1938	*The Coloured Lands* (Collected Essays)	Sheed & Ward
1940	*End of the Armistice* (Warnings on Hitler)	Sheed & Ward
1950	*The Common Man* (Collected Essays)	Sheed & Ward
1953	*A Handful of Authors* (Collected Essays)	Sheed & Ward
1955	*The Glass Walking Stick* (Collected Essays)	Sheed & Ward
1963	*The Man Who Was Orthodox* (Collected Essays) Compiled by A.L. Maycock, this is a collection of Chesterton's early essays from various magazines and newspapers which had not otherwise been preserved in book form.	Denis Dobson
1964	*The Spice of Life* (Collected Essays)	Darwin Finlayson

Poetry

A good modern edition is *Poems for All Seasons*, compiled by Stephen Medcalf, Random House, 1994.